ORRIN HATCH

**Challenging the
Washington Establishment**

Richard Vetterli

Regnery Gateway
Chicago

Published by Regnery Gateway
360 West Superior Street
Chicago, Illinois 60610

LC: 82-61024

ISBN: 0-89526-629-6

CONTENTS

PREFACE

In the spring of 1981 freshman Senator Orrin Hatch became Chairman of the Senate Labor and Human Resources Committee, one of the most important committees in Congress. Before his first term was out, he had become one of the most colorful and influential men in the United States.

I first became acquainted with Orrin Hatch in 1978. In him I saw an intriguing and multi-faceted individual. Although a newcomer to politics and virtually unknown in his home state before he entered the race, Orrin Hatch had skyrocketed to popularity and was elected to the United States Senate in 1976. In his campaign and election I found an exciting story and even some episodes of rich humor.

His adventures in Washington as a freshman Senator fascinated me. I came to see that this was no ordinary man, and he was certainly not a "typical" Senator.

At first, I began to see him in the role of Jimmy Stewart—"Mr. Smith Goes to Washington." It seemed to me there were a number of parallels between that grand old movie and Mr. Hatch's real life. I thought it would be challenging to write a book about Senator Hatch in that style. I began writing in late 1979. The book was written on *situs*—in Utah and Washington, D.C.

Yet as my research began to open up a wider understanding of this man and the complicated world of power politics in which he found himself, the content of my research outgrew Mr. "Hatch" goes to Washington. I began to see a deeper meaning in his life, a meaning that in one way or another touches all of us. This is not just the story of the rise from obscurity to national prominence of a United States Senator. It is the story of the metamorphosis of an important leader.

Orrin Hatch's story is intimately entwined with some of the most critical events at one of the most crucial times in our nation's history. The real question is not whether this or that program is enacted into law, or whether the budget total is $10 billion one way or the other. The fact is that the people of the United States are dangerously close to losing control of their political system. A citadel of power sits astride the Washington scene, often impervious to the genuine needs and desires of the American people. Energized and supported by the vast resources of government in a milieu of false political ideology and crass self-interest, it is glamorized by a sensation-seeking and sometimes irresponsible press.

The following, then, is the story of that citadel of power and one Senator's response to it.

Since many of the conversations recorded in this book took place over time, some of the statements and conversations herein recorded are of necessity approximations of the actual conversations or statements.

Part One
The Beginner

Chapter 1
THE CHALLENGER

"Look, Orrin, now just isn't the time. Even if all the other factors were favorable, you're starting late. It's April already. The other candidates are in full swing. And let me tell you something: Moss can't be beaten—at least not this time. You know, he's the grand old man; and that group of voters he calls his 'hidden constituency' is really out there. The opinion polls can't find them, but they're always there on election day. After all, he's been reelected twice. No, now isn't the time. If you go after the nomination for the experience, for exposure, that's one thing, but don't expect to win. Six years from now—well, that's another story."

This advice was given in April, 1976, by Vernon Romney, Attorney General of Utah, who hoped to be the Republican candidate for Governor. His words were deflating to Orrin Hatch. As Hatch left the Attorney General's office and walked rather aimlessly down the steps of the capitol building, he stopped a moment and looked out over Salt Lake Valley. The first signs of spring were becoming visible. The tops of the mountains that rose majestically to the east of the valley were still covered with snow, in marked contrast to the bright areas of green that were beginning to appear in the valley. To the west, the Great Salt Lake fairly sparkled in the morning sun. It was an exhilarating scene, and Hatch filled his lungs with the crisp, clean morning air, held it for a moment, then forced it out through clenched teeth. He wheeled about and bounded up the stairs, his long, athletic legs taking three steps at a time.

As a religious man, Hatch thought in long-range terms. Time and again during his political career his pioneer background would inspire him, energize him, force him back from discouragement and even despair; and it would temper him—something a man like Hatch, with his energy and quick response, needed. His decision as a young man to become a missionary for two years for his church, his decision to seek a law degree, even his choice of a wife—all were made with a mind single to making his life count. His ambition was born of a firm belief that what talent he had must be dedicated to more than those elemental indicators of success so generally recognized. He had an overpowering motivation to place his life on the altar of service to those ideals he held inviolate. He could not be passive. He had to make a difference. The space and time he took with his life had to mean something more than commonplace daily routine. In 1945 his brother had been killed in a bombing raid over Germany. The arrival of the telegram from the War Department and the anguish of his parents had left a deep impression on his young mind. That same evening Orrin's tough father had expressed his pride, through his tears, that if his son had to die, he could have given his life for no worthier cause and for no greater country. The following morning Orrin discovered that, during the night, several strands of his hair on the right side had turned grey. They remain so to this day.

For over a decade Hatch had believed that those who managed the current political establishment had sacrificed the principles of America's greatness to false and alien philosophies which threatened to lead the country to economic debacle, moral decadence and both domestic and international policies which would inexorably lead to war rather than peace.

There was a sense of urgency in his life that kept him uneasy and dissatisfied, even while he excelled as an attorney and a businessman. He could not understand, for instance, why the people of Utah, who of all people should know better, kept voting for Senator Frank Moss, an establishment-liberal Democrat. As the election of 1976 approached, the fact that Moss would probably be sent back to Washington for six more years became unthinkable to Hatch.

It was only after it was considered far too late for any sensible man to cast his hat into the senatorial contest that Hatch came to the conclusion that he should fight to face Moss the coming November. This was no ordinary man contemplating the pros and cons of candidacy. Hatch had a cause. He believed he could make a difference if elected to the United States Senate. He even believed periodically that he *could* be elected. His sense of urgency told him that the opportunity might never come again.

Still, he was not sure of himself, not at all certain that his gnawing sense of urgency and his near Quixotic need to play a conspicuous role in what he believed would be the battle for America's future were not blinding him to political realities, especially after his discussion with Attorney General Romney. Hatch's first impression was that he had let his enthusiasm and his zeal run away with him. After all, he reasoned, it was stupidity or undeserved arrogance to suppose that a newcomer to Utah's political scene with no political experience and no name identification whatsoever among the voters could suddenly decide at the eleventh hour that he was going to be the next United States Senator from Utah. It was absurd. Who did he think he was?

Yet as he paused to look out upon the beauty of the valley he was overwhelmed again with the sense of urgency that had kept him from fully enjoying what would otherwise have been a happy and successful life. This time the feeling brought with it the exhilaration that only a man of faith can understand. He did not stop to analyze the sense of urgency and of hope that now filled him. He just knew that he was not ready to give up yet. Vernon Romney was a well-informed man, he reasoned, but he wasn't the only person that knew Utah politics. That morning Hatch talked to a number of other people at the State Capitol, including State Senator Warren Pugh. All responses were negative. They centered on the fact that all the Republican candidates were well known, while Hatch was a newcomer, that Moss was probably unbeatable, and that Hatch had waited too long to begin. Still Hatch was not ready to concede that his was an impossible goal.

In the days that followed, without any political organization— without having given any thought to the modus operandi of running a campaign—Hatch talked with dozens of Utah's most prominent people. As yet no newspaper had mentioned his name, but the word was getting out that he was showing interest in at least entering the primaries. He began to receive calls from prominent Republicans. Some called to feel him out, others to give encouragement, still others attempted with varying degrees of intensity to talk him out of filing. He now began to experience the endemic gut-wrenching problem that all politicians sooner or later have to face—among all those willing to give advice, who had his interests at heart and who were motivated by other interests concealed behind the façade of concern?

On May 7, four days from the May 10 filing date, a prominent member of the Utah Republican Party Central Committee called Hatch at his office, and asked to speak with him as soon as possible. In their meeting that afternoon, Hatch was reminded what he had heard so often during the previous weeks. On the Republican side he was matching up with too many heavyweights—and with no political experience of his own. Jack Carlson was a former Assistant Secretary of the Interior, former assistant director of the Bureau of the Budget and former assistant to the director of the President's Office of Management and Budget. He also held a PhD in economics from Harvard. Sherman Lloyd was a former four-term U.S. Congressman from Utha's 2nd District, and a respected legislator. Desmond Barker, a third candidate, had been special assistant to former President Richard Nixon in 1971-72, and a consultant to the Secretary of the Treasury during Nixon's first term.

All of these candidates already had campaign organizations, and all were well known. Jack Carlson appeared the front runner. Political street scuttlebut had it that Carlson had already gained sufficient delegate strength to sew up the nomination. This well-liked, talented and experienced candidate seemed to possess all the positive characteristics one generally associates with political success.

"That's the way it is," Hatch was told. "And anyway," was the warning, "Moss may be impossible to beat this time around." But this party leader hadn't come to talk to Hatch about the Senate race. "Instead of butting your head against a wall, why don't you settle for a sure thing?"

"I don't know what you have in mind," responded Hatch, "but I'm sure of one thing, and that is that there is no such thing as a sure thing."

"Well, Orrin, this is as close to it as you'll ever come. I am here to offer you the nomination for the United States Congress, 2nd District. I can pretty well guarantee that you will be the only candidate to come out of the convention. What's more, our unofficial polls tell us that the incumbent Allan Howe can be beaten. He's weak and you'll tear him apart."

As events later proved, that offer may well have been the "surest thing" in Hatch's political career. A few weeks later, the Democratic incumbent, Allan Howe, was arrested by an undercover vice squad officer for allegedly soliciting sexual favors in Salt Lake City's tiny red-light district. His claim that he, too, was investigating the area—"under cover"—failed to prevent loss of his political support. In November he was trounced by Republican candidate Dan Marriott.

Nevertheless, Hatch balked. The offer was tempting, to say the least, but he had to think about it. That night—all night—he would appraise the situation in detail with a characteristic thoroughness that was to make him one of the best informed and articulate members of the U.S. Senate, and which often threatened to drive less motivated associates mad. First, there was the offer itself. Was it legitimate? Or was it an attempt to pull him off the Senate race? Did he really want to be a

Representative? Only a two-year term, and one vote among 435 other Congressmen. What about his Utah law practice? He had built this law practice from scratch, and all of his hard work was just beginning to pay off. His first year promised to bring in well over $100,000 in profit for him. And what about his family? Another move for what might well be just a two-year stay in unpleasant surroundings? They loved Utah, too. Maybe he shouldn't apply for anything right now. Perhaps it would be better to build the law practice, set down some deeper roots, and become better acquainted with the political community.

In the morning he was still undecided. That was Saturday, May 7. Sunday morning, May 8, he remained undecided. The weekend was filled with agonizing over his decision. On Monday, May 9, one day before the final filing date, he had at least reached one conclusion. "Sure thing" to the contrary, he would not run for the House of Representatives. This was not the typical politician, concerned primarily with what one must do to be elected in a particular setting; this was a man with a purpose. He would, he believed, be buried in the 435-member House, and his influence and impact on public policy there would necessarily be minimal. It was in the much smaller United States Senate where his vote would count more and his views and principles would be heard more clearly. It was as simple as that; he would "count" in the Senate. Any political expert will tell you that Senators carry far more prestige on the "Hill" than do the numerous members of the House. The responsibility of representing the entire state of Utah in the United States Senate was also appealing rather than serving a smaller segment of the population in the House of Representatives.

So that decision was made. Yet the situation of his timing still rankled. He shifted from feelings of certainty that it was "now or never," to a more common-sense attitude to "cool his heels" till next time. Never before had he vacillated so in making a decision. Never before had he shifted so rapidly from exhilaration to feelings of defeat. It bothered him that his ordinarily deliberate and crisp response to problems had eluded him. He did not at all like feeling insecure; he had too much to do with his life.

During that Monday, April 10, 1976, Orrin Hatch spoke with four people concerning his future, but with a sense of frustration over feeling that he had to rely on others to help him make this decision. Although they had discussed his probable candidacy many times, Hatch and his wife, Elaine, had a final heart-to-heart on whether or not he should file. As always, her answer was brief and to the point. "Whatever you decide, your children and I will stand with you."

That afternoon Hatch had lunch with the indefatigable State Republican Chairman Dick Richards in the Hotel Utah Coffee Shop. When Hatch repeated what he had heard too often, that if he filed he would be facing at least three popular candidates, all with extensive political experience in Washington, D.C., Richards responded emphatically, *"That's to your advantage!"*

"What?"

"That's right. Listen. This is going to be an election year of anti-Washington sentiment. It isn't just Watergate . . . and by the way, you can't tell me that Carlson's identification with the Nixon regime is going to benefit him now. There is a growing negative feeling for the whole business back in Washington. You're going to see some new faces in the Senate next year, and I'm convinced you can be one of them. I think the voter is looking for a nonpolitical type who can present an image of moral strength and who is willing to tackle the bureaucracy, the red tape, the over-regulation, and the corruption in the Washington scene. I think old faces are a detriment to the Republican Party today. You cut a fine figure. You're young and articulate. You can be a breath of fresh air to the Party, to the State, and to the Senate. If you have guts to pay the price of running hard and tough, I think you can win the nomination. And don't let anyone tell you Moss can't be beaten. He's tinged with 'Washington' just like Jack, Sherm and Des."

When they left the table, a few minutes later, Hatch had not touched his lunch. Arriving at his office a little after 1:30, he returned a call to Doug Bischoff, who was the State Senator from his District, chairman of the State Republican Candidate Recruitment Committee, and State Chairman for Reagan for President.

"Orrin," he began, "I've been trying to get in touch with you all day. I don't know what decision you have made about filing, but I want you to know that a lot of us believe you are the one to win. I know you have been under a lot of pressure to file for Congress. I say forget that. Go for the Senate."

"I have decided," responded Hatch," that I will file for the Senate nomination or not at all."

"Good! I want you to know something else. If you file, I will do everything in my power to see that you gain the nomination. It's not just for you. I honestly believe that only you can defeat Moss if he is to be defeated. It won't be easy. You're starting late, but then you know that."

Bischoff was right. Utah politics are unique. It is ordinarily essential to file application for the United States Senate at least six months to a year in advance of the mass meetings. At the mass meetings, delegates are chosen who go to the state party convention to select the nominees who will run off in the primary for Congressional and other races. Normally a minimum of six months is essential prior to these meetings for a potential candidate to find people who are dedicated enough to make an appearance at all of the legislative district mass meetings, and work to become his committed delegates at the state convention. In this process, Jack Carlson was a master. Many of the local political professionals agreed that he would probably get 70 percent of the delegate votes on the first ballot, thereby avoiding a primary runoff.

And then, of course, there was the matter of money. Campaigns do not run themselves. There have to be workers, some full-time paid; there must be television spots and appearances, radio announcements and mountains of literature, to say nothing of travel expenses. "How are you fixed for funds?" queried Bischoff.

"I don't have anything," replied Hatch with resignation. "I don't have any money, I don't have an organization, and I don't have any workers. Right now I just have myself."

"Well, that's a beginning. Do you know Ernest L. Wilkinson?"

"Yes, I've met him a number of times. I don't know if he would remember me."

"Orrin, I was just thinking—you and he believe a lot alike, and he's been known to give heavy financial support to selected candidates. Why don't you give him a call?"

It was late afternoon before Hatch reached Wilkinson on the phone at his Brigham Young University office. "Dr. Wilkinson, this is Orrin Hatch."

Silence.

"Ah, I have decided to file tomorrow as Republican Candidate for the United States Senate."

Silence.

"Ah, I was wondering if you would be kind enough to meet with me this evening for just a few minutes."

Interminable silence.

"Ah, Dr. Wilkinson . . . ?"

"If you can come to my office promptly at seven this evening, I will give you fifteen minutes."

"Thank you sir, thank . . ."

Click!

Few people felt ambivalent about Dr. Ernest L. Wilkinson. You either liked him very much or not at all. But whichever it was, you acknowledged him as a "mover." Wilkinson, already president of a multimillion dollar law firm, had been called to preside over Brigham Young University when it was still referred to as "that nice parochial school 50 miles south of the University of Utah." By the time he retired, Brigham Young University housed 25,000 students on easily one of the most beautiful and functional campuses in the United States.

Wilkinson was a conservative through and through. Throughout his tenure he fought pitched battles with government administrators who wanted BYU to accept federal funds. When informed by a member of an accrediting commission that not enough Keynsian economics was taught at BYU, Wilkinson responded that that was exactly what he intended, that free enterprise economics was to be taught there.

Wilkinson was a strong supporter of the Republican Party, and had run unsuccessfully for the United States Senate himself against Frank Moss. He was a master of turning conservative philosophy into common-sense declarations, and was a sought-after speaker all over the United States.

The first President of Brigham Young, Karl G. Maeser, once reported that if he were placed in prison he would use every means at his command to escape, but that if he drew a chalk line about himself on the sidewalk and gave his word not to step over it, he would not. The day Ernest L. Wilkinson became President of Brigham Young University, the "chalk line" became his symbol. Therefore, Hatch knew if he could get Wilkinson to promise his support, that support would be whole-hearted.

Yet, like every human being, Wilkinson was not without flaws. "I am afraid," he once said, "that I am a rather poor judge of horse-flesh." He had at times unnecessarily alienated certain faculty members who did not deserve his suspicion. And he had supported others who in one way or another let him down. "At times," said one of his close associates, "Dr. Wilkinson has taken some men at their word who didn't deserve his trust, and has been suspicious of others without cause." So, in this the twilight of his remarkable life, he had grown skeptical of his ability to discern true men from false.

This was the man whom Orrin Hatch was going to ask to provide the initial funds for his first step into politics. Little wonder he was nervous as he took Wilkinson's handshake.

"You're two minutes late."

"Ah, yes sir . . ."

The conversation was to have lasted 13 minutes, but it continued for nearly 2 hours.

Questions, questions, covering points of specific legislation to broad philosophical concepts. Never had Hatch felt his innermost thoughts and beliefs so penetrated by another human being. All the while Wilkinson's steel eyes never left him.

Finally, Wilkinson settled back in his chair. "Well, you say all the right things. But I've heard this kind of talk before. I can't remember a candidate I've backed who hasn't sooner or later disappointed me." He hesitated a moment. "Are you a man of principle? Are you a man of courage?"

Now it was Hatch's turn. He leaned forward in his chair and fixed his eyes on Wilkinson. "Yes, sir. I *am* a man of principle. I come from a humble background, with parents who taught me that a man's honor and his word are the most important things he possesses. I have had to work hard for everything I have attained. I appreciate hard work. I know the value of money, and I have never knowingly taken advantage of another human being. I spent two years of my life as a missionary of our Church, and I live according to its precepts.

"I feel as strongly as you do that our politicians are leading this great country into disaster because they either have no principles or espouse counter-productive ones. I believe I can make a great contribution as a United States Senator, and because I have had to be courageous all my life, I know I will be able to stand on principle regardless of the pressure."

Hatch hesitated a moment, then threw in the "kicker."

"Dr. Wilkinson, I know how much you wanted to be a United States Senator. Had you been elected I believe you would have made a difference. If I am elected, and I believe I can be, I will do what you would have done. We believe in the same principles, and we are both fighters. There is no one you could support who would better represent you."

Hatch hoped that Wilkinson would sense the sincerity that prompted his emotional response. When it was over, Wilkinson replied in a subdued voice, "I believe you have told me the truth."

When Hatch left the Wilkinson office at nearly 9:30 P.M. he had attained the former university president's unqualified endorsement, and snug in his pocket was a check for $2,000 (the limit imposed by the federal Election Commission on contributions from husband and wife in a federal election).

It was not until some time later that Hatch learned Dr. Wilkinson was under heavy pressure to endorse Jack Carlson, and that his daughter was not only a supporter of Carlson, but would give his nominating speech at the State Convention. Evidently, his meeting with Hatch had more than impressed the old gentleman with his possibilities.

When Wilkinson had told Hatch he would give him his support, Hatch saw that his authoritative countenance, so evident during the first part of their conversation, had suddenly become benign, even sad. In his eyes Hatch thought he saw a feeling of insecurity, undoubtedly over whether he had made the right choice, or whether his old nemesis, his measure of a man, would once again disappoint him.

Wilkinson had run for the United States Senate in 1964, a bad year for Republicans. Wilkinson followed Goldwater's coattails to defeat. It was one of the few times the State of Utah has gone Democratic in a Presidential race. He had planned to run again in 1970, but suffered a series of severe heart attacks. Now he was old. Soon he would die and he knew it. But this bright, intense young man who never smiled had caught his interest. Perhaps, he dared hope, he had found a candidate who espoused correct principles as he saw them and had the integrity to hold them above politics. Perhaps, he thought, this young upstart could, with his help, accomplish the dream he himself had longed for in vain.

As Hatch drove home he made a solemn vow to himself that Dr. Wilkinson would never have cause to regret backing him. That night, if he had not before, Hatch adopted the "chalk line."

Early on May 10, the last filing day, Hatch called the party official who had encouraged him to run for the House rather than the Senate.

He said, "I'm going for the big one!"

"It's your funeral."

"Well, send flowers."

"Orrin . . ."

"Yes?"

"Good luck. Really . . . . Good luck."

The walk from the parking lot to the office of the Secretary of State reminded Hatch of the feeling he used to get as a boy going to the dentist. To make matters worse the media were there. Hatch was very nervous. He went through the motions of filing numbly. He did not have the air of a professional politician that day. Once back in the parking lot he wondered if what he had mumbled to the press would come out all right over television that night and in the morning papers. He was certain he had appeared the hayseed.

This fear of appearing unprofessional stayed with him far into the campaign. His campaign workers despaired of his "stiffness" that hid his typical warmth and gregariousness and tried unsuccessfully for some time to get him to "smile a little, for hell's sake." One of his campaign advisors remarked with frustration that his picture on the first campaign brochure made him look like "Beelzebub."

At any rate, the great adventure had begun. The next few days were frantic for Hatch. With the money donated by Dr. Wilkinson and a few other close friends, Hatch opened up a small office in the Continental Bank building in downtown Salt Lake City, and had the first brochure printed with his "Beelzebub" picture on it. Within three days he had set up a phone bank, and a friend, who was a prominent *Democrat,* sent him a logo he had prepared for use in the campaign with the stipulation that his name never be revealed for having done so.

Hatch was greatly relieved, however, when he read the news items reporting his candidacy and the remarks he had made at the state attorney general's office. In the *Salt Lake Tribune,* under the caption "Last Hopefuls Sign in for Spot on Ballot," Utah residents read that among other last-minute filers, "A 42-year old trial lawyer, Orrin G. Hatch, calling himself a 'nonpolitician,' filed in the crowded field seeking the Republican Senate nomination to run against Senator Frank E. Moss, unopposed in his party in bidding for a fourth term."

"The old-line party professionals tell me I have no chance to win," Hatch was quoted, "or even to come out of the party state convention. But I'm used to impossible odds. That's the story of my life. . . . We need new faces, new blood, new thinking. It is time to turn out the politicians in Congress who have contributed to the failure of recent years."

Hatch was also featured, looking more like a funeral parlor director than an aspiring candidate, in an article from the Salt Lake *Deseret News* under the caption "Lawyer Seeks Seat in Senate." Again, after describing himself as a nonpolitician to the press, Hatch had launched an attack on the Washington politicians and "bureaucrats." The *Deseret News* picked up his remarks in some detail. "I have spent most of my professional life fighting the growing oppressive federal bureaucracy," he was quoted, "mostly for the working people." He flayed those "expedient politicians," who were "too busy running for President, building power bases, or feathering their own nests to provide the moral leadership this nation needs. . . ." Hatch was delighted that the article ended with his appeal to the Republican party structure: "We need new faces, new blood, new thinking, with new emphasis on honesty and integrity in Washington. I appeal to all GOP members to keep an open mind on the issues and judge the candidates on their capacity to win in November against incumbents who are part of the problem."

Finally, two days later, Hatch was pleasantly surprised to find himself featured in a special section of the *Deseret News,* "Today in the West." This coverage he had not anticipated. Although his late filing had disadvantages too numerous to contemplate, it had given him a tremendous lift in exposure. Since he was the only Senatorial candidate to file at the last minute, he was news. There was no way that Hatch could have purchased this much-needed exposure in the newspapers of the State.

Hatch was deluged with phone calls, letters, notes and even telegrams. The response was overwhelmingly supportive of his remarks against the "bureaucrats and politicians." A number of the most influential Republicans sent laudatory notes.

So, with a feeling of great relief, Orrin Hatch judged that he had not come off too badly in his first "appearance" before the public. However, in a few weeks, on May 17, he was scheduled to speak at the first county convention in Brigham City in Utah's northern Box Elder County, where he would appear with the other Republican senatorial candidates. He would no longer be the star of the hour, as he was in the coverage of his last-minute registration. The "beginner" would now be up against the professionals, the really polished and respected politicians. When asked if he felt like Daniel going into a den of lions, he replied, "No, just the opposite—like a lion going into a den of Daniels."

Of one thing Hatch was certain; he had hit a responsive nerve with regard to public sentiment concerning the Washington, D.C. scene. He was, in fact, reaffirming what was taking place all over the country. In effect, millions of Americans were looking for someone just like Hatch—a political virgin with class and integrity. Watergate, the tragedy of Vietnam, energy shortfalls, escalating inflation, the meteoric growth of government combined with its apparent inability to solve the nation's problems, the scandals involving Wayne Hays and Wilbur Mills—all of these had combined to engender a wholesale loss of confidence in the national government by a substantial percentage of the American people. The characteristic American optimism was beginning to give way to cynicism, directed toward the federal government. In a number of campaigns, past experience in Washington would cease to be an asset and would become a definite liability.

A Gallup poll conducted in the spring of 1976 indicated that most of the American people were unhappy with the way the politicians were running the government. Not a single presidential candidate appeared to inspire faith and confidence in a majority of Americans. Nearly half of those questioned in the poll stated they would prefer to have someone outside the world of politics become a candidate.

It may well have been this aversion to politicians, lack of confidence in government, and a longing for moral restoration among a substantial number of American voters that later put the "outsider" from

Plains, Georgia, in the White House. As James David Barber reported in the March, 1980 issue of *Psychology Today*, "Governor Jimmy Carter emerged preaching the common American values of decency and compassion and honesty. A nation ready for moral revival voted him in."

Looking back, there seems little doubt that this powerful sentiment was a major factor in Hatch's rise from obscurity to election. As it was, Hatch appeared as a nonpolitician, unblemished by service to the suspect federal government. He came across as a decent human being who could be a vanguard for the public in fighting government corruption, encroachment and usurpation.

Hatch was quick to perceive the connection, and it was not difficult for him to play it for all it was worth, since it did not involve a wrench to his conscience. Just prior to the first mass meeting at Brigham City on May 17, Hatch took out an ad in a number of local newspapers under the title of "Let's Win For A Change." The ad featured a picture of Hatch with his wife and six children. His wife and some of the children were actually smiling, although he, of course, was not. Beginning with "Your family and mine deserve better representation," he emphasized the line that was to carry him through the primaries and the general election. "He believes Utahns want a change away from big government and the ever-increasing domination of our lives by the federal bureaucracy. As one of Utah's leading lawyers, he understands the system and what it takes to make changes. He has the youth, vigor, experience, integrity and an intense desire to improve the quality of life for Utahns. HE IS THE ONLY CANDIDATE NOT ASSOCIATED WITH THE WASHINGTON ESTABLISHMENT."

During the hiatus between Hatch's filing and the first County Convention, Hatch worked desperately to set up some sort of campaign organization and to raise some much-needed money. Both were difficult tasks, and Hatch brought into his organization good friends, but none with extended professional political experience. Their loyalty and good intentions were not enough, and Hatch's loyalty in turn to his friends later made vital changes very difficult and drained Hatch's emotions.

In the beginning Salt Lake attorney Grey Nokes served as campaign manager and advisor for Hatch. Since there was no money to pay a campaign manager, Nokes had to keep his law practice going as well. He nearly worked his way into a hospital bed. Another friend who offered his help to Hatch was Frank Bailey, a retired Air Force officer, whose exactness and genius at coordinating the campaign office made him indispensable. Retired army Colonel Bill Barr and his wife Ellen joined the Hatch organization and worked tirelessly as Hatch's advance team. They prepared the tables, booths, banners and other paraphernalia at the convention sites prior to the mass meetings. Then, as time went on, other friends joined Hatch's team, such as David Fisher, a BYU Law School student who also worked as an advance man for Reagan. He had been on the campaign staff of Congressman Burton Talcott in Salinas, California. Bill Pingree, also on the Utah "Reagan for President" team, offered his services.

On the night Hatch's filing was announced over television, Flora Green Haddow was watching the evening news. When Hatch's candidacy was discussed she put her hands to her cheeks in surprise. She called to her son, Mac. In a few minutes Mac was on the telephone to Hatch. This proved to be an important call for both men.

The Haddows had been friends of the Hatch family in Pittsburgh. Throughout his early youth, Mac had turned to Orrin's father Jesse as a father-image. Mac's stepfather was an alcoholic, whose affliction left him little compassion for his wife's children, and Jesse Hatch was the only real father Mac ever knew. The tough union lather gave Mac a father's love, counseled with him, saw that he went to church on Sunday, from time to time stuffed a few dollars into the pocket of his scruffy Levis, and more than once cuffed him on the side of the head to temper his natural unruliness.

Flora Green Haddow had brought her family to Salt Lake City in 1968, a year preceding the immigration of Orrin Hatch. Mac began his freshman year at Brigham Young University but could not settle down. One day he walked off the campus, drove home, packed a quick bag, and went back to Pittsburgh. There he joined the United Steel Workers and went to work in the steel plants of Pittsburgh. That was in 1968–69, years of crippling strikes for Pittsburgh.

The Haddows had always been Democrats, so Mac quite naturally lent his energy and support to Democratic politics in Pittsburgh. Yet as time went by he became increasingly disenchanted with the wholesale corruption inherent in the unholy marriage of unions and the Democratic party in Pittsburgh. Finally, in disgust, he turned his allegiance to the political maverick Pete Flaherty. Flaherty, a reform-minded man of action, had been defeated as a candidate for Mayor in the Democratic primary of 1969 and had run as an independent in an unheard-of attempt to break the Democratic party-labor machine. His call for support to help clean up Pittsburgh city government brought Mac Haddow to his banner with all the enthusiasm the young steel worker could muster.

This was one of the greatest experiences of Haddow's life. He saw politics in its rawest form, learned the rudimentary forms of campaign organization and experienced the fundamentals of tough campaigning. Almost overnight he became politically "street-wise." This left him with a healthy skepticism about human nature tempered with the ability to recognize the worth of such men as Flaherty. But most of all the experience added dimension to his life. He was no longer a young man without purpose. His baptism into the fire of politics had taken place in the toughest of environments. He learned to stand, to commit himself to a cause in the face of overwhelming odds, even physical threats. (One evening two fellow union toughs attempted to "convince" Haddow that he was campaigning for the wrong side. The confrontation left the 230-pound Haddow with a badly sprained hand, but his adversaries crawled away, each with a broken jaw.)

When Mac Haddow returned to Brigham Young University the following year, he was a different young man than the drop-out who had once fled to the steel factories of Pittsburgh in an attempt to escape the commitment needed for academic success. As a freshman and again as a junior, he took second place in the National Forensic Society tournament and became National Champion in Persuasive Speaking. Also, as a junior he became National Champion in Parliamentary Debate.

Hatch, a complete newcomer to politics, was not aware of the worth Haddow could bring to his campaign. He only knew that a friend had offered to help, and it made him feel good to have Mac on board. Hatch put him in charge of coordinating his campaign in Utah County, but soon Haddow had moved to Hatch's head office in Salt Lake City. Finally, he moved to the directorship of the campaign.

Quite naturally Hatch found that raising money was very difficult. Most of the key Republican donors who were not already committed were holding on to their money until the State Convention had made its choice; some would wait until the primary contest, if there were to be one, was over. Hatch learned what so many inexperienced candidates have discovered—that the early money is the toughest to come by, and that there is often a wide margin between promises of financial support and the actual appearance of the funds. Hatch had to draw upon a campaign labor market that was all dried up; most of the party firebrands were already committed to other candidates. He would receive no help from the political "groupies" who always surface in the campaign years, for they too had been incorporated into other campaigns. There would be precious little help, personally or financially, available to a "Johnny-come-lately" candidate with so little hope of winning. Hatch was in the unenviable position of not only having to pick up support among what was left of the uncommitted, but actually having to change the minds of the already committed, if he was to have any chance at all.

Setting up a campaign organization is a difficult task under the best of conditions—but to attempt to set up a Senatorial Campaign organization with barely two months time before the candidate selection process at the State party convention was madness. The hundreds of representatives at the Convention who actually select the candidates had to be contacted personally by the candidate and his campaign staff.

In Presidential election years, such as 1976, the state primary conventions also select presidential electors, delegates and alternates to the party's national convention, and a national committeeman and committeewoman. So 1976 was to be an important political year in Utah. The fact that it was also a presidential year was eventually to prove crucial for Hatch, but for the time being he faced at least three other well-organized candidates who had been working from six months to a year to find potential delegates to the county mass meetings. And the State convention was two months away.

Jack Carlson had been particularly active in preparing for the mass meetings and the convention. He was well established among top party leaders, had a substantial early following, probably a majority of the delegates, and had developed a campaign organization that had already been functioning for some months. Many of those most knowledgeable about Utah politics expected that he would take the needed 70 percent of the delegates at the state convention on the first ballot. Generally, the media people expected the race for Senator to be between Carlson and Moss.

Obviously Hatch's strategy had to rule out winning the convention vote outright, or keeping Carlson from taking first place. His first hurdles were to: number one, keep Carlson from gaining the necessary 70 percent delegate vote; and, number two, beat out the other candidates for *second place*. With the two-candidate rule, Hatch would then have another shot for the nomination by the voters in the primaries.

To make matters worse, Salt Lake City's television Channel 7 (KUED) invited all the Republican Senatorial candidates to a "debate" on May 14. Hatch was not going to have the time he had expected to prepare to meet the other candidates. Throughout the presentations, Hatch was nervous and uncomfortable. Time and again, when he should have been concentrating, he found himself studying the other candidates. The only one he had met was Carlson.

Hatch had come to the studio with a somewhat negative impression of Des Barker, but after the debate was over, he saw Barker as an intelligent, impressive man, with a facile mind and a professional bearing.

Sherm Lloyd also impressed him. His past experience as a United States Congressman made him appear knowledgeable indeed in his responses and observations. But Hatch reminded himself that Lloyd was facing certain drawbacks. First, of course, was his association with Washington D.C. Also, Lloyd was 63 years of age. The epithet "One-Term Sherm" had been circulated widely throughout the State. Also, the former Congressman had an image of being haughty and arrogant. He had offended a number of former campaign workers who had now cast their support elsewhere. Hatch believed the accumulation of these handicaps would preclude Lloyd's winning the nomination. Ironically, as the campaign progressed Hatch gained immense respect for Lloyd. For whatever else Sherm Lloyd was not, he *was* a man of integrity. He was a man of truth who told all people at different meetings the same story. He simply would not lie or hedge a statement to gain political advantage.

It was, after all, Jack Carlson who had impressed Hatch as the candidate with the greatest chance to win. Carlson was playing it "cool." He apparently believed that he had acquired enough pledged delegates to win at the State Convention. Therefore, his style was dictated by this belief. The object was to "hold the fort," emphasize his own qualities and experience, and avoid mistakes.

Hatch, on the other hand, with an almost "born again" zeal, was out to make a difference in government. Political style did not interest him. He came to convince, to expound, to convert. He did not think of attempting first to please his audience, and when he did—with increasing regularity as time passed—it was incidental to his message that big government had ceased to be a servant of the people and had become their enemy, that unless Leviathan was soon cut down to size, the people would lose their freedom, and that those so-called "servants of the people" who were contributing to this enslavement ought to be turned out of office.

The debate itself on Channel 7 turned out to be more of an introduction of the candidates to the television audience than a debate. Hatch was nervous, too stiff, too serious. He certainly did not outdistance his political rivals that night, *but neither did they bury him.* When Hatch first appeared at the television studio, obviously ill at ease, he sensed, perhaps inaccurately, that the other candidates looked at him with an air of haughtiness which seemed to carry with it an unspoken interrogatory, "What on earth are *you* doing here?"

However, when the affair was over, several in attendance in the studio remarked that the other candidates seemed a bit shaken. Apparently they had, that evening, developed an incipient respect for Hatch. But if the other candidates appeared a bit shaken, then they simply matched the appearance of candidate Orrin Hatch. It was not until morning that he became convinced that the inability of his opponents to annihilate him politically over television was a major victory. No, the consensus of his friends would not go so far as to say he had won the debate, but he had *held his own* on his first outing with some highly experienced and smoothly polished professionals. For Hatch this was an important milestone. He realized that his opponents were just human beings after all, and that he could challenge them in extemporaneous speaking or debate without being embarrassed. This revelation did a great deal for his confidence. At the very next candidate meeting in Box Elder County on May 17, Orrin Hatch became a true challenger.

Hatch's skeletal campaign organization had been able to get his original brochure to a large number of the county delegates before the meeting, and his office counted over 60 telephone responses, all positive, the day of the meeting. This was very encouraging to Hatch. Nevertheless he faced the Herculean and necessary task of attempting to personally meet and talk to each of the county delegates and those new state delegates that were to be selected at the county conventions.

The mass meeting in Box Elder County began the exhausting round of 29 county conventions with 29 candidates for various offices. Each candidate was given only two minutes to speak before the county convention. Ostensibly, the idea was to have the candidates appear before the 2,512 state delegates in competition for their support and vote. In fact, many of the delegates were already committed to Hatch's opponents who had been campaigning for months. Many of them were friends of certain candidates who had attended the mass meetings and conventions with the express purpose of supporting additional delegate votes to their candidate. Carlson, Lloyd, and Barker had been working on getting committed delegates elected at mass meetings for some time.

Hatch finally came to the conclusion that he had no way of even meeting all of the delegates. He had to devise a worthwhile method of contacting them all, but he was at a loss to know how.

As the county conventions wore on, however, Hatch began to feel that his two-minute discourses were making some impact. He sensed he was on the upswing. He doggedly kept at his original anti-politician, anti-Washington line. He took personal pride in that he believed fervently in every statement he uttered. While speaking before an audience of students and faculty at the University of Utah, he was asked his stand on abortion. His statement against abortion and especially federal funding of abortion came through loud and clear—and he lost a lot of potential votes that day.

But he was making converts elsewhere. In the last analysis, if one rules out timing and luck, Hatch's greatest asset was himself. He had a charismatic personality ensconsed in a slim, tall, masculine body, topped off by a handsome face, an attractive sprig of grey hair over his forehead, and a fluent tongue in his mouth. All of this which, in giving him a striking appearance, served to accentuate his obviously heart-felt message to his audiences. It was, in fact, not only what they wanted to hear, but it was presented in a way that stirred them. The other candidates began to sound flat, even tedious, in comparison. Hatch, after starting out slow, soon began to outclass his opponents in presentation.

In the beginning he had not realized how difficult it would be to articulate his feelings. A belief in certain principles, even strongly held, will remain sort of an amorphous mass of sentiments until it is verbalized, and extensively. At first, Hatch's remarks did not adequately express his intense feelings. Taking his ideology from sentiment to coordinated, precise and coherent verbalization was far more difficult than he had imagined. But as this became easier, so too did his belief and confidence in what he was saying. There developed a blending of thought, words and dedication to the ideals he expressed. Just as linguist and United States Senator from California Sam Hayakawa wrote in his *Language in Thought and Action,* before a person can make a thought truly part of his value system he must articulate it, verbalize it so that it becomes a commitment to that principle or value. So, with each opportunity to express himself, Hatch became increasingly able to touch his audience with a moving, consistent, and flowing masterpiece of speech.

Soon he began to make inroads in that group of delegates who were uncommitted or fence-straddling. Then, amazingly, he began to *convert* (in every sense of the word), delegates who had previously been committed to the other candidates. In Utah County, Mac Haddow had been working on a close friend and teacher who was a committed delegate to one of the other candidates, but to no avail. Then that teacher heard Hatch at one of the candidate meetings. He went to hear him again at another meeting. At the Republican Party Convention he voted for Hatch. Zenda Hull, Vice Chairman of the Republican State Party and a fan of Jack Carlson, switched her allegiance to Hatch after hearing him speak but once. She was very open in her belief that he would be the next United States Senator from Utah.

The entrance of Hatch into the 1976 campaign had brought a new dimension into a field dominated by experienced association with Washington, D.C. None of Hatch's political opponents was prepared to face opposition from an inspiring non-politician who would be able to capitalize on an anti-Washington mood among the voters. While Hatch's lack of experience and paucity of political credentials would ordinarily be a detriment to the perceived legitimacy of his candidacy, they had now become an asset.

By attacking the Washington monolith this new and exciting political candidate put each of his Republican rivals—and later Senator Moss—in a defensive posture they could not control. It was the devastating impact of this posture, suddenly foisted upon them by an increasingly believable and untarnished candidate, with which they were unable to deal effectively.

Suddenly, the ordinarily positive points each could make on his political experience and expertise turned sour. As Carlson's campaign continued to emphasize his political and administrative background, the message, in "ordinary" times a very positive input, proved to be a detriment to him.

Hatch increasingly came across as a fresh and competent alternative to a Washington scene that had become suspect to a great number of voters.

With each new convention under his belt, Hatch began to feel more competent in his presentations. After each presentation he made a special effort to get down on the convention floor and shake hands with all the people he could. While of course this was good political strategy, it was not contrived; Hatch loved people. When after the Morgan County convention Hatch learned that all of that county's delegates had decided to vote for him at the State Convention, he was delighted, and the word now began to spread through the unofficial Republican party grapevine that this bright, fresh, appealing nonpolitician might just be the only one who could beat Moss in the general election.

Still, the impossibility of the Hatch organization to contact all of the Republican delegates personally, given the time constraints, rankled. Day after day and night after night Hatch searched his mind for a means to reach the delegates in a personal way.

Hatch had noticed that at all of the conventions the meticulous Carlson taped his own talks for later review and critique by him and his associates. One evening, as the delegate talks were in process, and Hatch happened to again notice Carlson's tape recorder, an idea came to him. He could hardly contain his emotions. He *could* reach all of the delegates to the State Convention; not personally, but via the next thing to it—tape recordings.

The next morning Hatch wrote out a 14-minute speech covering his beliefs and feelings. That afternoon he recorded his presentation at Bonneville Recordings in a half-hour sitting. Then, 2,512 cassette tapes were made of the recording. The Hatch campaign organization had red, white and blue labels printed with Hatch's picture (unsmiling again and looking as if he had just stepped in something). The following morning the tapes, together with a parchment transcript of the tape, was sent to every delegate. All of this was accomplished in about three days, at a cost of a little over $3,000 of borrowed money.

The response was electrifying, with hundreds of favorable responses from delegates all over the State. There is no doubt that what later became known among some of Hatch's opponents as "the tape connection" proved important. It is doubtful that the two-minute talks at the conventions would have given him sufficient delegate votes at the State Convention.

In spite of his late entrance, Hatch had some things going for him. First was his appearance (in spite of his unsmiling pictures). Wherever he spoke, he came across as bright, articulate, honest, and attractively masculine. His approach as a nonpolitician and antagonist of the Washington establishment was also an important factor. To be sure, the other candidates took their swipes at the bureaucrats but somehow it did not carry the weight nor ring with the authority of this modern David standing before Goliath. Finally, of course, was "the tape connection." Soon, the idea was being discussed in political circles all over the country. But most important, Hatch was informed that his fellow Republican challengers were very upset over the response given the tapes.

It was at the "Meet the Candidates Night" at a high school in the city of Pleasant Grove, just a few miles north of Provo, that Hatch caught another element that was to greatly influence the future of the campaigns. Each of the candidates was asked whom he supported for the presidency, Ford or Reagan. The first candidates hedged and there was not much response from the audience. When Hatch was asked, he responded, "I give my unqualified support to Ronald Reagan, and I believe that, if he is nominated, he will be our next President." The audience broke out in wild applause.

The last to respond was Sherm Lloyd. He had heard the applause, but he stated, "I know what you want to hear; I could tell you I was for Ronald Reagan if I wanted to pander for your vote. I have served in the United States Congress with Jerry Ford. I saw him come into Congress each day well prepared to do a good job. He is a good friend and a good President. I give him my support.''

At the end of the debate Hatch worked his way through the crowd and took Sherm Lloyd by the arm, leading him aside. ''I would like to shake your hand,'' he said emphatically, ''Ever since this campaign began I have witnessed evidence of your complete integrity. You are a great man and I am proud to appear at these meetings night after night with such as you. I am only sorry we have to be combatants at this time.''

From that point on Hatch and Lloyd developed a friendship. After Lloyd had lost the primary convention vote he contacted Hatch with an offer to help. In the last days of the general election Lloyd made several strong endorsements of Hatch over the radio. He was also responsible for energizing the liberal wing of the Republican party in support of Hatch by insisting that Hatch, while a strong conservative, was not an ideologue, but a man of principle, and that he was ''his own man.''

After the Pleasant Grove meeting, the State Chairman for Reagan for President, Doug Bischoff, told Hatch, ''You did the right thing tonight by endorsing Reagan. We are convinced that Utah will give all of its delegates to Reagan at the State Convention. For the most part this is 'Reagan Country.''' During the rest of the county conventions Hatch made it a point to speak in favor of Governor Reagan. The response was always overwhelming. Not only did it gain him support among the many audiences, but also secured him the backing of the top Reagan supporters in the State, many of whom were prominent in the Republican party.

Hatch had now added the final ingredient to a campaign that had developed piecemeal and almost by accident; one which he found compatible, for he really did support Governor Reagan for President.

The Hatch campaign organization, however, was having its problems. Apprehension, loss of sleep and overwork gradually began to take their toll. Spats and arguments erupted, especially when it appeared that things were not going well. Hatch wanted to step in and ''lay down the law.'' Perhaps he should have, but he never did. He loved them all so much for their loyalty and dedication he could not bring himself to be critical. It was this conflict within his own ranks (however natural) that proved the greatest drain on Hatch's emotions. Hatch was working from 18 to 20 hours a day, and as the campaign wore on, it began to tell on him. He was exhausted most of the time, more from emotional than physical strain, and was having great difficulty in getting ''up'' for some of the meetings. At the Salt Lake County convention he was placed in such an inconspicuous place on the platform that it was impossible for him to meet or be seen shaking hands with the two honored guests:

Senator Paul Laxalt from Nevada, and Utah's Senator Jake Garn. Hatch became very upset. When he noticed that his hands were beginning to shake, he forced himself to calm down. One day he would take such setbacks stoically, but now they put additional stress on an already strained nervous system.

Finally, the day of the State Convention arrived. That day, only nervous energy and sheer determination kept Hatch on his feet. He was perspiring profusely and was nauseated. He shook his head when he compared the sophisticated booths of his opponents with the one Colonel Bill Barr had put up for Hatch. With virtually no money, Barr had done his best. Hatch's booth looked like it might have once been a Shriner's Club parade float—red, white, and blue, with bright colored streamers. While Carlson's booth had instant play-back video machines with tapes of Carlson speaking in montage sequences, Hatch had to yell over the din to crowds sometimes numbering over a hundred that gathered around to hear him. Several times his voice gave way. He was not at all sure he was going to be able to give his five-minute talk that afternoon before the whole convention.

The other Senatorial candidates provided food, hors d'oeuvres, and other expensive delicacies. In Hatch's booth they gave out popsicles with a little inscription on them—"Lick Moss, vote Hatch." Someone handed a popsicle to Hatch. When he saw the inscription on it he smacked his forehead with the heel of his hand and blurted in agony, "Good grief!"

As the evening wore on Hatch's nausea increased. He terrified himself by imagining his getting up to speak before the delegates and throwing up on the dais. He had been scheduled as the last to speak among the senatorial candidates, which gave him some comfort. At least, he reasoned, he would have a chance to rest, regain his voice, calm his nerves, and tailor his speech, if need be, by what the others would have said. When he was informed at the last minute that he had been switched from last to first—he would be first and Carlson would be last—he found it extremely difficult to hold his temper.

By this time he was fighting off a sense of doom. Ernest L. Wilkinson had expressed a desire to give Hatch's nominating speech. Many of Hatch's workers tried to caution him against Wilkinson. "Wilkinson is controversial," they told him, "and you can't afford that at this point. Get someone moderate, better, even non-political, but not Wilkinson!"

But Hatch had decided to go with Wilkinson. It was Wilkinson who had launched his campaign, Wilkinson who had expressed such genuine faith in him. So, whatever the outcome, the grand old gentleman would give the nominating speech.

As it turned out, Wilkinson gave an outstanding speech. As it also turned out, this was his last hurrah. Soon he would pass beyond the veil. It was, perhaps, fitting that his last political oratory should be the nomination of a young fighter in whom he saw the staying power and the same tenacity and guts that had characterized his own life.

The seconding speech was given by the beautiful Alice Buehner, a former Mrs. America. She, too, was well received. Then Orrin Hatch, reaching for that reservoir of inner strength that had so often in his young life given him an extra boost of courage and energy; walked boldly to the stand, grasped the podium firmly, and for five minutes issued a speech and a challenge—forcefully, articulately, and without a stammer or a pause—just as if his knees weren't shaking.

Whoever had changed the order of speakers had not done Carlson a favor. By the time he stood to speak, the convention was literally worn out. Few heard him. Hatch's speech had no peer that night.

Finally, after several false starts with the electronic machinery, the delegate vote was tallied. As expected, the highly regarded Carlson won the total vote with 930. However, Hatch garnered an amazing 778 delegate votes. Then followed Sherman Lloyd with 442, Desmond Barker with 250 and Clinton Miller with 28. Jack Carlson had failed to get 70 percent of the delegate vote. He would have to face Orrin Hatch in the primaries to see who would be the Republican standardbearer to face Senator Frank Moss in November.

Chapter 2
THE CONTENDER

Hatch left the convention numb with exhaustion. By the time he got to his home he had difficulty remembering what had happened between the announcement of the official delegate tally and his stepping out of a car in his own driveway. Without a word he went into his room and collapsed on the bed; after which, of course, he lay awake all night. At three in the morning he shuffled into the den and watched the last of the late-night movies. He was being baptized into the world of politics.

It wasn't so much the fact that he had ended his first round in politics $13,000 in debt that pulled at his "innards." Orrin Hatch was, and remains to this day, a purist, indeed, the most pristine kind of idealist. His kind of idealism frustrates those who would compromise on principle infuriates the crass realists who see mankind from its worst side. Hatch and his kind are easily hurt, hurt deeply, when people, friends, public figures, don't measure up. To those who wheel and deal he appears arrogant and uncompromising, his sincerity mistaken for pride, his humility for self-righteousness. It was inevitable that Hatch would become both a loved and a hated Senator in Washington.

An example of his stubborn reliance on principle can be taken from his first job offer straight out of law school. Law school was no cinch for him. He and his wife of a few months, Elaine, lived on his parents' place a few miles outside of Pittsburgh in what was once a chicken coop. Orrin and his father remodeled it, plastered the inside, put a one-room heating unit inside to make a remarkably cozy two room chicken-coop cottage, in spite of the fact that the Pittsburgh humidity turned the walls black in the winter. On the coldest nights, the sewer line would freeze and clog, and the room without the stove became cold and clammy.

Upon graduating from Brigham Young University, Orrin had been granted a full honor scholarship to attend the University of Pittsburgh Law School. Along with his scholarship, he was able to make ends meet by working summers as a lather with his father, a job foreman. At first his fellow lathers resented Orrin, certain that he was hired only because he was the foreman's son. They did not realize that Orrin had been a master at the trade since he was 16. Soon his speed, strength, and professionalism, along with his good-natured tolerance of their ribbing and teasing, gained him their respect and friendship.

During his last year in law school, Hatch's family had grown to the point that he needed additional money. He secured a job as an all-night desk attendant in a girls' dormitory at the University. He was the only young male so trusted. Having once been a missionary, dormitory officials considered him a minister. During this time he averaged about four hours of sleep a day. His greatest battle that last year was to stay awake in class.

He graduated with honors. It was a great day for his wife—and for his three children born while he was in law school. They were going to get out of the chicken coop. It was also a great day for Orrin. The largest defense firm in the city of Pittsburgh, asked him to come in for an interview.

From the outset Hatch was informed that the firm wanted him, that he had been checked out pretty thoroughly and appeared to have the style, ability, and appearance they were looking for.

Difficulties arose when he was asked to sign an agreement not to compete, however. This agreement would have prohibited him from competing for any of the clients of the firm for five years should he ever resign. Hatch stiffened his back. He told them that he believed such an agreement to be unethical. Now, the agreement may not have been legally unethical at all; and many prominent law firms around the country may have such agreements. But that made no difference to Hatch. He thought such agreements were *morally* unethical—therefore he wouldn't budge.

The two partners were speechless for a moment. "Why, Mr. Hatch," one partner broke the embarrassing silence, "every attorney in the firm has signed this agreement."

"Really," responded Hatch. "Well, I have to tell you that were I in your shoes I wouldn't hire an attorney who would be willing to sign such a contract."

The law firm wouldn't budge either. Professionals to the end, his interviewers did not close the door. Hatch was asked to think it over, talk with some of his law professors, then give them a call the next day. He agreed, but he already knew what his answer would be. He walked out of the plush law offices demoralized and frustrated. He rather aimlessly walked up Grant Street, past the City and County Building. What was he going to tell his wife? Oh, there were other law firms, but few, very few, like that great firm.

He stopped for a moment on the corner by the City and County Building wondering what he would do next. At that moment someone called his name.

"Orrin, Orrin, is that you? What a miracle! I have been trying to reach you all day, and here I bump into you in the center of town and you looking like a lost puppy."

The man behind the voice was John Chaffo, Hatch's law school preceptor and a great admirer of Hatch. "Good news, Orrin. I got a call early this morning from the law firm of Pringle, Bredin and Martin. They are very impressed with what they have heard about you and have asked me to bring you in for an interview—any time, just any time. This is the firm for you. They are the most ethical, tough, trial lawyers in Pittsburgh. It's a very small firm but one of the most respected, and one of the oldest, if not the oldest, in the city."

Incredibly enough, that very afternoon Hatch was being interviewed by three of the partners of Pringle, Bredin and Martin. When that interview was over he was guided into the office of Samuel W. Pringle, the man who made the final choice on appointments. Pringle talked to Hatch for about a minute and a half. He then turned to the others and said, "Hire this man."

Now, no one could convince Hatch that everything that had happened that day was pure coincidence. Hatch would tell you that when you do the right thing, the honorable thing, things always turn out all right. It is often difficult to deal with such a man.

So it was that after the Republican Convention, Hatch experienced ambivalent feelings. His sense of victory was dimmed. In his idealism he was more hurt than exhausted. He did not like the political world into which he had plunged. He did not enjoy battling fellow Republicans. And he didn't at all like being "barbed" by them. As a historian and political scientist, however, he knew he would have to get used to it. He reminded himself that American politics were adversary politics, made rough and tumble under the protection of the many freedoms the system enjoyed. Carlson was no second-stringer. It was going to be a tough campaign. "Don't take it personally," Frank Bailey encouraged Hatch, "it's all part of the game.'' Hatch was reminded of Harry Truman's crisp wisdom in reference to the peculiarities of the American political process: "If you can't stand the heat, stay the hell out of the kitchen."

The sensitive Hatch was also deeply concerned about his once unified campaign organization whose members had worked so hard for him for so little. By the time of the convention, loss of sleep, worry, frustration, and round-the-clock activity had so frayed the nerves of his campaign workers that their working together further was an impossibility. It would take time for the wounds of harsh words and unintended accusations to heal. In a while they would all be friends again—even laugh over what now seemed a nightmare. But for the time being Orrin Hatch was without a campaign organization.

Hatch surmised that if he were to win the primary, he desperately needed three things. First, he needed money. Second, he needed a professional campaign organization, or at least some professional guidance. And finally, as he saw it, he needed the endorsement of Ronald Reagan, who was Utah's runaway favorite for the Republican nomination. Utah was Reagan country, and his endorsement, if it could be gained, would mean a great deal. (But then, of course, eminent political figures simply do not endorse candidates during their party's primary.)

Indeed, Hatch had set out some extremely difficult tasks to accomplish. The Monday after the Utah Republican Party Convention, he had lunch with Chuck Bailey, a respected political field man for the Republican National Committee, who had been assigned to the Senatorial campaign in Utah. For the most part, Bailey had assumed the posture of meeting with both Republican candidates, while waiting to see the outcome of the primaries. But he had come to the conclusion that not only could Hatch win, but that he would probably be the better candidate against Moss. At any rate, Bailey suggested to Hatch that he contact a Paul Newman, an executive of DMI (Decision-Making Information) in California. Newman is considered to be one of the brightest political minds in the country. But Newman charged $300.00 per day, plus expenses, and Hatch was already a full $13,000 in debt. Hatch balked at the cost, but Bailey was insistent. "Orrin," he reasoned, "without some kind of really professional help, you're going to end up a loser in debt. Believe me, it's much better to be a winner in debt."

Finally Hatch agreed to hire Newman—for one day! So, Mr. Newman's services were purchased for 24 hours. (According to Hatch, that was one full day.) Newman, of course, was booked solidly, but promised to give Hatch his one day as soon as possible. It was not until three weeks later that Hatch met him at the Salt Lake City airport. Paul

Newman stepped off the plane—all five feet two and one-half inches of him—dressed in bell-bottom dungarees, a white shirt, unbuttoned to the stomach, alligator cowboy boots, beads, and a bouffant curly hairdo.

Physically, Mother Nature had perhaps not smiled upon him, but his bouncy, congenial manner put everyone immediately at ease. Too, he had an air about him one caught almost at once that he knew what he was about. He was deliberate without being offensive, in command without appearing arrogant, brutally frank, but with a twinkle in his eye.

During the ride from the airport to the Hotel Utah in Salt Lake City Newman questioned Haddow in great detail about the campaign. It did not take him long to become aware of Haddow's native savvy and his quick, perceptive mind. During the next several hours Newman interviewed Hatch and what was left of his campaign organization. Hatch became aware that Newman had done his homework. Between the time Hatch had contacted him and his arrival in Utah three weeks later, Newman had become an expert on Hatch and on Utah politics. That evening, among other things, he told Hatch to hold on to Mac Haddow. Haddow must, he insisted, head Hatch's campaign. And he insisted that the "highly organized" Frank Bailey remain as director of systems.

He outlined a victory program, cautioning Hatch to follow it to a tee, even if he felt it was unproductive or unnecessary. "It's not the isolated point that counts, my boy, it's the whole bundle, coordinated and interlocking, each playing upon the other, reaching a crescendo by election time. You will undoubtedly get other suggestions on how to run the campaign and some of them will be very good suggestions. You must resist the temptation to follow any of them. There just isn't enough time. What I have told you to do will take all your time and then some; but if you follow it faithfully you have a good chance of landing in the Senate. You have made it this far in spite of yourselves. Now I think with a little luck and a little professionalism you can pull it off."

Haddow began to incorporate Newman's game plan into the campaign the following morning. His biggest task was to get the voting districts organized with Hatch supporters. Each district was to have a captain and a committee. This committee was to have several important functions. First, there was the communication with other people living in the district, thereby developing a near-constant promotion of Hatch on a one-to-one basis. This method has great value in enlisting voters who are uncommitted or unsure. Each committee member was to have a packet with information about Hatch, his brochures, and a list of questions and answers that the committee members were most likely to be asked.

The committee members also had the responsibility of setting up phone banks in each of the districts. The phone banks had four major uses: first, by asking a few questions about the election, the caller could usually ascertain which candidates the voter was going to support in the coming election and simultaneously identify those not registered. Second, if the voter was undecided, the caller would have a chance to sell Hatch; and third, on the day of the election, the committee would call only those registered as voters known to be for Hatch—once in the morning, and once in the late afternoon or early evening to make sure they voted. Then, if there were time, one could always take a final swipe at those who were uncommitted but who seemed to be leaning toward Hatch. Finally, telephone lists were also used for the "voter-drops"—Hatch literature plus a reminder to vote—just before the election.

Haddow called in his brother, John, to coordinate the district committees, dubbed "Hatch Victory Squads." Both were pleased and a little surprised to find a large and growing number of people throughout the State willing to be members of the Victory Squads. Some, who had heard about the committees called Haddow and asked if they might organize their particular districts. Amazingly, with just six weeks to go until the primary election, Haddow estimated that of the 1,690 voting districts in the State, Hatch Victory Squads had been organized in over 1,100 of them. To be sure, some of these committees were weak, and not all performed well. Nevertheless, it was a remarkable feat.

Paul Newman had told Haddow to "make a big thing" out of the district committees. There was nothing to hide. If Hatch's opponents had professional direction they had already organized their own; if not, there was not enough time, at least for Carlson, to find out what they were all about. Announcing to the press or in speeches, for instance, that Hatch had organized 25 or more districts would, according to Newman, demonstrate to the public and to the Hatch workers that Hatch had *momentum*—very important for an underdog.

The Carlson organization had for some time advanced the claim that superior Carlson district organizations were primarily responsible for his large delegate count at the Convention, and would assure him victory. For the time being the Hatch organization was running scared. At the same time, however, continued announcements concerning the growing numbers of Hatch Victory Squads proved demoralizing for Carlson workers.

Newman instructed Haddow to organize a media campaign, concentrating on a profile of the voter groups Hatch needed to attract if he were to win the primary. "You do not use the media the same during a primary contest as you do for a general election," he pointed out. "The object of political advertising is not just to reach the widest possible audience indiscriminately; you must concentrate as well on certain groups that are crucial for this particular primary election. In order to win, you need to mobilize only a relatively small number of enthusiasts."

The Republican primary voter will tend to be more conservative than the general election voter, and this is particularly true in Utah. Primary voters in two-party states are generally more emotionally involved than the average voter, and tend to be more ideologically attached to party symbols. In short, they tend to be more politically active. Generally, so-called "independents" and weak party identifiers do not vote in primaries. Split-ticket voters generally do not vote in primaries. And, for a number of decades, Utah has had a high level of split-ticket voting in the general election, a situation which has produced Democratic governors and a Republican-controlled legislature.

The socioeconomic profile of the typical politically active Utah Republican voter in 1976 revealed an urbanite who earned $15,000 per year and above, and had at least some college experience. His employment tended to be in the professions or mid-management. For the primary election, then, this was Hatch's number one target group.

For the primary race, in furtherance of Newman's plan, Hatch decided to place the bulk of campaign money in radio rather than television. First of all, the cost of extensive television commercials would have been prohibitive. Secondly, for this particular primary campaign it was much easier to get targeted groups with some assurance through radio. This meant that campaign funds would be more efficiently spent through that medium rather than television. What television time was purchased appeared between 7 and 9:30 P.M., around and during the news broadcasts; prime time for the particular audience Hatch wanted to reach.

The Hatch organization purchased a great deal of radio time on station KWMS, although that station had the lowest rating of any of Utah's major stations. It was the perfect station for the target group; it was an all-news station, heavily patronized by the target group in their automobiles going to and from work, between 7:30 and 8:30 A.M. and 4:30 to 6:30 P.M. Haddow called this his "prime time—drive time."

Newman's second targeted group for Hatch was Utah's farmers. While less than 4 percent of Utah's working force is in agriculture, farmers in the state are heavy voters, making their political impact larger than one would assume by their diminishing numbers. Prime time to reach farmers over radio is around 6:00 and again between 9:00 and 11:00

in the morning. The latter period Haddow called "lag time." This was when the farmer was generally in and about the barns doing "chores," and typically listening to the radio.

The third targeted group for the primary was the senior citizen. Here Hatch needed help. In Utah, senior citizens are both numerous and active—a phenomenon attributed to Mormon health practices which preclude liquor, tobacco, tea and coffee, and the Mormon family that tends to revere its elders and promote their continued activity and feelings of worth. Chase Econometric Associates rate Utah as one of the most desirable retirement areas. A Utah politician ignores that audience only at his peril. In recent years, older citizens have become increasingly active in elections and influencing new laws. By 1978, slightly over 60 percent of people between 65 and 74 voted, substantially above the national average. What is more, this group is diversified in thinking and political philosophy. It is probably an exaggeration to suggest that as people become older they become more conservative; in recent years at least, they have not tended to vote in blocs. A political appeal to this group must be prepared with a great deal of thought, for while they see inflation as their number one enemy, and while they are reluctant to support tax increases for new programs, they also vigorously resist suggestions to reduce their benefits from federal programs. So if those senior citizens voting in the Republican primary tended to be slightly more conservative than their peers who would vote in the general election, Hatch still had to be careful when attacking Behemoth Government not to give the impression that their existing benefits would be in jeopardy. Therefore his ads during the news on television, and "fringe spots" on late-night programming— considered prime time for this group—had to be carefully portrayed and worded.

Finally, an attempt was made to reach the party "firebrands" by advertising on certain of Utah's talk shows—especially KSXX—where the more politically ideological exchanged views with the commentators and talk show hosts. Again, these intensely interested voters will tend to vote in a primary.

Newman believed that proper scheduling was often a major key to victory in close elections. Hatch was to be tightly scheduled "from six A.M. till midnight, six days a week," he insisted. There must be constant movement within the Hatch organization, again, to provide the image of upward movement—momentum—to the organization and to the public. It was like selling cars; if you had a good product, the more people you talked to the more cars you sold. Newman reminded Haddow that Hatch had every quality of the dream candidate—he was tall, attractive, intelligent, informed, a superior, moving speaker whose sincerity was obvious; and he was not tinged with the brand of "politician." "That boy's got charisma," said Newman. "Now, nobody can explain to you what that is; you only know when someone has it, and Hatch has it. It brings an audience into the palm of his hand. They will believe him, they will trust him, they will like him. I tell you, Orrin Hatch is the finest political candidate I have seen in 15 years. If you can get the people of Utah to see him and hear him, he'll leave Carlson and Moss in his dust. So, get him before the people. *Get him before the people!*"

Finally, Newman worked with Haddow and Bailey in setting up a budget. No one had to tell them that Hatch needed money. What hurt most was the realization that even in a political campaign it often took money to make money, and one often had to go into debt. In the weeks ahead, the Hatch squads were very instrumental in bringing in money, and as Hatch came more and more before public scrutiny, contributions increased commensurately. Newman was right. The image of momentum and political contributions were intimately connected.

Newman left Hatch his list of prominent Republicans and patriotic organizations all over the country as a source of further funds. "Nothing wrong in going out of the state for funds," insisted Newman. "People all over this country would thank God to have a man like you in the Senate, no matter what state he was from. Once in the Senate your vote is for all of us. This country is in trouble, son, because of the lack of men like you in Washington. You write a good letter explaining what you stand for and you'll get a few bucks in."

By phone, Newman put Hatch in touch with multimillionaire Richard A. Viguerie, the master of direct mailing who revolutionized modern campaigning. Viguerie's company, RAVCO is headquartered in Vienna, Virginia, where computing machines have digested countless mailing lists of every form imaginable. Viguerie agreed to sell the Hatch organization a formidable list of the nation's conservatives—ones known for their generosity to conservative candidates and causes.

But this process is more complicated than one might expect. First of all, printing and postage costs involved in direct mailing are, of course, high. Then, too, Hatch was starting late. Many who would receive the request for funds would have already donated to other candidates. Nevertheless, it was worth a try they thought.

This experience with direct mail for campaign funds was both a fascinating and a frightening adventure for Hatch. When the last of the tallies were in, the process had netted Hatch over $280,000; but it had cost his campaign nearly $200,000 to get it. Hatch spent many a worried hour over that one. He was relieved that, at this late hour, it had worked out as well as it had.

Hatch also began to receive funds through the recommendation of an organization called *The Right Report*. At Viguerie's suggestion, they had recommended that conservatives give funds to Hatch. But, in attempting to get Hatch's mailing address, someone had mistakenly put down the address of the other senatorial candidate from Utah—Jack Carlson. Yet, even this error was to work to Hatch's advantage.

Finally, Newman had suggested that Hatch fly to Kansas City during the Republican National Convention to meet officials of certain conservative organizations. And, as Newman predicted, it was not difficult for Hatch to convince them that he was knowledgeable, responsible and bright. When he returned to Salt Lake City he had gained, among others, a pledge for help from the Committee for the Survival of a Free Congress, directed by the brilliant Paul Weyrich.

At this point, Hatch was somewhat bewildered. His campaign organization could still best be described as chaotic, yet they continued to make the right decisions and do the right things, moving right along with the assuredness of sleepwalkers. If they appeared at first as the "blind leading the blind," soon they would be taken seriously—very seriously indeed.

Most important, the street-wise Haddow proved to be a necessary antidote to Hatch's simplistic love of people and his naïve willingness to take almost anyone at his word. Hatch wanted to believe in people.

However, his new life in politics was teaching Hatch what Haddow had learned much earlier. In politics, it is good to be Christ-like, but it is also necessary to be "wise as the fox." At the mid-point of the primary campaign the Logan city newspaper, *The Herald*, featured a "Primary Voters' Guide" in which statements and background of various candidates appeared. The articles had been composed from questionnaires sent to each primary candidate; but under the name Orrin Hatch was the statement: "Did not return questionnaire." This statement was untrue, Hatch had submitted a detailed answer to each of the questions.

That afternoon Hatch and Haddow drove the 80 miles from Salt Lake to Logan. Hatch wanted to confront the editor, Cliff Cheney, a prominent spokesman of Utah's liberal left, face-to-face.

Cheney defended the omission by pointing out that Hatch had not properly filled out the questionnaire. (Hatch had appended typed statements to the questionnaire indicating to which questions they referred).

"Mr. Cheney," responded Hatch, "I am not here to argue with

you. You are nitpicking and you know it. You saw a chance to eliminate my response on a technicality and then went so far as to print that you had received nothing at all from me. Not only have I lost a forum in your paper that you granted to other candidates, but you have made it appear that I wasn't interested in the people of Logan. You have allowed your political biases to condone a dishonest act. I believe that you are basically an honest man, and I am here to demand that you do the honorable thing by printing my statements."

From behind his desk, Cheney looked steadily at Hatch. Finally, he said: "I'll take care of it."

A week later the statements of Orrin Hatch were featured in the Logan *Herald*. Again, what might have been a setback turned into a boon for Hatch. He was featured singly without having to share space with other candidates, and closer to the election date.

The campaign itself took the posture of Hatch gaining momentum and growing exposure and Carlson tending to drift. It appeared that the Carlson campaign had financially exhausted itself by the series of television ads featuring Carlson in clips from the State Republican Convention. The Carlson organization had spent a great deal of money on television ads. During the State Republican Convention a number of films were shot of Carlson, emphasizing his winning the largest delegate vote. Carlson also made substantial use of billboards. These strategies were probably a mistake, since saturation techniques are better suited for a general election. Television spots are expensive, and it is questionable whether billboard advertising enlists new votes. Its chief benefit is probably to reinforce those voters already committed to the candidate. In a campaign where large numbers of Republicans were undecided, Carlson's money could have been better spent.

As Hatch struggled to popularize his name and zero in on the target groups, Carlson began to lose an increasing percentage of his natural constituency. The Carlson organization was counting, for instance, on help from the many graduates from the Freeman Institute. The founder of this organization, W. Cleon Skousen, had been an FBI agent and a university professor. The purpose of the Institute is to promote an understanding of the United States Constitution and the basic principles of the American Founding Fathers.

In Orrin Hatch, however, increasing numbers of Freemen graduates saw a strong and articulate exponent of Constitutional principles they had been trained to recognize; and to the dismay of the Carlson organization, began to offer their support to the Hatch campaign, adding materially to Hatch's growing strength.

Carlson was in the right place but at the wrong time. Hatch's entrance into the race had changed the whole complexion of the campaign. As the campaign intensified, Carlson's organization became increasingly aware of the fact that they were being moved inexorably to a defensive position with the rise of Hatch's popularity. It was not just the perceived need to change strategy. Given the timing of the political climate and the charisma of Hatch—two phenomena they could not control—there existed few alternatives. They had been backed into a corner.

With their game plan thoroughly disrupted, the Carlson organization was forced into secondary tactics which were disjointed and often counterproductive. The attempt to isolate Hatch by concentrating on Moss' legislative record, for instance, did not take because Hatch was appearing as an increasingly legitimate candidate. Then there was the attempt to copy the tactics of California Governor Edmund G. Brown against Ronald Reagan. There was a concerted attempt to paint Orrin Hatch as a "Bircher extremist." This caused Hatch his first feelings of outright anger in the campaign. Ironically, several of Carlson's campaign people had been actively seeking support from individual John Birch members (the John Birch Society does not endorse candidates for political office). Some were undoubtedly delegates.

As the apparent underdog, Hatch did the usual thing by publicly challenging Carlson to a series of debates to be scheduled in various parts of the state. And Carlson did the usual thing; he would like to debate Hatch but thought his challenge to Moss for a series of debates was more important. After all, he reasoned, here's where the real difference of opinion was. And the Carlson campaign organization naturally found numerous conflicts on the dates suggested by Hatch. Also, Carlson's organization didn't like the open format suggested by Hatch. No, the ground rules would have to be modified. Wisely, Carlson was not about to give Hatch additional exposure. It was all very routine—avoid the debates without appearing to do so. Moss was giving Carlson the same treatment.

Hatch, on the other hand, needed to demonstrate that he, as a conservative, held different views than Carlson who was also a conservative. He played Carlson's reticence to the hilt. On July 29, the *Salt Lake Tribune* reported Hatch's concern over the stymied debates. "The issues dividing myself and Mr. Carlson are many," he was quoted, "and his desire to debate Senator Moss is not only premature but lacks in knowledge of political reality. I will meet the people of our State and forthrightly answer their questions on any subject—on any issues. If Jack

Carlson won't debate the issues before the people of Utah, how can we expect him to fight for us in the U.S. Senate?''

So, as expected, the debates never came off, but Hatch was still getting his name in the press. In his sparring with Carlson he was gaining legitimacy as a responsible candidate and he was getting name recognition—so vital for a ''dark horse.''

When numerous letters from *Right Report* subscribers containing contributions for Hatch's campaign, but mistakenly addressed to Carlson's campaign headquarters arrived, they were promptly returned to sender. This left an opening for Hatch that was worth more to him than the money in those envelopes. On September 5, the *Salt Lake Tribune* printed the following under the title ''CHARGES FLY AS UTAH POLITICS HEAT UP'': ''Republican Senate candidate Orrin Hatch has attacked his primary election opponent, Jack Carlson, for not having the 'courtesy' to forward mistakenly addressed mail containing campaign contributions. 'I am really surprised that Jack decided to send the letters back to the senders when both of us live in the same neighborhood, our campaign headquarters are just a block apart, and we see each other virtually every day,' Hatch said Friday.''

All along the campaign trail Hatch mentioned the returned contribution letters and Carlson's refusal to debate. It was corny, but among many Republican voters, Hatch was gaining the image of injured innocence.

Then there was the attempt to paint Hatch as a ''carpetbagger,'' an outsider, rather than a native Utahn. Even ''Letters to the Editor'' were exchanged on the subject. One such letter by a Mr. England was particularly hard hitting, referring to Hatch as an immigrant from back East.

The Hatch reply was geared to capture the ''fairness'' emotions of the electorate. If Americans generally subscribe to unwritten ''rules of the game,'' then Utahns are doubly sensitive to such guidelines. In 1970, a highly respected Lawrence Burton had brought in an ''outsider'' to run his campaign (against incumbent Senator Moss), who was not as knowledgeable about the character of Utah's electorate as was Paul Newman. He devised one television spot featuring a burning ROTC building on a campus in the eastern part of the United States. Included was a paragraph from a letter signed by Moss indicating his sympathy for the emotions faced by students because of the Vietnam War. Actually, the Moss letter—an open letter—was written to the students of Utah, and had nothing to do with the student riots to which he, on numerous occasions, had indicated his opposition. Moss was able to make a great deal of the issue, and there is no doubt that Burton was seriously hurt by it.

On September 10, in "letters to the editor," in Utah's prominent *Deseret News,* Orrin Hatch's mother wrote from Midvale, Utah, under the title *"Her Fault Hatch Not Born In Utah"*:

> After reading Mr. England's letter in Tuesday's *Deseret News,* I feel so badly that I am the culprit—the reason Orrin Hatch was not born in Utah.
>
> His father and I met in Hiawatha, Utah, where I had been living with my father and stepmother. Orrin's father is of old pioneer heritage. His great-grandfather was sent to colonize Ashley Valley near Vernal, Utah. His other great-grandfather marched with the Mormon Battalion in the war with Mexico.
>
> My mother wrote for us to come to Pittsburgh as there was a building boom. Always my husband, a native Utahn, had a deep longing to return to Utah, but by the time Orrin was born we had a large family and the depression was so severe we even lost our home.
>
> I am now thinking of Utah's early greats—how they came from New York State, Vermont, Pennsylvania, Canada, and overseas such as Widtsoe [former Mormon Apostle and renowned scientist] and Maeser [the first president of Brigham Young University]. Also, our Latter-day Utahns have become great men in other states.
>
> Orrin has lived seven years in Utah plus four at Brigham Young University. Orrin has had many hard knocks—he struggled to gain an education. He was a history major and loves this country and Utah very much. I would not wish my boy to win without merit.

"It was through no fault of some of my opposition," Hatch reminded his audiences, "that they were born in Utah. I had a choice. I came to Utah at a substantial loss in salary because I wanted to live here and because I wanted to raise my children here. I love Utah by choice, and, if it takes love to represent you, no one could represent you better."

Also self-defeating to the Carlson campaign was the claim that Hatch had not served his country in the military, while Carlson had a distinguished service record. Imagine the heart-felt response when Hatch told his audiences that he had been exempt from the Korean War because he was the "sole remaining heir." With passion and sincerity he told of the day during World War II when the family received word of his brother's death. He recounted the feelings of overwhelming grief by his parents, tempered only by their deep religious convictions and their pride that their son had given his life for his country.

All during the campaign, Carlson was emphasizing his claim of fiscal conservatism while Assistant Interior Department Secretary for energy and minerals in an attempt to counter Hatch's anti-bureaucrat stance. At first, the naïve Hatch let the claim pass, but not Haddow the fox. Through a series of long-distance calls to Washington Haddow was able to ascertain that, in fact, the budget for his Department was substantially less during his short tenure as an executive officer than before or after. However, Haddow was informed that since budgets for the various departments are established annually and since Carlson's tenure had been from August until February of the following year, the budget for his department had been created eight months before he assumed a leadership position. What one needed to do was to compute the economic performance of the Department for the subsequent six months after Carlson had left. That could have given some indication of his fiscal record. In fact, the authorization outlay when Carlson was in control (though perhaps through no fault of his own) had gone above the savings of the previous period.

Three weeks before the primary election, hearings were held in Salt Lake City concerning federal restrictions of mining on government-owned land. In attendance was Dr. William Fisher, then the Assistant Secretary of the Interior. When the Hatch organization was informed that Carlson had called a press conference with Fisher directly after the hearings, Hatch was concerned and called the Carlson headquarters. He was assured that the press conference was to be related solely to the hearings and would in no way be political. Haddow even called Fisher and received the same answer. Again Hatch was satisfied—*but not Haddow*. While Hatch's immediate response was to take the Carlson organization at their word, Haddow began with the Madisonian concept that all politicians must at least be assumed to be rascals.

Members of the Carlson organization who attended the press conference were visibly disturbed when they saw Haddow come into the room. For, just as Haddow had expected, the purpose of the press conference was to have Dr. William Fisher vindicate Carlson's fiscal conservatism while an Assistant Secretary in the Interior Department. Dr. Fisher assured the press that under the Carlson regime the budget had decreased 23 percent.

Then Haddow broke in. "I think," he stated loudly, "that the press ought to be aware that Dr. Fisher is giving Mr. Carlson credit for a budget he had no part whatsoever in making." He then gave the press a short lesson in government budgeting, with the appropriate dates of Carlson's tenure thrown in.

One should not suppose, however, that the inexperienced Hatch did not spend time trying to pull his foot out of his mouth. He was taking some lumps, too. He was learning that any idle word, even in jest, might be picked up and used against him. During one speech he chided Carlson's Harvard background, stating tongue in cheek that he understood all Harvard graduates were liberals. Two days later he was hit with a letter to the editor from a Mr. Heath, who denounced the statement, and reminded Hatch that Ernest L. Wilkinson was a Harvard graduate. "Many of Mr. Hatch's fellow attorneys," the letter continued, "would also be appalled to know that he considers their distinguished degrees from Harvard as detrimental to sound political thinking."

As the days passed, the Hatch organization began to feel that they were making a great deal of progress. But, of course, there was no way to tell for certain. Just how far Hatch would have to climb the popularity poll to victory was indicated by the results of a local television (Channel 2 "Newswatch") poll that had been conducted between June 5 and 27, and involved 400 potential Utah voters. The question asked was, "Which of the eight listed candidates would you like to see win the election as U.S. Senator from Utah?" The results were released August 5th, after the Republican State Convention, and included the names of those who had lost the delegate vote as well as Hatch and Carlson. The responses were, Frank Moss (D), 48 percent; Sherman Lloyd (R), 23 percent; Jack Carlson (R), 4 percent. All the other Republican candidates, including Hatch, received but 2 percent of the poll each, with the remaining responses in the undecided column.

What the poll indicated was that the Republican Convention delegates probably should have gone for Sherman Lloyd, but that even he would have had little chance against the incumbent, Moss. Mac Haddow, however, was unconvinced. He acquired a copy of the poll and studied it with his usual intensity. "Look," he told Hatch, "this poll was anything but professional. It was conducted before the Republican Party Convention, with a whole field of candidates. Naturally the response was going to be based on name identification, and obviously, the two that had served as Senator and Congressman, respectively, were going to get the most response. Since Moss was the incumbent, it was natural that he would get the largest response at that time." However, Haddow was certain that Moss was vulnerable. After 18 years in the public eye, Haddow pointed out, Moss should have done better. Haddow's analysis also indicated that Moss did not do that well among the people most likely to vote—the 35-

to 44-year-olds or among active Mormons. Anyway, the fact was that Lloyd, the apparent stronger Republican challenger in June had been eliminated at the Convention, and Carlson at that time seemed to be not much better known among the voters than Hatch. For the time being, he was the man to beat. Moss could wait until after the primaries.

The fact was that Hatch *was* rapidly moving up not only in name recognition but in the confidence of the Republican voters in the State. Americans, especially Utahns, feel an affinity for the underdog. This fact gave Hatch more press than he probably would have had otherwise been favored with. Being new in the political arena, a number of newspaper writers probed his background, adding a good deal of public interest information about him. In a candidate review, the *Salt Lake Tribune* of August 12, had this to say about him: "Orrin Hatch was born in Pittsburgh and grew up there, but his social and religious ties were in Utah. At 16, he was apprenticed in the metal lathing trade and became a member of the AFL-CIO. He has great regard for the working man and owes his higher education to the training he had in a trade. It helped pay his way through college. He earned his juris doctor degree at the University of Pittsburgh, then became a member of one of the nation's oldest law firms. In four years he was a full partner in the firm and he eventually became an officer in five eastern corporations. With the desire to raise his children in Utah the decision was made to come west. In the court room he has defended many clients—successfully more often than not. As one of his major victories, he assisted in making it possible for the 5M Co. to gain access to the Kaiparowits Plateau in order to mine 25 million tons of coal that had been stymied by the Bureau of Land Management."

Much has been written about "peaking" in a political campaign. No one really knows beforehand when a campaign is going to peak, but most professionals can tell you if a campaign peaked too soon or too late. Apparently Carlson's campaign peaked shortly after the Republican Convention—much too soon for this election. It may well have been that the Carlson organization spent too much of the hard-to-come-by primary funds on those TV spots right after the Convention. In contrast, Hatch seemed to make a steady rise, peaking just before the election. In this particular election, when there were undoubtedly many Republican voters who were undecided, this worked out well for Hatch.

On September 10, the *Salt Lake Tribune* issued the results of a statewide poll which had been conducted by Bardsley and Haslacher, Inc., concerning the Senate race. Here appeared a significant difference over the June poll. The results gave Hatch a 4 to 3 lead over Carlson. However, the poll also indicated that one out of four Republican voters was still undecided. This meant that whoever made the greatest political impact during those final days would probably take the election. Also significant were the poll results indicating that either Hatch or Carlson would enter the general election only a slight underdog to Moss—another change from the June poll. "Since both Mr. Carlson and Mr. Hatch are holding Senator Moss to a bare majority or below," commented the *Salt Lake Tribune,* "it looks like a hot fight lies ahead."

Also on September 10, Orrin Hatch gained the "icing" on his political "cake." For weeks he had been actively seeking the endorsement of Ronald Reagan. He believed if he could just talk to Reagan, he could succeed in persuading him to grant his support. Although Reagan had lost by a narrow margin to Ford at the Convention, Hatch knew that Reagan still carried great weight among Republicans in Utah. But how to get in touch with the man? One influential Republican told Hatch it would be next to impossible to contact Reagan, even more difficult to get his endorsement. After all, you simply did not ask a national political figure to make an endorsement during a primary campaign where two loyal members of his party were in contention.

For several days, however, Hatch had been talking long-distance to Reagan's high-level campaign strategist and personal friend, Mike Deaver, in California. Finally, Deaver had become convinced that Hatch was Reagan's "kind of man." He relayed the information to Reagan who was vacationing in Mexico and, for all intents and purposes, *incommunicado.* After some discussion Deaver was able to get Reagan to talk directly with Hatch's office from Mexico, where he reached Haddow. In rapid fire, this time with the added support of Deaver, Haddow pled Hatch's case. His hands wet with perspiration, he wasn't sure he heard correctly when Reagan said, "Tell Hatch I will be happy to endorse him."

"Say that again, sir."

"Tell Hatch I'll be happy to endorse him."

"Mr. Reagan, would you be so kind as to send us a telegram confirming our conversation for the press."

"Well, yes. When do you need it?"

"The minute I hang up, sir."

Reagan laughed. "All right, Deaver will send it to you immediately."

"Thank you, Mr. Reagan. Mr. Hatch will be happier with this endorsement because of his respect for you than he will for the political help it will bring him."

"Tell Mr. Hatch 'Good luck and God Speed.'"

Shortly afterwards a weary candidate Hatch walked into his campaign office. Haddow grabbed him by the shoulders and said in an amazingly calm voice, "You have got it!"

"What do I have?"

"You've got the endorsement by Reagan!" the whole office staff cried in unison.

"What? Are you sure? What proof do you have?" Hatch hardly knew what he was saying. When he learned it was indeed really true, he almost smiled.

Reagan's message arrived at Hatch's office late in the afternoon. Haddow wanted the news of the endorsement out immediately and had called for a press conference. If the telegram had not arrived, Hatch could still claim endorsement and offer the proof the following morning. The important thing was to catch both the evening television news and the morning newspapers. As it turned out, the telegram arrived five minutes before the press conference convened. That evening Hatch appeared on television reading the telegram.

The reaction from the Carlson camp was immediate. One of Carlson's campaign spokesmen claimed that the endorsement coming at this time was fraudulent, since Reagan was vacationing somewhere in Mexico and could not be contacted. Hatch had received the endorsement on Friday, September 10, before the Tuesday primary vote. When, on Sunday, a full-page ad appeared in the major newspapers in Utah showing a picture of Reagan and the telegram, the Carlson people became quiet. One can imagine their frustration. This was both a devastating and an unexpected blow.

The heading for the ad pronounced in bold letters, "A TELEGRAM FROM RONALD REAGAN TO ALL THE PEOPLE OF UTAH." To the left of the title was a large picture of a smiling Ronald Reagan. The telegram read: "To my many friends in Utah, I want to express my gratitude for the outstanding support I received from the people of Utah in my bid for the Presidency. Now the time has come for me to do everything I can to endorse a man of quality, courage, discipline and integrity; a man of demonstrated ability, strength, and vision; a man who believes in individual freedom and self-reliance. With these qualities in mind, I enthusiastically endorse Orrin Hatch for U.S. Senator from Utah. Orrin Hatch has the quality of leadership, the forthrightness of purpose, and the personal honesty needed to turn this country to a proper course. This is Ronald Reagan asking you to elect Orrin Hatch to the United States Senate. Good luck!" The telegram was dated September 10, 1976.

Finally, the coup de grace occurred when Reagan returned to California and Paul Smith, commentator on Utah's most prestigious radio and television network, KSL, called Reagan by phone. Reagan stated that he was happy to clarify his endorsement of Hatch, adding that he believed Hatch was the one to beat Moss. That conversation was repeated time and again on the radio on the Monday before the election.

In the meantime, the frustrated Carlson organization had been claiming an imminent endorsement by President Gerald Ford. Actually, they had asked Ford if he would endorse *the Republican Candidate* from Utah for the United States Senate and Ford had sent a telegram stating he would be happy to do so. But, of course, Carlson was not yet the candidate.

Haddow shifted into high gear in an attempt to keep the Carlson camp's claim of an immediately impending endorsement from Ford from undermining the publicity Hatch was getting from the Reagan endorsement. Robert Dole, Ford's Vice-Presidential running mate, was scheduled to arrive in Salt Lake City on the Monday morning before the Tuesday primary. Haddow made contact with Dole's advance people and informed them what the Carlson camp was attempting to do. They, in turn, informed Dole. Then Haddow contacted those reporters from Utah's press and television who were to meet the Dole plane at the Salt Lake City Airport. He persuaded them to make their first question to Dole: "Are you and the President endorsing Jack Carlson *at this time* for the United States Senate?"

"No," was the reply, "we are not!"

On September 14, 1976, Orrin Hatch, described by *Tribune* political editor, Douglas Parker, as "the unknown trial lawyer turned politician," beat Jack Carlson handily, 104,351 votes to 57,092. Indeed, Hatch had peaked well; and all agreed, even Hatch, that riding the crest of that peak was the endorsement by Ronald Reagan. "I simply do not run well against Ronald Reagan," said Carlson sadly to a *Tribune* reporter.

Chapter 3
THE CHAMP

On September 16, 1976, the *Deseret News* Washington Bureau reported that "Utahns were puzzled at the margin by which Orrin Hatch defeated Jack Carlson in Tuesday's GOP Senate Primary. While Hatch had been expected, during the last week, to take a narrow victory, his 47,000-vote win had both Republicans and Democrats scratching their heads."

Two days later the *Salt Lake Tribune,* summed up the primary campaign by stating that, "Mr. Orrin Hatch, a 42-year-old lawyer, presented a fervent, rapid-fire debating style to grab the enthusiasm of the Republican ranks, and garnered 104,351 votes to Mr. Carlson's 57,092."

As had been reported, a substantial portion of the Republican electorate was undecided down to the wire. Undoubtedly, Hatch's ability to capture the undecided vote during the last week or so led to his lopsided victory over Carlson. In the last analysis it was Hatch's ability "to grab the enthusiasm of the Republican ranks," combined with Governor Reagan's endorsement, that orchestrated his decisive victory.

Reagan's endorsement of Hatch was nearly unprecedented. An endorsement by a national political figure of one primary candidate over another of the same party is a political taboo of long standing. Hatch had supported Reagan from the beginning and had presented himself as an unabashed conservative rather than a fence-sitter. Furthermore, his intelligence, his hard-hitting style of debate, and his uncanny ability to convert his audience to his logic as a speaker and to himself as a person, made him a credible candidate. Reagan, smarting from his loss to Ford at the convention and his desertion at the last minute by some "fair weather" conservative delegates, looked upon Hatch with a great deal of respect. Here was a man he could support without qualification, and—breaking precedent—he did so during the Utah Republican primaries.

Hatch's victory in the primary added immeasurably to his name recognition. A *Tribune* poll shortly after the election showed Hatch with an amazing 90 percent name-recognition factor. Hatch was placed ahead of Moss by 13 percent. Senator Moss correctly pointed out, however, that since he had not participated in the primaries, being unopposed, and since Hatch had been in the limelight, it was only natural that his political stock should go up. The Senator was also accurate when he informed the media that his Republican opponent had always been ahead just after the primaries, and that he had predictably moved ahead of his rival to be the winner at election time. Too, pollsters always had trouble predicting Moss's support. Typically, Moss ran ahead of his constituency response to polls. He called it his "hidden constituency," but one prominent Republican said that Moss's "hidden constituency" was made up of people who wouldn't admit to a pollster, or anyone else for that matter, that they were going to vote for Moss. However, in the privacy of the voting booth they came through for the good Senator.

Nevertheless, Moss must have been troubled by Hatch's extraordinarily high name-recognition factor. Equally disturbing was the revelation by the pollsters that Moss enjoyed only a 44 percent approval rating within the state of Utah. Moss immediately began an intensive and very costly media campaign, including a prodigious number of ads in the state's newspapers. He hired Napolitan, the New York Democrat media genius, and saturated prime-time television with expensive and obviously professional ads. From whatever source, Moss was well-heeled. The Hatch organization supposed that organized labor was giving Moss a fortune, some outright and some by contributions through various individuals and organizations and by sending into the state dues-paid political operatives to man the phone banks and conduct get-out-the-Moss-vote drives. Haddow had appeared at a number of Moss functions incognito (which was some trick given his size). Among those mingling with the Moss entourage were a number of people Haddow had not seen before. He noticed one particularly "spiffily" dressed and dapper-looking gent at a number of these functions, and struck up a conversation with him.

"You from around these parts?"

"No, I'm from Washington, D.C."

"Really!"

"Yes, I work on the Budget Committee for Senator Muskie, I'm, ah, sort of on vacation and helping out Senator Moss here."

"The hell you say!"

"Yeah, what do you do?"

"I'm a poet," Haddow called back over his shoulder as he walked away.

The Hatch campaign, on the other hand, was broke—flat broke. For the first three weeks after the September 14th primary victory, Hatch and the few hands that remained on board had to do everything without financing. For his part, Hatch kept up the gruelling pace of meeting the people and speaking before groups, large and small, as he had during the pre-convention and the pre-primary days. He spoke several times a day, sometimes four, five and even six times in one evening. He was on his way by 6:15 each morning and usually returned around midnight. He was constantly tired. He learned to take "cat-naps" as he was driven or flown between engagements. Soon his metabolism adjusted somewhat to the pace and these little snatches of blessed sleep actually began to refresh him. He was not under the same emotional tension as he had been before the primaries. He was adjusting to the vagaries of politicking. His exhaustion was a result, now, simply of lack of sleep—not the sickly, sweaty, exhaustion of headaches, nausea, heart palpitations and the stiffness of tension. Earlier in the year, before he decided to run, he was smashed from behind in an automobile accident which seriously injured his neck and low back. He had constant pain throughout the race.

Hatch was pleased with the response he was getting at the various engagements. His philosophy, his oratory, and his abnormal ability to remember vast amounts of facts and figures had blended magnificently into presentations that were startling in their content and delivery. Moss suffered by comparison just as had Jack Carlson.

Hatch rigidly held to the issues during the campaign. Where he attacked Moss, it was over the issues that had stood him in good stead during the primaries. It was not difficult for Hatch to demonstrate inconsistencies in Moss's voting record and to show that Moss was out of step with the prevailing mood of the Utah voter.

However, Hatch, too, was suffering from a certain amount of disaffection within the Republican ranks. Former Utah Republican National Committeewoman, Madge Fairbanks, had reported that she would campaign against Hatch. Hatch, she complained, was just too conservative. She finally organized a "Republicans for Moss Committee." Its membership was miniscule, but Madge's ability to organize a number of press conferences made her and the committee inordinately visible.

In certain important ways, Senator Moss, the Democrat, faced the same disadvantages in facing Hatch as a challenger as had Jack Carlson, the Republican. First of all, both Moss and Carlson had been tinged by service in Washington, and this election was conducted during a period of apparent extended anti-Washington sentiment. As *Deseret News* political editor, Dexter Ellis, surmised, "The Senate race between Senator Frank Moss and Orrin Hatch may well hinge on the answer to this question: That is, whether the current anti-Washington, conservative mood of Utah voters is an overriding force or a political element of more superficial influence."

Moss was more at a disadvantage when faced with Hatch's inimitable speaking and debating style than Carlson had been, for he lacked Carlson's youthful appearance, his "macho," and his style. In both his TV ads and his debates, he appeared old and cross.

In every conceivable way Hatch had the advantage when appearing with Moss. His youthful, virile appearance served to emphasize Moss's age. While in law school Hatch had developed his own system of cramming, a process which helped him survive during his final year when he was forced to work all night and go to school and study all day. During his campaigns he resurrected the process and quickly memorized hundreds of facts and figures. In the debates, both Carlson and Moss were demoralized by Hatch's seemingly brilliant and razor-sharp mind, and endless knowledge of technical aspects of the issues, which he spit out with the rapidity—and the devastation—of a machine gun.

But most important was Hatch's ability to communicate energy. When he got in front of an audience there was an almost incredible reaction. Like an evangelical minister, he converted his audience to the political gospel according to Hatch. Moss soon learned that his new opponent was not at all like Congressman Lawrence Burton, whom he had defeated in 1970 and that he was a vastly more formidable opponent than even Ernest L. Wilkinson, whom he had defeated in 1964.

Moss's previous Senate votes favoring the use of federal funds for abortion (Moss finally voted against federal funding of abortion the year of the election) and his support for the Common Situs Picketing Bill (this would have enabled union subcontractors to picket or secondarily boycott a complete construction site and force unionization on all other non-union subcontractors even though their dispute may be with only one other minor subcontractor on the job site; too, it would have been legal for members of any other unions on the site to walk off the job) were weak spots in his campaign. So, too, was his support of federal land use planning and federal strip-mining legislation. Mac Haddow also produced numerous statements made by Moss favoring the repeal of Section 14(b) of the Taft-Hartly "right-to-work" statue—all of these were sensitive issues to the people of Utah, with a majority opposed to Moss's stand on them. It remained for Hatch to keep these issues before the public.

But most damaging to Moss was his voting record on fiscal policy, making him, as one conservative periodical stated, "one of the biggest spenders in Congress." Hatch hammered away at his "flagrant disregard for the taxpayer," and his "consistent contribution to irresponsible spending by the Federal Government."

Newspaper headlines demonstrated Hatch's attack: "CANDIDATES TANGLE ON JOBS, BUDGETS"; "ORRIN HATCH ATTACKS UNIONS, BUREAUCRATS"; "HATCH RAPS GOVERNMENT IRRESPONSIBILITY"; "MOSS DEFENDS FOOD STAMPS, HATCH ATTACKS SPENDING"; "MOSS, HATCH AT ODDS ON U.S. DEFICIT"; "HATCH ATTACKS MOSS VOTING."

Moss seemed unable to shake a "spendthrift" image. His recourse to "humanitarian" motives in explaining his voting record did not seem to take. Too, his endorsement by a number of unions may have done him little good. In fact when, on October 5, the *Deseret News* reported that Moss had received $54,777 in political contributions from the unions just through September 1, public reaction was hardly positive.

Another cloud casting its shadow over Moss's reelection possibilities was one which deeply troubled him but one over which he had no control. Democratic Representative Allan Howe, who had been arrested for allegedly soliciting sex from an undercover policewoman, obstinately refused to step down from his candidacy in spite of pleas from party leaders that his appearance on the ticket might jeopardize the election of other Democrats. The party ranks were seriously divided over Howe's continued candidacy and his pathetic refusal to accept guilt. "If we hadn't split the party in two, we would have a big blitz on by now," Moss told a *New York Times* reporter midway through October. "Howe is like having a big cancer in your stomach. I'm sort of caught in the middle." In the past Moss's electoral success was due, to a large extent, to his popularity in the Democratic party. Now he was not certain how much enthusiasm he would be able to muster in a party with a nasty taste in its mouth.

To add to his problems, Moss's researchers indicated a continued drift to the "right" in Utah, accentuated by Vietnam, and a growing public frustration with "Washington politicians." And Moss also faced the near certainty that Utah would go heavily for President Ford on November 2. No coattails for Moss there.

Finally, the capable Jack Carlson, by ignoring his Republican rivals during the struggle for delegates and the primaries, and going directly for Moss's jugular vein, had left Hatch with a backlog of sophisticated attacks against Moss that had already taken their toll before the general election campaign had begun. In effect, this phenomenon was placing Carlson as a particularly important asset to Hatch, one to which Carlson was not averse.

Especially biting was Carlson's charge that Moss's committee assignments were not the most significant, thereby making his seniority insignificant. Hatch picked up on this. "Seniority is important," retorted Hatch, "but that seniority is only as important as the votes that are cast. Senator Moss's votes are fiscally irresponsible, and often dictated by his attachment to organized labor." When Moss boasted at one debate that he was chairman of the Senate Aeronautical and Space Sciences Committee, Hatch pointed out that in the new Senate reorganization plan the committee was scheduled to be abolished. With that humiliating revelation constantly revived by Hatch, Moss's membership on the prestigious Senate Budget Committee somehow lost its luster. "We may have gone down the wrong track in stressing my seniority and my service to the state," said Moss to the *New York Times*. "If so, I'm going to start counterpunching."

And counterpunch he did. Moss took the offensive. The tenor of his campaign changed by the second week in October. He and his media ads moved to the attack. The Moss organization began to study every word Hatch uttered, probed his past and investigated the source of his growing financial contributions.

Utah houses an inordinate number of federal employees. Moss's organization sent letters to them asking their support, warning that they would lose their jobs should Hatch be elected. "Had we sent such letters," retorted Hatch, "I would probably have been put in jail."

Responding to Hatch's contention that Moss's voting record "has made us the laughing stock of the eastern liberal Washington establishment," a Moss ad began: "Who is this young upstart from Pittsburgh who calls us Utahns the laughing stock of the nation?"

Early in the campaign, the popular conservative brewer Joseph Coors sought to extend to Hatch $1,000 from the Coors Political Action Committee. At first Hatch demurred. "I am a Mormon bishop," he told Coors, "I do not drink beer, nor could I ever give you any support for your particular product other than that coming indirectly from my strong belief in free enterprise."

"Mr. Hatch," was the reply, "I would never compromise your beliefs nor would I ever ask you to be anything but yourself. My support for candidates has nothing to do with anyone's support of beer-drinking.

Rather, with their belief in that political and economic system that guarantees my right to make and sell a product on the free market.''

Hatch accepted the $1,000 and Moss was not long in taking Hatch to task over this one. He went so far as to claim that Hatch was accepting large amounts of money from Colorado ''Beer Barons,'' and implied they were running his campaign.

But the Senator got nowhere with the Coors donation. His overreacting proved unbelievable, and he failed to make it an issue. Actually the Mormon people, who are almost always ''teetotalers,'' but seldom ''stuffy,'' gave the Coors donation little attention; and for many in the non-Mormon community, Hatch's acceptance of the ''beer'' money caused him to be more credible. While he was visiting the Geneva Steel Mills near Provo, several of the workers hailed him and cried out ''Yea Coors!''

And, again with information researched by an improving staff, Hatch actually turned the incident to Moss's detriment. When Moss brought up the Coors donation at one of the ''Candidate Night'' debates, Hatch responded lightly, ''Senator Moss, I must say that it is a little hypocritical of you to accuse me of having my campaign run by a man from Colorado whom I don't even know and have never formally met, merely because he gave me some money, when you have received $9,600 from the Marine Engineer's Benevolent Associations. I don't know of any deep water ports in Utah.''

Again there was laughter at Moss's expense. That quote went all over Utah. Hatch kept bringing it up, adding to it the fact that Moss had received $85,000 from organized labor, probably most of it from out of Utah. Hatch hammered hard at labeling Moss a ''tool of organized labor'' in a ''right-to-work'' state.

In the beginning Moss's television ads had the aura of professionalism, showing him as a leader of the ''little people,'' and one of the leaders in establishing national parks in Utah. Just prior to the campaign, Moss figured prominently in the exposure of the Medicaid scandals. He masqueraded as a poor Medicaid recipient and was examined, treated, and photographed. He got front-page coverage across the country. Curiously, however, the escapade made little impact on the people of Utah. Perhaps many felt it to be a political gimmick. Others undoubtedly felt as was expressed in an editorial in the *Wall Street Journal,* where he was criticized for acting beneath the dignity of a U.S. Senator. Whatever the reason, Moss was not materially benefited by his efforts.

Hatch's first debate was with Don Holbrook, Moss's campaign manager, before the Salt Lake Kiwanis Club. Holbrook is one of Utah's most prominent attorneys, a senior partner in Jones, Waldo, Holbrook, and McDonough. He is a dignified man, who had himself run for various political offices, but without success. He remained, however, a kingpin in the Utah Democratic party. He was an experienced debater with a keen mind.

On this day, however, Holbrook was shocked. He had clearly underestimated Hatch—his incredible ability to memorize facts and figures, and his hard-hitting verbal style. Holbrook appeared unprepared and frustrated. When he turned to attacks on Hatch, he lost his audience. The Moss organization was quick to learn, as had the Carlson organization before them, that being on the same program with Orrin Hatch could be a devastating experience.

When Hatch met Moss before the Salt Lake Rotary Club on October 6, the Senator was obviously and uncharacteristically nervous and high-strung. When Hatch commented that organized labor would put somewhere between $50 and $100 million, directly and indirectly, into the 1976 campaigns throughout the country, Moss retorted, "I hardly think that they would do that . . . at least not where it's visible."

Moss caught his breath, but too late. The Rotarians almost brought the house down. Later, when Moss was asked about the right-to-work issue, he responded, "I am for every man's right to work." Again, there was laughter from the audience. When the Senator left the Rotarian luncheon he was visibly shaken.

From that point Hatch had the advantage when meeting Moss in debates or "Meet the Candidate" nights. Time and again Moss missed these events and had others appear in his place—sometimes Holbrook, sometimes Moss's son Brian.

But if Hatch was a "runaway" winner at the debates, Moss's early television ads were relatively successful—especially since the Hatch organization began the campaign broke and his media campaign began slowly and late. The only television ad the Hatch organization was able to mount between September 15 and October 10 got sidetracked. They had selected a time midway through *Butch Cassidy and the Sundance Kid,* but the ad finally appeared eight minutes after the movie was over.

Ironically, however, Hatch's original lack of funds for television space turned to his advantage. The Moss organization had purchased television time early and had spaced the ads rather evenly over the campaign period. Hatch, on the other hand, had to wait far into the campaign before he had accumulated enough money for any sustained television campaign. When he finally had enough money, television salesmen from

Utah's television networks informed him that there were no prime-time spots left. Haddow went to the stations with his sleeves rolled up. The result was that during the last week of the campaign, Hatch got a prime-time media blitz at a cost of over $34,000. The sheer volume of the ads diminished the impact of the Moss ads.

On October 6, a Salt Lake television poll (KUTV) gave Moss a slim lead over Hatch, 45 percent to 43 percent. On that same day, however, a *Deseret News* poll conducted by Dan Jones Associates of Logan, Utah, showed Hatch with 48.5 percent of the votes and Moss with 39.5 percent. Most ominous for Moss was an affirmation of his greatest concern—his continued ability to hold the Democratic party close to his political breast. The poll showed that Moss held support from only 65 percent of the Democrats interviewed. "Although Moss could override Hatch's primary election impetus," stated Jones, "he needs to do better in the traditionally Democratic areas of the State." This news from a respected pollster caused some consternation in the Moss camp.

Ironically, also on October 6, the DMI pollsters from California released the results of a Utah state-wide telephone sampling. The results—63 percent of the respondents said they believed Moss would win a fourth Senate term.

Near the end of October a "plum" fell into Moss's lap. Months earlier the former heavyweight champion George Foreman had brought suit against Hatch and a whole host of others for $5,000,000 in damages in an exaggerated complaint filed by the celebrated Melvin Belli. This was the type of suit typically brought against doctors and lawyers. Hatch had prepared a perfectly legal private placement memorandum for a businessman in Salt Lake City. Foreman had subsequently invested $300,000 in the venture. The money had then been invested by the promoter-contractor. When the contractor went broke, Foreman, in a typical "shotgun" action, sued a whole host of persons, including his own attorneys as well as Hatch.

At first Hatch gave the suit only passing attention, but Haddow was worried. Such a nuisance suit was easily explained, reasoned Hatch. "Not so," insisted Haddow. "You're in trouble. In the first place, both the plaintiff and his lawyer are celebrities. Secondly, just the fact that you are sued brings a negative connotation to a public, most of whom will never understand the nature of the case, nor your explanation, however logical. Finally, this gives those reporters who hate you an opportunity to distort the issue in such a way as to make you look like John Dillinger."

"But," responded Hatch, beginning to see the implications of Haddow's words, "Carlson didn't bring it up in debates."

"You were damned lucky," replied Haddow," He probably didn't know about it."

Actually, Carlson *had* known about the Foreman suit. He had, however, rejected the idea of attempting to make it an issue against Hatch. Carlson was a tough campaigner who asked no quarter and gave none. But he considered using the suit "hitting below the belt." Had Hatch done something dishonest or illegal, that would have been another thing. Carlson had too much integrity to imply an immoral act by Hatch where his common sense told him none had been committed. Carlson wanted the election, but not so much that he would undeservedly damage Hatch's reputation.

The Moss organization had known about the Foreman suit for some time. They were waiting for the right time to deliver Hatch a "knockout" blow. However, on the Evening of October 26, just days before the election, Holbrook blew whatever timing advantage Moss might have gained by releasing the information at the "last minute." Channel 2 had invited Holbrook, representing Moss, and Republican State Party Chairman Dick Richards, representing Hatch, to a televised debate.

The debate started off inoffensively. It was almost boring. Then accusations began to fly concerning the integrity of the candidates. After Richards had imputed impropriety in Moss's labor support, Holbrook angrily brought up the Foreman suit.

This turned out to be unfortunate timing for Moss. Governor Ronald Reagan had agreed to come to Utah to campaign with Hatch for a few days starting on the 27th. And, Reagan was big news in Utah. Not only did his arrival blunt the news of the Foreman suit, but it allowed both Reagan and other Utah celebrities to respond, adding legitimacy to Hatch's claim that bringing up the suit was a "smear tactic." The very respected Utah Senator Jake Garn, for instance, was quoted as stating he had been sued 50 to 60 times just while he had been mayor of Salt Lake City; even Governor Reagan told the Utah press that he had also been sued before. And, as luck would have it, the endorsement of Hatch by President Ford was released to the press on the 27th.

Again timing seemed to be on Hatch's side. Had Moss revealed the suit closer to election time, Reagan would not have competed with it for media space; and Hatch would have had less time to explain its nuances.

When Hatch heard Holbrook had discussed the Foreman suit over television, he got that same sick feeling he had experienced during the primaries. On the evening of the 26th, Hatch called Reagan and explained the situation. Hatch left Reagan an out. He felt he owed him that.

"I will understand, Governor, if you think it would be better for you not to come to Utah at this time."

"Orrin," was the reply, "stop worrying. I'll see you tomorrow."

Reagan campaigned tirelessly for Hatch through October 27th and 28th. Hatch was impressed with his seemingly boundless energy, his enthusiasm and his graciousness. He always went out of his way to sign autographs and shake hands with the young people that met the entourage at each stop.

Most important for Hatch was the excellent press given Reagan's visit, which tended to overshadow the bad press concerning the Foreman suit. And the fund-raising dinner at the Salt Lake Hilton on the evening of the 27th netted him $18,000.

In the morning Salt Lake Channel 4 interviewed Reagan prior to his departure to the airport. He was told by the newsman that one of Ford's campaign workers had intimated Ford's displeasure that Reagan was campaigning in Utah for Hatch when he should have been campaigning in Texas. Reagan, who had campaigned in several states for Ford, was deeply hurt. (The fact that Ford lost Texas in the general election was to add to the breach between the two that had smoldered just beneath the surface since the primaries.)

On this rather sour note, Reagan left for California. Hatch actually felt guilty over Reagan's trip to Utah. First the Foreman suit, then the anger of Gerald Ford—he was haunted by the thought that Reagan might have been sorry he came to Utah.

In the meantime the polls were shifting back and forth between Hatch and Moss. A scant few days before the election, the polls began to show Hatch inching ahead, varying from 1 to 4 percentage points. The Moss organization was arrogantly optimistic, however. Such a small lead by Hatch would be insufficient, they contended, to overcome Moss's traditional "hidden constituency" that always showed up at the last minute to confound the pollsters and annihilate the opposition.

Hatch was "running scared" and kept up a torturous schedule and a relentless volley against Moss's voting record, his alleged fiscal irresponsibility and his antipathy to Utah's "right-to-work" climate.

Hatch was concerned over the possible outcome of the last TV debate on Salt Lake's Channel 2. There were many undecided voters and it was conceivable that this final debate would make the difference. Hatch knew he could "take" Moss in the debate. What was worrying him was the inevitability of Moss's making whatever he could of the Foreman suit. There was no doubt that suit had hurt Hatch politically.

Both candidates were nervous as the last-minute preparations were made for the debate. Five minutes before they were to begin, Mac Haddow burst into the studio and handed Hatch an envelope, winking with that certain degree of self-satisfaction as he did so. Hatch went to a corner, opened the envelope, and read its contents. Several of Moss's entourage were watching him intently. They saw Hatch's eyes enlarge to the size of saucers. Otherwise his face remained taut and expressionless.

Sure enough, as the debate became increasingly heated, Moss suddenly brought up the Foreman suit, intimating that voters should think twice about supporting a man who was being sued for securities fraud. Hatch, he claimed, had an obligation to tell the people of Utah about the suit. He had not done so, and thus remained suspect.

Then it was Hatch's turn. He looked intently at Moss for several seconds without speaking. His hand was in his coat pocket, confidently patting the message given to him by Haddow shortly before air time. Finally, he asked Moss, "Senator, have you ever been sued?"

Moss was taken aback. "Of course," he replied haltingly, "all attorneys get sued sooner or later. Anyone can bring suit by just paying $15.00 to file a complaint."

"Have you ever been sued for land fraud, Senator?"

The color drained from Moss's face.

"Well," said Hatch, slowly bringing the envelope and its contents out of his coat pocket, "I have here a copy of the complaint where you were sued for land fraud two years ago by your former top campaign worker."

Moss slumped in his chair and said nothing. Hatch waited a moment to let his coup sink in, then he unleashed a verbal barrage against the tongue-tied Senator.

Senator Moss never regained composure. After silently listening to Hatch's attack for some time as if his thoughts were elsewhere, he suddenly screwed up his face, and with his right hand, reached across in front of the commentator, Lucky Severson, and pushed against Hatch's chest as he cried out, "Would you please hush up and let me say something!"

Hatch sat back in his chair and calmly clasped his hands in front of him and said words to the effect that, "Certainly, I'll always hush up for a United States Senator."

While the debate was continuing, Haddow was calling reporters at television Channels 4 and 5 to tell them of the suit against Moss. The reporter at Channel 5 had been a supporter of Moss. He was incredulous. "Haddow, you had better be able to prove what you are saying. If I come down there and find you're feeding me a bunch of baloney, I won't take kindly to it."

"If you will come down here," responded Haddow, "I will give you a copy of the complaint."

When the bewildered Moss left the Channel 2 station, reporters from both Channels 4 and 5 were waiting for him, cameras and all. The reporter from Channel 5 held up a copy of the complaint against Moss and asked him about it. Moss was beside himself. He instinctively grabbed for the papers and bellowed, "Check with my attorney."

Moss made another mistake that night—he agreed to go to Channel 5 to be interviewed. After all, the reporter was his supporter. *And the reporter roasted him.*

Moss emerged bloody from his nightmare, but he was a professional. He was, in his eyes at least, not yet beaten. The Moss organization struck back ferociously.

At approximately 6:30 P.M. on Friday, October 28th, an employee from the *Salt Lake Tribune* made a call to Mac Haddow. "You had better get down here," he warned Haddow, "and look at the full-page ad Moss has taken out against Hatch for Sunday. It's really nasty."

Late that evening Haddow was admitted to the *Tribune* newsroom and shown a copy of the ad. It was indeed "nasty." Hatch was accused of being bought and controlled by Colorado "Beer Barons." He was also accused of accepting illegal funds from right-wing contributors, and other clandestine sources.

Early the next morning Hatch had a meeting with former BYU President Ernest L. Wilkinson, in which they discussed the Moss ad. Wilkinson was very upset. After studying a copy of the ad for some time, the former Washington attorney dictated a three-page telegram to the editors of Utah's major newspapers, in which he claimed Moss's ad was scandalous and libelous. He further claimed that malicious intent could be drawn from the ad, and that Hatch would sue every newspaper that had the temerity to print it.

After the telegrams were sent, Wilkinson began to make blistering phone calls, as only he could, to various newspapers. He was angry and emotionally distraught. To him the possibility of Hatch losing to his old political enemy Moss was unthinkable.

That afternoon, while attending a football game at Brigham

Young University, Ernest L. Wilkinson suffered a heart attack. The fact that he was in the company of his son, a prominent heart specialist, prolonged his life for yet a short season.

On Sunday, October 30, the major newspapers of the state came out as usual. The Moss ad had been deleted from all of them.

On election day, Orrin Hatch and his wife spent the morning in the Mormon Temple, the only place they could be alone and out of the political arena. In the late afternoon they voted, then went to the Hilton Hotel to await the election returns.

During the campaign the Hatch organization found television Channel 4 to be the most fair and balanced in news reporting. Hatch had decided that, win or lose, he would give Channel 4 his initial statement. At 8:15, he drove to the station, leaving Haddow to represent him at the hotel. The first person Hatch recognized at Channel 4 was Dan Jones, the expert pollster from Utah State University. With only 1,200 votes in from across the state, Jones had declared Hatch the winner. Simultaneously, the Channel 5 pollster, Jim Mayfield, a University of Utah professor, was also claiming victory for Hatch.

Back at the Hilton, Senator Moss was refusing to concede defeat before a barrage of questions from overbearing reporters. He was certain that his "hidden constituency" from Salt Lake and Weber counties would pull him out. Then the returns began to come in from those areas. Hatch was running nearly even with Moss in Weber County, a traditional Democratic party stronghold, and early returns showed Hatch winning Salt Lake County. Moss's "hidden constituency" was not going to materialize.

Moss supporters were stunned. The Moss "victory party" (ironically convened at the same hotel as the Hatch victory party), had been celebrating boisterously since about 6:00 P.M. The booze and braggadocia flowed copiously until about 8:45. Then a telling silence fell over the crowd.

In the Four Seasons Room, where the Hatch supporters were milling about, there was, from the first minutes of the evening, an air of victory one could feel just by being in the room. As the minutes passed, the confident chatter grew in crescendo as the returns began to come in. *Deseret News* staff writers Costanza and Spencer reported that "an electric mood of victory filled the election night headquarters of Republican Orrin Hatch even before the returns and projections began. It was as though the will of the huge Hatch crowd standing in an ornate Hilton Hotel conference room was stronger than mere vote tallies soon to come."

At 9:00 P.M. Mac Haddow was anxiously pacing back and forth at the Hilton entrance, awaiting the return of Hatch from Channel 4. When he arrived, Haddow broke away, waded through a crush of people to the podium of the Four Seasons Room. He raised his arms for silence, then cried out, *"Our new Senator is coming!"*

Pandemonium broke loose. It was some minutes before Hatch could find his way through well-wishers to take the stand. When he passed the Moss conference room, Senator Moss had just conceded the election before the television cameras. He then turned and tucked his head under Governor-elect Scott Matheson's chin and sobbed with all the anguish of his broken heart.

Hatch momentarily felt deeply for Moss and strained to look at him over the pushing crowd. But soon the euphoria of victory consumed his own emotions. The cheering crowd swept him past the Moss congregation to the Four Seasons Room podium. He stood for a moment just looking at his joyous, rollicking supporters, wondering if it was all a marvelous dream. . . . Then, Orrin Hatch smiled.

Part Two
The Neophyte

Chapter 4
ORIENTATION

Hatch arrived in Washington while the 94th Congress was still in session. After purchasing a home in Virginia, he visited the office of the man he had unseated to pay his respects. But Moss was inconsolable. Twice he said, ''I can't believe the people of Utah would do this to me.'' His eyes periodically welled with tears.

Occasionally the victorious challenger will be offered the office of the defeated Senator, while awaiting his permanent office assignment. Not so with Hatch. He suspected that Moss had refused to allow him to use the office. Too, Hatch was listed 98th in seniority. For his first months in office he was ensconced in the basement of the Russell Building, in room 15B with some auxiliary rooms alongside.

When Hatch and his staff opened the steel metal doors to the stark atmosphere of 15B and its accompanying offices, they all had a good laugh. The rooms were dingy, scarred and nearly barren. Open pipes hung from the ceiling.

Hatch's staff organized into special furniture details to scour the Senate Building for chairs and desks. Someone noticed that there were several pieces of old-looking furniture in the outside halls of both the Dirksen and Russell buildings. Just junk, they thought, probably to be thrown out. At any rate, no one would miss these scarred pieces. Thinking this was rejected furniture, Hatch's aides absconded with enough pieces to furnish adequately 15B and the two other companion offices. They did not realize that this furniture, some of it original furnishings, was decorative and had been marked by the Sergeant at Arms. The furniture was reported mysteriously missing. Not until Hatch changed offices was the mystery cleared up. Hatch was red-faced and hoped, but in vain, that the story would not circulate through the Senate. Most embarrassing of all was the Hatch office's inability to recognize the nature of the furniture they had "liberated."

After several weeks, Hatch was moved to a suite on the backside of the Sixth Floor of the Dirksen Building, the farthest possible walk from the Senate floor. The offices were small and the furniture was "a beat-up modern." Human nature being what it is, Hatch and his staff soon grew to miss the "old days" of 15B.

Those first few days prior to and subsequent to his swearing-in were very important for Hatch as he became acquainted with his new colleagues. At a seminar sponsored by the Committee for the Survival of a Free Congress at the Washington Sheraton Hotel, Hatch met Senators Paul Laxalt again, Dick Schweiker, Bob Griffin and others.

Hatch was singularly impressed with Senator Barry Goldwater. Hatch described him as "a crusty, irreverent fighter, who lived by principle, was always anywhere and everywhere the same, with a coherent and consistent moral-conservative philosophy that never deviated from the high plane of his integrity. He could be neither bought, threatened, nor cajoled." Goldwater reminded Hatch of "an old wounded eagle" he had once seen high in Utah's Wasatch mountains—bloody with the scars of battle, but undaunted. Goldwater was the kind of man that men when they are young want to become; the kind of man that men when they are old wish they had been. From their first meeting Hatch and Goldwater were bound by a camaraderie that only men who devoutly share a cause can understand.

One Senator, Robert Dole, filled Hatch with compassion. Dole seemed down and unsure of himself. He was being pushed to run for Senate Minority whip but he was hesitant. To a close friend he confided, "I cannot take another defeat."

As Vice-Presidential candidate under Gerald Ford, Dole had taken a severe pummelling from the national press. Only those who have experienced the verbal invective that can be applied by the national press can understand its nerve-wracking impact. Sometimes these tactics become little more than smears launched against certain public figures because of intense dislike of their philosophy and politics. These smear tactics used against such undeserving recipients as former Secretary of the Treasury, William Simon, Howard "Bo" Calloway, former Congressman and Secretary of the Army, and Maurice Stans, former Secretary of Commerce, are but a few examples.

Now some elements of the press were implying he was the cause of Ford's loss. All of this had taken its price on Dole, and his spirit seemed to be momentarily broken. When Dole first came to the Congress he was a "fire-eater." "He was so exciting," said one Senator, "that we felt he would be one of the greatest people ever to hold office in this country."

On this afternoon, however, Bob Dole looked a long way from there. He was bloodied and his head was bowed. He seemed to have been intimidated and it was taking its toll on his spirit and leadership.

That evening Hatch wrote a letter to his oldest son describing the excitement of the day's events, in which he expressed his personal like for Dole, called him a man of *vivre* and moral substance. "We have not heard the last from Bob Dole," he predicted.

In that same letter Hatch also wrote of Senator Strom Thurmond, the Democrat turned Republican who once ran for the presidency under the Dixiecrat Party rather than support Truman, "You just had to admire this straight-backed older gentleman who is married to a 30-year-old beautiful girl and with whom he has fathered four children. He has to be one of the more impressive people in the Senate."

Hatch was also impressed by Bob Griffin, another candidate for Senate Minority leader. Of freshman Senator Malcom Wallup, Hatch wrote, "this man looks like one of the more steady conservative and dependable people. He is a rancher of English descent. He is a big man, a rough man, but nevertheless, a very articulate person."

Hatch was taken by the clever personality and extraordinary intelligence of the 70-year-old "Sam" Hayakawa. At informal gatherings and Republican Conference meetings, they were to seek out each other's company, although the California Senator frequently "snoozed" during these meetings.

Later, during Jimmy Carter's State of the Union message, Senator Hayakawa was snoozing when a reporter with a camera began to pan in his direction. Ted Stevens leaned over to Hatch and whispered, "Orrin, wake him up, wake him up, the cameras are on him." Hatch poked his elbow into Hayakawa's ribs. The startled gentleman jerked up in his seat and cried out, for all to hear, "I'm awake! I'm awake!" Although his snooze prompted press criticism, Hatch quipped on a later California trip that "One Sam Hayakawa asleep is worth two Tunneys awake."

Of the Democratic Party freshmen, Hatch was most impressed with the flamboyant Daniel Patrick Moynihan whose public life had led him to lend his expertise to both Democratic and Republican administrations. Hatch measured him as an intelligent and stubborn man whose conscience would cause him to vote against the Democratic majority more than once during the days ahead, especially over defense and foreign policy.

Hatch met arch-liberal Democrat Hubert Horatio Humphrey only once before the new Congress began, but, like almost everyone else, he immediately liked him. In the next few months Hatch's admiration and respect for Humphrey grew. It was not just his kindness, his class and his friendliness. Senator Humphrey was, using the modern rather than the traditional vernacular, a *true* liberal.

As Hatch gained experience in the Senate he learned to differentiate between liberals. There were the "interest-group" liberals, those Senators tied closely to special interests which demanded special legislation or government largesse on their behalf. Such liberals are willing agents of these groups, where votes and favors are exchanged for electoral support and substantial campaign contributions. Often there is a third entity involved in, to use the term of Theodore White, the "Iron Triangle"—a bureaucratic agency or bureau which looks upon the interest group as its clientele, and the entangled Senator as a power broker in its behalf. The main purpose of this troika is mutual support and political survival. These alliances were to spell doom for any substantive attempt by Carter to bring the runaway spending of Congress under control, and thus relieve the pressure of inflation.

Hatch had placed Humphrey and some of the other Senate liberals in a different category from those he branded "interest-group liberals." Hatch felt that these were men of integrity, self-styled progressives, who saw liberalism as an ideology of progress on the one hand, and a means to solve complicated social programs on the other. They were "their own men." They were honest, not self-seeking in their beliefs. If they supported a social measure or voted for a bill favorable to a powerful interest group such as the AFL-CIO or the NEA, it was out of conviction rather than self-interest. Hatch could understand this, for he was an "honest conservative." Here was an identity in spirit. In Senator Orrin Hatch, the venerable Senator Hubert Humphrey had a sincere friend and admirer until the day he died. It is interesting that in Hatch's first freshman year in the United States Senate, among the men he respected most were Barry Goldwater and Hubert Humphrey, Senate spokesmen for opposing philosophies.

Early one morning Orrin Hatch began a pilgrimage around Capitol Hill. He was alone with his innermost thoughts. It seemed impossible to him that he should be there; that he should have frustrated a "sewed-up" Utah Republican Convention; that he, an unknown, should have emerged victorious in the primary over a candidate with the experience, the ability and the charm of Jack Carlson. He had to smile when he thought of his political näiveté in boldly asking for the endorsement of a national Republican figure—Reagan—during a primary of two Republicans. It just wasn't done, but Reagan had granted that endorsement. And, the burying of Moss under 50,000 votes—Hatch shook his head. It seemed a dream.

It was good to be alone. He passed a few people at that early hour. No one knew him. He was just another American citizen renewing and reviewing his heritage. There was an invigorating chill in the air that morning. On the lawns surrounding the ''Hill'' there were patches of snow. The day would have been much colder had it not been overcast. But occasionally the morning sun broke through with a startling brightness that caused the snow to sparkle and brought a brilliant sheen to the wetness of the walkways.

As he passed the monuments, as he stopped to ponder the shrines, the events of the nation's history flowed in profusion through his mind. Events that he had once read about and long ago forgotten broke through his memory. Never in his life had it all been so real, so believable, so inspiring.

It was dawn when Hatch began his pilgrimage at the Lincoln Memorial. The great tree-lined pool, stretching a half-mile from the Lincoln Memorial to the Washington Monument sparkled in the sunlight.

Above the great statue of Lincoln were the words: ''In this temple as in the hearts of the people for whom he saved the Union the memory of Abraham Lincoln is enshrined forever.''

On each side of the great hall were four Doric columns. Beyond the columns on the south wall was inscribed the Gettysburg address. Hatch found himself reading the words aloud: ''Four score and seven years ago our Fathers brought forth on this continent a new nation conceived in liberty and dedicated to the proposition that all men are created equal . . .''

On the north wall Hatch read Lincoln's second Inaugural address. It thrilled him to read and repeat again, ''With malice toward none, with charity for all, with firmness in the right as God gives us to see the right . . .''

Feeling invigorated, Hatch jogged to the Jefferson Memorial, its northeast entrance facing the tidal basin of the Potomac. As Hatch passed from the plaza up the steps toward the memorial room, he looked up, above the entrance where was engraved the figure of Jefferson standing before the Committee selected to write the Declaration of Independence.

Above the four colonnade openings and interior forums upon which the dome rests, is an inscription: ''I have sworn upon the altar of

God eternal hostility against every form of tyranny over the mind of man."

To the right, ahead of the statue Hatch, once again found himself reading aloud from the inscription. "God who gave us life gave us liberty. Can the liberties of a nation be secure when we have removed a conviction that these liberties are a gift from God? Indeed, I tremble for my country when I reflect that God is just, that his justice cannot sleep forever."

The next stop in Hatch's pilgrimage was the Washington Monument. To Hatch its great size was impressive while its simplicity was eloquent. As he perceived the panorama from the base of the monument he was impressed with the symmetry of the Capitol City—the Capitol, the White House, the Mall with its long tree-bordered pool; the Washington Monument and the Lincoln Memorial on the west axis of the Capitol; and finally the Jefferson Memorial on a line with the south axis of the White House.

From the Washington Memorial, Hatch walked to the old Library of Congress, then the Supreme Court Building. Majestic in appearance it was set off by a double row of four Roman columns each. Above the massive entrance were engraved the words, *Equal Justice Under Law*.

From the Supreme Court building, Hatch crossed the park to the Capitol building. High atop the Capitol dome Hatch recognized the bronze statue of *Freedom*.

Finally, freshman Senator Orrin Hatch of Utah stood in the Chamber he had reserved for last—the United States Senate.

For some minutes Hatch stood almost motionless contemplating the chamber first as an entity, then in its constituent parts. Near the ceiling, around the gallery, were busts of famous lawmakers. Hatch recognized Thomas Jefferson, John Adams, John Calhoun, George Clinton, and others. Between each bust, high in the gallery was a bronze torch holder.

At last Hatch moved into the Senate floor in search of his desk. His chair was located in the third row, second seat from the aisle on the Republican side of the Chamber (left side). The chair of the President Pro Tempore was directly in front. "Good," Hatch thought. "I'll be right in the middle of any action on the Floor." Since his chair was toward the back of the room, Hatch surmised he would be in a good position to see all that was going on.

Hatch reverently reached out and touched his dark red mahogany desk with fingers that were shaking slightly. The colonial style of the desk seemed quite fitting to Hatch. From each desk hung a microphone. Hatch wondered what it would be like to address "Mr. President" for the first time.

He sat down at his desk. He was surprised at how close the desks were to each other. He was also pleasantly surprised at how comfortable the cushioned dark mahogany chair was. Everything looked so stately. On the upper edge of the desk was a pen well. In it lay an old-fashioned pen with a metal tip beside a small container of black ink. Covering the desk were copies of bills that had been considered as the 94th Congress worked out the last days of its existence. Also on the desk was the previous day's *Congressional Record*.

Slowly Hatch opened the desk drawer. There he found a few pieces of legislation and a Congressional directory. Then he saw the names of the Senators who had occupied the desk, written by their own hand. There were the names of ex-Presidents McKinley, Kennedy, and Truman. Also, carefully written in order of occupancy, Hatch read the names Muskie, Tower, Humphrey, Church, Percy, Thurmond, Schwiecker.

Hatch carefully closed the drawer. Then his fingers touched a brass plate on the top of the desk. On it was neatly engraved "Senator Orrin G. Hatch."

Then the spell was broken. For some time during that early morning he had felt almost in a detached state—as if he were not really there but perceiving it all looking as one would at a film, or from outside through a window. The atmosphere and the quiet emptiness of the room lent itself to the euphoria.

Now chattering and laughing Senate pages burst into the Chamber. One of the Pages rushed to Hatch's desk and in all the sincerity of youth grasped him by the hand and cried out, "Welcome, sir, you must be Senator Hatch."

Hatch sniffled embarrassingly and cleared his throat. "Ah, ah, yes, thank you young man. It is good to be here."

Late that evening Hatch wrote an impassioned piece in his diary in which he expressed wonder that men could have walked where he had walked this day and then by their actions default the legacy that had been so carefully left to them by the sacrifice of blood. That same evening he wrote a personal letter to each of his five children—even to those who were at home—explaining to them his feelings of this day.

Orrin Hatch was sworn in as United States Senator on January 4, 1977. As he looked about his surroundings, the term "these hallowed halls" rushed through his mind time and again. He was awed by his presence there, humbled by its history, inspired by its origin. He sensed that he was at the threshold of a great and important adventure, and he promised himself for the hundredth time that he was going to count.

Shortly before the swearing-in ceremonies, Senator Hatfield of Oregon asked Hatch to follow him outside the Chamber. "There is someone who wants to meet you," he said.

In a few moments they were entering the office of the Vice-President of the United States, Nelson Rockefeller. Rockefeller was pacing up and down. Hatch thought he looked very dejected. He got the feeling that this man was very lonely. Nevertheless, the Vice-President was cordial and friendly. "Well," he said taking Hatch by the hand, "you are to be congratulated on your stunning victory." After a short discussion, the three walked back to the Senate together.

Once back in the main Senate chamber, Hatch was seated in the front row, third seat from the far right. Sitting immediately to his right was Bob Packwood, from Oregon, and to his right Bob Griffin of Michigan and principal candidate for minority leader. Seated to Hatch's left was Strom Thurmond.

The Senators marched up in rows of four to the Vice-President's desk where Rockefeller administered the oath. Each time the oath was administered, everybody in the chamber, including all those in the gallery, applauded. It was a deeply moving experience for Hatch.

When Hubert Humphrey went up to be sworn in, he looked like a ghost. He was at that moment recovering from a cancer operation performed in New York City. After Humphrey signed the Senate roll book, he received a sustained ovation from those in the Chamber, by Democrat and Republican alike.

Then Orrin Hatch walked forward. He raised his right hand, and was read the oath.

"Do you solemnly swear that you will support and defend the Constitution of the United States against all enemies, foreign or domestic; that you will bear true faith and allegiance to the same; that you take this obligation freely, without any mental reservations, and that you will well and faithfully discharge the duties of the office on which you are about to enter, so help you God?"

"I do—so help me God."

Chapter 5
THE "COMEUPPANCE"

Prior to the beginning of each new Congress, the Congressmen meet with their respective parties in Conference (the Democrats use the term "Caucus"). Here the party leadership is selected and preparations made for the awarding of committee assignments.

At the Republican Conference, Carl Curtis was re-elected as Chairman. To Hatch's complete surprise, Curtis had asked him to offer his nominating speech. It was a singular honor, and an unprecedented one. Hatch was the only freshman who nominated anybody for a Conference position.

Texas Conservative John Tower won the Chairmanship of the Policy Committee, which serves as a forum for discussion, communication and sometimes helps to work out compromises among differing Senate Republicans. Bob Packwood won the Chairmanship of the Senatorial Campaign Committee, which attempts to help Republican senatorial candidates to be elected, and incumbents to be re-elected.

At first, Jack Danforth was the only freshman to be granted a position on the Policy Committee. Hatch and Hayakawa were listed on the Senatorial Campaign Committee. Then Goldwater, backed by other conservatives, suggested that more freshmen ought to be on the Policy Committee. This suggestion caused a series of events that proved quite beneficial to the young conservative newcomers. Conference Chairman, Carl Curtis, in a surprising move, selected Utah Senator Jake Garn as Chairman of the Select Committee on Committees. Garn immediately stepped down from his position on the Policy Committee and recommended that Hatch be appointed in his place.

73

All of this did not sit well with liberal Senator Jacob Javits, who had served as the Select Committee on Committees Chairman the previous year. Javits was not one to take lightly what he supposed to be a personal affront and a conservative ploy. That evening he called Carl Curtis and read him the riot act. He also went to other leaders of the Republican Conference to express his displeasure. Finally, Secretary to the Minority Bill Hildenbrand came up with a precedent showing the chairmanship to be a rotating chairmanship. At that point, Javits, a man whose character was above pettiness, apologized to Curtis and supported the rotation.

The change in this important committee's leadership was to prove a boon for the new freshman conservatives. Assignments to Congress's standing committees are crucial for the political future of new Senators. It is in the standing committees where the real work of the Congress takes place. They serve as a means of screening the legislature's business, and a process, often involving the use of subcommittees, of considering legislation in some detail, tasks impossible for any chamber as a whole to perform. The committees bring specialization to the consideration of the inevitable complexities in the content of legislation, and provide committee members the opportunity to gain expertise in the subject matter of their respective committees. Here they can earn respect, deference and power.

But some committees have more prestige than others. Some committees are more actively involved in the momentous decisions that affect the nation. Some committees see more action and more important action than others. Therefore, for the new freshmen conservatives, the fact that conservative Jake Garn, rather than liberal Jacob Javits, was chairman of the committee which made an important contribution to standing committee assignments, was fortuitous.

Hatch had studied the Senate standing committee system in great detail and had selected the committees of which he wanted to be a part even before he had arrived in Washington. Because he was a former member of a labor union and because he believed big labor bosses were serving neither the working man nor the country at large and because he believed that public welfare was the most abused area in national government, Hatch wanted to be selected as a member of the Senate Labor and Public Welfare Committee—under the new reorganization, the Labor and Human Resources Committee. He felt the most important domestic legislation would be coming through this committee.

In addition, Hatch desired to be placed on the Judiciary Committee. He had calculated that another 20 percent to 30 percent of the important legislation considered in the Senate would come through it. The Judiciary Committee is a specialized committee with substantial power. Therefore, from his first day in Washington, Hatch campaigned with Republican party leaders for positions on these committees. His instant prestige in Washington, plus his new friendship with Goldwater and other substantial Republican conservatives, not to mention Senator Garn's selection on the Select Committee of the Committee on Committees, all combined to grant Hatch his wishes.

The President of the Senate, of course, is the Vice-President. However, this peculiarity in the checks-and-balances system does not carry with it much authority. Although the Vice-President may preside, he may vote only to break a tie. And since his presence in the Senate is understandably erratic, custom has provided the President *pro tempore,* a member of the Senate majority party, usually a member with long seniority—the "grand ole man" of the majority party—to preside in his absence.

The primary respective party leadership in the Senate falls to the majority and minority party or floor leaders and their respective whips. With no formal power constitutionally granted to these party leadership positions, their authority rests upon the willingness of their colleagues to follow their leadership. The relative independence of the United States Congressman through the peculiar American electoral process, especially the primary system that has served not to involve more people in the democratic processes, but also to divest political party leadership from the selection of candidates, has caused party loyalty to become only one of many influences affecting one's behavior and one's vote—from personal philosophy, to interest group alliances, to the nature of the home constituency.

Typically, floor leaders stand near the ideological center of their Congressional parties, are experienced parliamentarians and have leadership abilities that are respected by the Senate membership. The most recent giants among the Senate floor leaders have been Lyndon Johnson and Everett Dirksen.

To be selected floor leader by one's peers is indeed an honor—with some reservations. It is an expression of confidence since the whole Senatorial party will suffer with an inept floor leader. It is the job of the respective floor leaders to guide their party's program through the Senate. Since major government policy proposals now originate in the Executive branch, only the party whose man is sitting in the White House will tend to have a detailed program. The Congressional party without a President of their political persuasion will be relegated largely to an obstructionist role, that is, as a critic of the proposed legislation of the other party.

It was in the contest for Republican minority floor leader that Hatch experienced his first defeat as a Senator. The two front-runners for the position were Howard Baker and Robert Griffin. Hatch admired both, but leaned toward Griffin. One reason was that Griffin was up for re-election in 1978 and might well have needed this honor in order to keep his seat in Michigan. "There are too few of us left," Hatch reasoned to himself, "to take a chance on losing any more." Another consideration was whether to have a spokesman (Baker) or a tactician and procedural expert (Griffin).

Behind-the-scenes campaigning between contestants is common, and this case was no exception. Republican Senators were approached by both Baker and Griffin. Among the freshmen all but Hatch and Wallop opted for Baker. It was difficult for Hatch to tell Baker that he had committed to Griffin, but he did so, directly and truthfully. Baker appreciated this forthrightness that was to give Hatch a quick reputation for integrity. As Baker turned to leave he hesitated and looked back at Hatch. Then he said, "Mr. Hatch, I like you. Yes, I like you."

"That goes both ways, sir," answered Hatch.

Baker won 19 to 18. It was a tough defeat for Griffin, but he took it in style and immediately threw his support behind Baker. Interestingly, but, not untypically, *both* Baker *and* Griffin had gone into the vote with a *majority* of Republican Senators verbally committed to each. No wonder, thought Hatch, that Baker had appreciated a quick, unencumbered, and honest answer from him.

After the party leadership has been organized, the job of reconstituting the various committees begins. The chairmanships always go to the majority party, and these chairmen are blessed with a majority of their party on each committee, supposedly by "rule of thumb" roughly in proportion to their numerical percentage in the full Senate.

Seniority is crucial. Although there are some exceptions, and although both parties have attempted to modify the custom, committee chairmanships are almost always granted automatically to the ranking member of the majority party on each committee.

In spite of this nearly automatic selection process, committee chairmen typically maintain a high level of prestige and exercise substantial authority over legislation assigned to their committees.

Thus, seniority is a vital ingredient in the power structure of

Congress. It is this fact of congressional politics that was behind the month-early resignation of Republican Senator Wallace F. Bennett in 1974, allowing his Republican successor, Jake Garn, to have a few weeks' seniority jump on his fellow freshmen. Then in 1978, when "Sam" Hayakawa upset Democratic incumbent John Tunney, the latter, in an extraordinary beau geste, resigned a few days early and petitioned Governor Jerry Brown to appoint his opponent, thereby giving Hayakawa an edge of seniority over his freshmen colleagues.

When Senator Moss was asked if he would extend the same favor to Hatch, he declined. He referred to Hatch's campaign statements which implied that Moss's 18-year tenure and committee standings were of little importance to Utah because of his liberal voting record. Too, he added, he did not want to put his loyal staff off the federal payroll until absolutely necessary, an utterly inappropriate assertion, since staff are kept on until the end of the year even if a Senator resigns early.

From the very beginning, some of the Republican professionals looked upon the so-called "new conservatives" from the West, especially Hatch, with some misgivings. They did not sit well with some of the Republican Old Guard for their refusal to be apprentices. Theirs was also a proclivity to be less tied to the party for party's sake alone. To make matters increasingly touchy, virtually overnight the freshmen had become a new coalition in the Senate. Their conservative philosophy and their zeal had made them as a group a difficult challenge for the Republican party leadership, who had to balance some major philosophical differences in the party. They were not mavericks in the sense that they stood independent of the Republican party. Theirs was not a contentious nor an uncooperative spirit. Still, it was obvious that they would not back party directives for expediency's sake. This includes not only legislation, but support for particular Senate leaders and even party-supported candidates for administrative positions. Soon prominent newsmen such as the remarkable and controversial Jack Anderson were calling them the "untouchables."

At the head of what the media was calling the new "Rocky Mountain Conservative Coalition" of 1976 was Utah's newest Senator, Orrin Hatch. His political näiveté gave him no hint that he and his new young conservative Senators and Congressmen-elect were the vanguard of a conservative swell that just four years later would give every appearance of a possible political re-alignment that might approach that of the 1930s.

Hatch was amazed and not a little concerned at how quickly he was moved into the limelight. It was something he had neither planned nor even anticipated. Yet within days of his arrival at the nation's capital, the media was postulating his future.

His appearance, his charisma, his philosophy and the surprising facts of his election combined to propel him in print to a position of leadership in the "New Right," a movement he had not even known existed before he had arrived in Washington.

The *Congressional Quarterly* of November 6, 1976, while claiming no real perceptible difference in the party makeup of the Senate, pointed out that "some of the more clearly identifiable voting blocs will be getting some new blood. The 'new right' group, led in the past two Congresses by Republicans such as Jesse A. Helms of North Carolina and James A. McClure of Idaho, will be getting a possible new leader in Orrin Hatch (R-Utah), and may also embrace Republicans Malcom Wallop of Wyoming and Schmitt of New Mexico.

"Hatch will be one of the most intriguing new figures in the Senate. . . .

"Hatch proved to be a born campaigner, with unusual stage presence and oratorical skill. Conservative interest groups are already counting on him as a spokesman in the 95th Congress, and some are even talking about him as a possible presidential candidate."

In February 7, 1977, under an article entitled "Moving into the Spotlight," *U.S. News and World Report* reported that "Conservatives may have found a new national leader in Utah's freshman Senator Orrin G. Hatch. . . . Today Conservatives across the nation are taking his measure as a potential successor to Barry Goldwater and Ronald Reagan."

To be sure, the spokesmen for the "New Conservatives" were delighted with this new political celebrity who appeared out of nowhere. The National Conservative Political Action Committee (NCPAC) called Hatch "one of the most attractive political newcomers in many years. He is a seasoned debater and a born leader." The February 1977 *Conservative Digest* called Hatch "the Senate's newest star. . . . Even before his election to the U.S. Senate, Utah's Orrin Hatch was touted by seasoned political observers as 'perhaps the most dynamic Conservative newcomer.'"

To the chagrin of some of the Senate Republican Old Guard, freshman Senator Orrin Hatch was gaining a great deal of attention even before the new Congressional session began. It did not take them long to perceive Hatch as an emerging spokesman for what was being called "The New Right." This disturbed them more than it did the Senate

Democrats, most of whom treated the emergence of the New Conservatism rather cavalierly. It would, they predicted, self-destruct, just as had the "old" Conservativism.

But to the Republican godfathers, this aggressive new conservatism offered the possibility of pulling the Republican Party out of the voter mainstream—what former UCLA political scientist Ivan Hinderaker called "The Big Reasonable Middle"—to an extreme position. Too, it was obvious that the new conservatives had a message to deliver and the philosophical content and brazen determination to deliver that message. Apprenticeship and party loyalty were going to be secondary with them. The old Senate custom of, "go along, get along" was not congenial to their character.

Shortly before the Congressional Session began, a prominent Republican Senator took Hatch aside, politely, and with the demeanor of fatherly affection. "Orrin, I want you to know how happy we are that you are going to be with us in the Senate. Of course, we're happy to have any new Republican. But it's more than that. I believe you have everything it takes to become a great leader in the Republican Party and in the Senate. You'll move to the fore quickly and we'll all benefit by it.

"All I want to say is, take your time. Don't push too hard too fast. A little apprenticeship never hurt anybody, and, well, it's kind of expected, you know, a tradition, sort of.

"It doesn't take much for anyone to see that the Republican Party is in trouble. We just took another bath at the polls and now we're stuck with that damned peanut farmer from Georgia, more than likely for eight years. Every time this happens we get some of our people excited and they want the Republican Party to get out of the 'rut' as they call it. They want us to move way over to the right. Don't get me wrong, I'm a conservative myself, but you have to see this thing rationally. If we move this party to the fringe in our frustration, we could kill it off as a national political force. You can understand why some of us are a little concerned about this New Conservatism business. We just don't want to see some of our new members get involved with coalitions that would divide our Party in these critical times."

Hatch waited respectfully and without interrupting before he answered. Finally, he responded. "Senator, I do so much appreciate your counsel and your concern. But I must tell you that I believe the people of Utah have sent me here to do a job and that I am going to expend every ounce of energy in this stewardship they were kind enough to grant me.

"Furthermore, perhaps the American people need to hear conservative Republican Party principles loud and clear. There is really nothing in these last election results that tend to demonstrate that the Republican Party as a whole is swimming in America's mainstream.

"And you'll have to forgive me. I don't know what the New Conservativism is. All I know is this: Our nation is on the brink of disaster under its present political leadership; the Conservative philosophy of the Republican Party is the key to averting that disaster; and I feel that it is my obligation neither to sit around and fiddle while Rome burns nor to throw fuel on the flames. I'm here to try and do something about this deplorable condition—and if that means I'm a New Conservative, well, so be it."

Hatch learned that day that not all of his political antagonists would be sitting on the other side of the Senate. His refusal to acknowledge certain aspects of Senate tradition would not set well with some of the Old Guard. And sooner or later there would be personality irritants with some of his colleagues. Hatch's charisma was bound to incite jealousy, and his principled determination would cause some to curse what they believed to be his crass arrogance. But his sense of urgency overruled all other considerations.

Even after Reagan had become President and the Republicans had captured the Senate, this group of new Senate conservatives, whose members had been elected between 1974 and 1980, continued to reject the "go along, get along" pressures of Senate politics. Yet, while sometimes causing their own party leadership great difficulty, they (along with their ideological counterparts in the House) were able to forge new avenues of communication and cooperation with conservative Democrats who proved absolutely essential to the legislative success of President Reagan's economic program. The leadership of the New Conservativism had created the statement, "Better to work with a *good* Democrat than a *lousy* Republican." Some of the conservative political action committees continued to anger certain Republican party leaders by actually supporting conservative Democrats over more liberal Republicans for both Senate and House seats.

The New Conservatives came to Congress with a sense of mission. It was not their intention to measure up to the Republican Party; the party, to retain their support, was going to have to measure up to *their* ideals of political and philosophical integrity. Jack Anderson gives us an example of this in his *Washington Post* article concerning Orrin Hatch entitled "The Misreading of a Senate Untouchable." Although the event happened as Hatch was finishing his first six-year term, it serves to portray an attitude he and others had brought with them to the Senate and never lost:

The heroes in the drama of government are sometimes damned by the press and public along with the rascals. But the honorable men and women in public life deserve to be noticed. Such a legislator is Senator Orrin G. Hatch (R-Utah), a feisty lawyer, a former construction worker, a card-holding member of the AFL-CIO and an erstwhile bishop in the Mormon Church.

Though an unabashed conservative in his political philosophy, his sense of personal rectitude has made him just as tough on Republicans as on Democrats when he suspects wrongdoing by government officials.

But apparently two Senate colleagues, . . . both . . . Republicans, had the impression that Hatch belonged to the "go-along-to-get-along" crowd.

According to my sources, it took a stormy face-to-face confrontation in Hatch's office to instruct the two senators . . . that Hatch won't back off an investigation merely as a senatorial courtesy.

Yet for all his verve, enthusiasm, and determination, Orrin Hatch was almost completely unprepared for what he faced as an inexperienced freshman Senator. Hatch supposed that he and his new conservative colleagues would join with such stalwarts as Goldwater, Garn and Laxalt to make an immediate impact on the Senate, indeed, the whole of Congress. In this he became faced not only with disappointment, but with the greatest frustration of his life. Nothing he had ever experienced or learned was to prepare him for what he was to encounter. He found himself caught in a web of an unConstitutional and morally indefensible hierarchy of power and politics he didn't even know existed.

Almost from the moment he was elected, a number of special interests, long since accustomed to the wholesale national trend of trading political support for special favors, began their pressure, deftly playing the political game while dangling before him the carrot of future political support (or suggesting obligation for past support). Before he left Utah he had listened to great numbers of demands and complaints. He was painfully unaware of the extent to which millions of Americans had come to look upon government as the dispenser of special favors and government officials as brokers of those favors. No sooner had Hatch arrived in Washington, then exponents of special interests descended on his office like a swarm of locusts. Like every other member of Congress, a large portion of his staff was exclusively involved in answering letters, chasing down complaints and doing research into the substance and reliability of demands. The pressure was so insistent that Hatch had difficulty not becoming cynical.

One late afternoon Hatch's secretary informed him that three rough-hewn Utah ranchers had been waiting to see him. After the introductions Hatch bluntly asked, "What can I do for you gentlemen?"

"Not a damn thing," was the smiling reply. "We're just on vacation here with our families and wanted to drop in and say we believe in you and what you're doing. If we can ever be of help to you please allow us to have that privilege."

Hatch's eyes welled with tears as he embraced these leathery cowboys.

It took only a few weeks for Hatch to discover the arrogance and the intransigence that existed in many areas of the federal bureaucracy, that vast army of public employees which has grown geometrically to manage the endless social programs enacted by Congress during the past 50 years. Like the equally naïve Jimmy Carter, Hatch had found this labyrinthine pyramid of departments, agencies and bureaus to be virtually impregnable. President Carter had initially attempted to fulfill his campaign promise to curtail the size of the bureaucracy, to make it more responsive to political leadership, and to bring some vestige of economy into its operation. He was not yet through his first year in office when, in utter frustration, he abandoned the attempt altogether. So it was that the federal bureaucracy actually increased in cost, size, and its control over the private lives of the American people under Carter's Presidency, just as it had under nearly every President of this century, Republican and Democrat alike. A humbled Carter actually declared that in his administration no federal bureaucrat need fear for his job.

Hatch found that many of these massive bureaucratic organizations had long since ceased (if they ever had been) performing the role of servants of the people. They were primarily concerned with survival and "empire building." This was the essence of the politics of the federal bureaucracy—the incessant, day-by-day, hour-by-hour, manipulation of the power centers of government, the penetration of the budget-making process, and the enticement and/or threat to the myriad of society's enterprises and interest groups, many of whom owe their existence, relative power and growth to government patronage. This power was wielded by unelected and largely faceless government officials. Theirs is the power to promote certain interests by creating favorable rules and regulations that inhibit competition, while at the same time establishing other rules and regulations which frustrate innovation and enterprise in other, not-so-favored interests. All of this was reprehensible to Hatch.

By 1980, the Federal Register, which records the rules and regulations promulgated by the Federal agencies, contained 87,000 pages. William E. Simon reports that in the last two days of the Carter Administration, a thousand pages a day were added.

Waste and inefficiency, the introversion of the various agencies which precluded concern for the government, the public, or the system as a whole, literally infuriated Hatch. It seemed to him that the separation of powers and the checks and balances system provided by the Constitution was being replaced by a bureaucratic *fourth* branch of government of unelected and largely unaccountable public employees who exercised legislative, executive and judicial power with impunity directly over the people of the United States.

But most frustrating of all to Hatch was the realization of how widespread the influence powerful interests, many with supporting bureaus or agencies within government, held with individual members of Congress. This was especially pronounced among liberal Democratic Congressional veterans. It seemed to Hatch that the longer these men sat in Congress the more susceptible they became to the blandishments of special interest, and the more narrowly defined became their perspective of the purpose of government and their place in the larger scheme of things. This meant that some of the most momentous and far-reaching decisions made by the Congress of the United States were being influenced, not so much on the merits of the issue, not so much in relation to social or economic needs or realities, as from political pressure—the exchange of political power for political support. Hatch was almost willing to accept the caustic comment of a disenchanted New Dealer that the components of the modern Democratic Congressional party were "little more than agents for special interests." To the extent that this was true, the vast body of "unorganized" Americans were restricted in both their political influence and their representation. Even though they went to the polls they were to a greater or lesser extent disfranchised.

The sad commentary is that, in the last analysis, it is once again the weaker entities in our society which suffer most from government intervention and gain the fewest benefits—the unorganized and dispersed citizens and the relatively weaker economic, social and/or political interests.

In any publicly financed program, therefore, principle beneficiaries will be relatively affluent people or groups who can make an impact on the influence system and enjoy leverage in the governmental system, including, of course, the bureaucratic cadres called upon to administer the program.

It is the same with the distribution of federal aid benefits. To be sure, there are some redistributionist effects, but the aid tends to follow the lines of political influence more readily than those of economic necessity as a single criterion.

The numerous poverty programs tell a tragic story of funds flowing to a generation of intermediary poverty hucksters who have made a lucrative living passing as representatives of the poor. Audits have shown that substantial amounts of these funds have just disappeared. This, of course, flaunts the program design, directs funds away from those who genuinely seek to ameliorate poverty, defaults the needy recipients, and cheats the taxpayer.

Hatch had come to Washington at a crucial time when the sponsors of the collective state were to make a decided push for an all-out authoritarian welfare state. The idealistic Washington liberals saw their utopian dream of a benign socialistic system meeting every human need a real possibility. They were joined by the "Iron Triangle," the coalition of bureaucratic departments, associated interest groups, and tangential congressmen, all using the force and economic largesse of government, the demands of special interest, and electoral coalitions to secure and bolster their individual political influence and power. According to George Gilder, writing in his *Wealth and Poverty:*

> During the seventies, these enterprising bureaucrats gathered, bringing all their human capital and entrepreneurial aggressiveness to the ventures of the state. Many of them were lawyers, because governmental expansion is best achieved through exploiting the fertile chinks and fissures in the tomes of federal regulation. They joined with Congressmen in mobilizing constituencies of private interests that could be profitably served. The programs multiplied, the money supply grew, inflation raised taxes, and the spurious yield of federal programs—which often gave no valuable service—and of government bonds—which often financed waste—remained as high or higher than the real profits of private capital.

It was obvious, then, that the growth of government had not been matched with dedication to public service. Hatch's experience with the Washington bureaucratic system left him with the belief that many government officials had become, or were rapidly becoming, the *rulers* rather than the *servants* of the people. There was no doubt that the liberal worship of centralized planning countenanced central government coercion, while reflecting a systematic bias against free choice, especially in local government and private economic activity.

With dismay, Hatch also came to believe that with some Congressmen helping the "poor" and "needy" had never been a serious moral objective. With them it was purely a matter of numbers, of garnering a persistent base of political support—put bluntly, a simple matter of buying all the votes possible.

It did not take Hatch long to learn that the welfare state was most beneficial to those in whose hands it was created and administered. Its creators generally receive the political support of those groups who are selected for benefits; and, much of the funds apportioned to welfare programs end up as high salaries paid to what Robert J. Ringer calls "middle-class-elite government employees." The liberal philosophy had attributed to the welfare state humanitarian goals, but Hatch saw something sinister beneath this façade of benevolence. In the process of attempting to alleviate the human condition, the liberal community had opened a Pandora's Box of consequences that heightened Hatch's sense of urgency. He was most concerned with the widely-held faith in the power of government to solve problems through political coercion and bureaucratic ukase.

In all of this Hatch saw the spectre of authoritarianism under the label of progressivism; of a centrally controlled society by a monolithic central government under the term "liberalism" (which once meant opposition to what it now sponsored); and a collectivized and regulated mass population under the misnomer of democracy.

It is significant that the political philosopher Walter Lippman wrote of the same concern in his *The Good Society* 33 years earlier, when Hatch was but a small boy:

> Throughout the world, in the name of progress, men who call themselves communists, socialists, fascists, nationalists, progressives, and even liberals, are unanimous in holding that government with its instruments of coercion must, by commanding the people how they shall live, direct the course of civilization and fix the shape of things to come. They believe in what Mr. Stuart Chase accurately describes as "the overhead planning and control of economic activity." This is the dogma which all the prevailing dogmas presuppose. This is the mold in which are cast the thought and action of the epoch. No other approach to the regulation of human affairs is seriously considered, or is even conceived as possible. The recently enfranchised masses and the leaders of

thought who supply their ideas are almost completely under the spell of this dogma. Only a handful here and there, groups without influence, isolated and disregarded thinkers, continue to challenge it. For the premises of authoritarian collectivism have become the working beliefs, the self-evident assumptions, the unquestioned axioms, not only of all revolutionary regimes, but of nearly every effort which lays claim to being enlightened, humane, and progressive.

Now, a generation later, Senator Orrin Hatch saw the reality of Lippman's observation in all its profusion, power, and pervasiveness. The results of this utopian thinking Hatch found on all sides. It had assumed the proportions of a religion with its "true believers," apparently oblivious to the growing recalcitrance of the bureaucracy, the multiplication of the federal debt, or even the consummate dishonesty of the self-serving coalitions that made up the "Iron Triangle."

In foreign affairs Hatch found an alarming propensity to divorce foreign policy from the realities of international power formations, ideologies, or national self-interest. He became alarmed with both the substance and the administration of American foreign policy, much of which he came to believe was inimical to the best interests of the United States as an entity and as a world leader. Here he felt that liberal foreign policy precariously bordered "peace at any price," and near-"unilateral disarmament." He was particularly concerned about SALT I, since he viewed it as primarily a one-way street to the benefit of the Soviet Union.

The policy of "mutually assured destruction (MAD)," whose goal was to bring the Soviet Union and the United States into such strategic juxtaposition that each country would be able to destroy the other also rankled Hatch. Theoretically, through using the respective populations as virtual hostages, nuclear war would logically be unthinkable, since each side knew itself to be vulnerable to destruction. In reality the United States had deliberately and by design been placed in a situation where it could be destroyed.

It was Hatch's belief that this policy was indeed "MAD." Not only had it sacrificed America's once clear military superiority to an obvious aggressor, but it obviated clear thinking on the subject. There was not sufficient concern with the possibilities of technological breakthrough in weaponry which would make current modes outdated. And there was no doubt in Hatch's mind that the relative military parity inherent in MAD placed the United States in a very vulnerable and disadvantaged position vis-à-vis the Soviet Union with respect to aggressive acts by that country short of nuclear war. Here the United States was placed in the unenviable role of having to judge at which point it would risk annihilation in order to stop that aggression. Too, the supposition that men always act rationally, even in the face of disaster, was a chimerical notion not borne out by Hatch's knowledge of history.

In fine, everything he had learned or experienced as a freshman Senator reaffirmed his earlier conclusion that *modern* liberalism had long since been removed from the moral, political and economic principles of *traditional* liberalism, and that its legacy would surely be disaster to the American people.

It was not that Hatch doubted the sincerity of what he called the "honest liberals," of which he imagined Hubert Humphrey to be the most perfect example. He could respect that because of his own strongly-held philosophical positions. What he could not understand was the almost total unwillingness of the liberals to come to grips with the myriad of obvious problems their political philosophy had created. He could not understand their unprotesting acceptance of the tactics of their fellow-travelers who made up the "Iron Triangle."

Hatch began to feel distressed and politically impotent. The liberal "establishment" seemed to be confidently in control in every phase of national government decision-making. President Ford had fought valiantly against a host of costly legislative proposals with his use of the veto. And, although there was not enough Republican power in Congress to mount a positive legislative program, Ford's vetoes helped keep inflation at a manageable level. Now he was gone and Jimmy Carter was President. Hatch soon learned that Carter was going to be a weak President, hardly one who would long stand independent of the liberal "establishment" which provided much of the Democratic Party leadership.

So, it was going to be business as usual—a new dose of deficit spending, a resumption of the rise of inflation, and more complications in America's foreign policy.

It was at this point that Hatch was brought near to the point of despair. He became convinced that only a miracle would stop the current juggernaut from tumbling into national disaster. The liberal leadership of government, he reasoned, was so caught up in its utopian dream as to be oblivious to reality. They could not be reasoned with, for they believed that history, science, and the realm of good intentions had proved them right—in theory at least. They would have to be replaced. The power of the "Iron Triangle" would have to be overthrown. Only then would this nation have a fighting chance to return to moral leadership. But how? In order for this to happen the American people had to be awakened to a realization of their awful situation, and the small minority in Congress of which Hatch was a part had to, like David facing Goliath, take on the Establishment with all their heart and strength.

Hatch plunged into the legislative battle with all the finesse of a Golden Gloves heavyweight, swinging wildly in every direction. While his mind, functioning like a computer, stored vast amounts of facts and figures on a hundred different issues, he fought as if there were no tomorrow—attacking here, debating there, speaking, encouraging his colleagues to rally on each issue as if there were 40 hours in each day and as if all shared his energy and his razor-sharp views.

There was so much to do, so much to learn, so many pieces of legislation beginning their flow through the governmental process. Read, read, study, study, question, question, call, call, debate, debate—Hatch's days grew longer and longer. A 20-hour workday was not uncommon. He rarely saw his family, began skipping meals, and on a rare occasion would not remove his clothing in a 24-hour period, sustaining himself by health food snacks, and his 5- or 10-minute catnaps. What sleep he did get was troubled. His nerves were getting taut.

Hatch, with all the exuberance of a Christian martyr, had thrown himself into an arena where the professionals were waiting to eat him alive. With fangs bared they pounced upon him, only to be driven back in amazement by his broad understanding of each issue on which he debated, combined with a rapid-fire debating style that often left his detractors groping for words. This alone allowed him to retain some substance as a new Senator. His opposition would have to be content with watching him become insufferably overbearing and burning himself out. He was not going to destroy himself by appearing the fool.

Orrin Hatch was suffering from the "Oh my God!" syndrome, made more severe by his already heightened sense of urgency. It happens often enough. Men of principle gain intimate knowledge of the workings of Washington, and they become shocked. "Oh my God," they cry, "why isn't something being done about this mess? Are we to go under before we do anything? Time is running out! The people of this country must know what's going on here!"

Within two months after the beginning of the 96th Congress, members of the Hatch office had been drained to the point of exhaustion. They were fighting among themselves as their frayed nerves broke out in invective. Hatch had put an insurmountable burden both upon himself and his staff. It would have been bad enough if Hatch had jumped from issue to issue ignorant of the subject matter of each. But he was not a "grandstander." He was, in effect, on fire. He was a man to whom every minute was a measure of his dedication and impatience. By the time he spoke or reacted to a measure, he had fairly become an expert on the subject. His incredible photographic memory and his ability to get by on catnaps again sustained him. He digested prodigious amounts of information and in the process wore his staff to a frazzle doing research.

Hatch pounced on every issue. He felt obligated to make an impact on every major bill, to say something about each presidential appointee (those who needed senatorial approval), to be involved in almost every debate. To his fellow Senators he appeared ubiquitous. Many admired his dedication, some shook their heads in disbelief at his naïveté made more obvious by his seeming relentless energy and spunk. Still others saw him as arrogant and overbearing, especially so because of his freshman status. Since principle, not party, was his primary motivator, his "stepping out front" with such bravado, combined with his relative aloofness from the Republican Old Guard, served to put a number of Republican noses out of joint. One Republican said of Hatch, "He's like Bronco Nagurski, he wants to take the ball and smash through the line on every damn play." A number of Democratic professionals in the Senate wrote him off as a "flash in the pan." Hatch would, they suggested, burn himself out in six months. He would be out of clout, out of friends, out of supporters, and out of breath.

It was at this point that Frank Madsen, his Administrative Assistant, began to move to the fore. Madsen is a calm, organized individual who has an unusual ability to work with people in kindness and consideration and who, most importantly, had Hatch's complete trust. Upon Hatch's arrival in Utah, Madsen had immediately sensed the character, strength, and inherent goodness of the man and had called him to serve as a counselor to him in his position as a Bishop over a Ward (parish) in the Mormon Church. Hatch had performed so well in that capacity that he became the Bishop after Madsen's call to serve in another church administrative post. They were very different in their personalities, but nevertheless became close friends. Their devotion to Utah as a state and a people bordered on the fabled Texan's pride in his State. Too, they both shared grave concerns over the moral, political, and economic conditions of the country, and spent many hours discussing these subjects.

When Hatch was elected U.S. Senator, he talked to Madsen the next morning. The question: Would he come back to Washington? "Frank," he had confided, "I'm determined all right, but I'm scared to death. I need you back there with me."

Frank Madsen was a member of a prominent Utah family and a graduate of the University of Utah (BS, MBA, JD). He and his family were in the midst of rebuilding a successful small business. He loved his work, his church calling, and his life in Utah. He really didn't want to go back to Washington. And yet he agreed with Hatch that the country was in desperate trouble, and someone had to try to change what was happening. For three weeks after the election, Madsen agonized over Hatch's appeal that he join him in Washington. Each day he had said "no" to Hatch. Finally he accepted the challenge, as he knew he would from the beginning. He knew Hatch could make a difference—perhaps even the essential difference. He immediately began organizing a staff for Hatch and closing down his personal affairs.

The frenetic pace of the first several months was hard on Madsen as well, and he sensed the necessity of bringing a feeling of calm resolution and purposeful cooperation to the office. He asserted himself with the staff and with the Senator, and he began to exercise an increasing measure of control over what had become an explosive situation. At times Madsen was the only glue that held the staff together. Still his loyalty to and faith in Hatch never diminished. And Hatch's respect for Madsen kept their relationship from reaching the breaking-point. With Madsen, Hatch knew when to back off.

Mac Haddow, on the other hand, preferred the rough and tumble of campaigning. He began to weary of the pressures of staff responsibilities. He longed to return to Utah and to stake out a political career. When Frank Bailey, then the Director of Hatch's Utah offices, was called to be a Mission President in Ohio for the Mormon Church, Haddow jumped at the chance to return to the politics of Utah. Soon he would leave Hatch and strike out on his own—always to be a friend but always his own man, with his own ways, and with his own separate destiny. No one in the Hatch organization was surprised at his decision to run for the Utah State Legislature.

Madsen gathered the staff around him and began to regroup. He pushed the young Senator to slow down the pace and to pull away from the continual confrontations. But Hatch wasn't listening. He needed more.

If a young, freshman Congressman can find a professional who respects him enough to take him under his wing, he can count himself lucky. Learning the politics and procedures of Congress is an education in itself. There are unwritten "rules of the game," mores, and behavioral expectations that have become custom. They are learned by common sense, the dear lessons of experience, by astute observation, or through the advice of friends.

Senator Orrin Hatch of Utah

**Senator Hatch being sworn in by the late Vice-President Nelson
Rockefeller.**

A firm believer in strong public schools, Senator Hatch gets refresher course in penmanship from a junior constituent.

Still a union member as well as being Chairman of the Senate Labor Committee, Senator Hatch is particularly interested in the problems of the working man.

Tom Perry, Hatch's chief legal counsel, and Senator Hatch prepare to take on Senator Kennedy and his swarm of staff assistants.

The Senator visits one of Utah's beautiful wilderness areas.

One of the more pleasant duties of office — Senator Hatch meets Miss Utah, Jean Bullard.

...with Barry Goldwater.

As members of the Senate Labor Committee, Senators Hatch and Kennedy often find themselves in adversary positions, but this doesn't prevent them from enjoying an occasional light moment together.

An articulate spokesman, Senator Hatch is much sought after by representatives of the news media.

It was obvious that Hatch was skating on thin ice. The only Republican who had tried to talk to him about it in those first days had been rebuffed. No one else wanted to take on the chore of reasoning with this human dynamo. Finally it was a Democrat who brought Hatch to his senses.

One of the Senators Hatch had come to admire most as the months of the new Congress passed was the Democrat James Allen of Alabama. In a letter to his son at Brigham Young University, Hatch described Allen as a "bulwark for conscience." In fact, Allen was often referred to as "the conscience of the Senate."

Allen was not only a substantial moral leader. He was also without question the best parliamentarian in the Senate. Hatch was so impressed with this that he vowed to develop the same skill. He literally memorized the Senate rules and devoured a dozen other books and pamphlets on the vagaries and precedents of parliamentary procedure. The most knowledgeable parliamentarians in the Senate became James Allen, Robert Byrd, Jesse Helms, and Orrin Hatch. This technical knowledge was to serve Hatch well in the years ahead.

Allen admired this brilliant and determined young Utahn. In him he saw the seed of greatness. He made it a point to become acquainted with Hatch. They became close friends and ideological companions. Since both served on the Judiciary Committee, they were able to communicate often.

So it was that this Democrat was the one who took upon himself the chore of bringing this hyperactive fledgling down to earth. After several attempts he got Hatch to come to his office.

"Come in Orrin and sit down."

"Thanks Jim, but I can only stay a minute."

Hatch began to move about nervously. It was obvious to Senator Allen that his mind was far away.

"Sit down, Orrin! For heaven's sake sit down! I have something important to talk to you about."

Hatch was embarrassed. He sat down and folded his hands on his lap.

For an interminable minute Allen looked steadily at Hatch, perceiving the tension that obviously weighed heavily upon him, the darkness under tired eyes. "Orrin, do you have enough insurance to take care of your family when you're gone?"

"Is this some sort of a joke, Jim?" Hatch was untypically irritated.

"Yes, Orrin, a cruel joke. Look, I don't want to interfere in your life, but I look upon you as a particularly gifted Senator with the philosophy that this nation must turn to if it is to survive."

Hatch was not taking the compliment graciously. His irritation was becoming more pronounced. "What has this got to do with insurance policies? Come to the point, I've got a dozen appointments this afternoon."

"Orrin, that's the trouble. You're driving yourself into the ground. No man, not even you, can keep up the pace you have set for yourself. Have you taken a good look at your staff lately? The word is out. Half of them are ready to quit, and the other half support you out of sheer loyalty. They are already nearly burned out. They are sniping at each other. They are getting sick—they are physically and mentally exhausted."

Hatch's voice was shrill. "The people of Utah elected me to . . ."

"They elected you to use your common sense," interrupted Allen, "not to kill yourself and drive your staff up the wall. Can't you see your effectiveness has got to be decimated, that the strength of your entire organization is being drained before the real battles have begun? Listen to me. It took Congress nearly half a century to bring this nation into its present crisis. Do you think you're going to restore us in one session of Congress and all alone?"

Hatch sat back, his brow furrowed, looking intently at Allen and not wishing to reply.

"Who do you think you are? You cannot be a spokesman for every issue! You cannot ride out like Don Quixote to right every wrong!

"Don't think for a minute that I do not appreciate the serious conditions we face. I am the first to admit that this onslaught against American democracy and traditional moral standards is running almost uncontested. But I believe with a little luck and some intelligent action, we can reverse this trend.

"The debauching of our currency and economic system by my colleagues is about to run its course. Inflation is going to get out of hand, and the American people are beginning to see through the dishonest rhetoric of the 'Great Society.' They are coming to see that they have been the patsy to political ambition and a false political philosophy. Believe me, a reckoning is coming.

"Our chance is coming, and I do not hesitate to say that this chance may be the last for all of us in this country.

"Good Lord, Orrin, I'm lecturing you, and I apologize, but I tell you in all sincerity that in the years ahead you are going to be one of the most important people in this country to lead us back to integrity—that is, if you're smart. Right now you're showing the wisdom of a shave-tail lieutenant experiencing his first combat. You're going to get yourself killed and carry your troops down with you."

Allen hesitated a minute, looking down at his feet. "Orrin, I'm sick. I may not be here long, and I want you to . . ."

Hatch was on his feet. "Jim, what . . .?"

"Listen to me," Allen broke in, waving his hand as if he could make his previous words disappear. "I can take that in stride. What I can't abide is someone like you literally committing suicide."

Hatch was humbled. As such, he was teachable. "What must I do?" His voice was no longer testy. He was not condescending. He asked the question in all seriousness.

"Good man, Orrin. Pace yourself. Choose your issues carefully, Then marshall your troops and your reservoir of energy selectively. You don't have to be an expert on every bill that comes through Congress. Use your time and your energy and your staff wisely. A general has only so many troops and only so much ammunition. I suspect the outcome of more battles than not has been decided on the method of *deployment* rather than by sheer force of arms.

"One thing more. Join forces with those who share your views. Don't *push* them, *lead* them! Some of us have been fighting the battle while you were still a 'Young Philadelphian' in law school. Now you can help unify us. One day you'll help lead us. We need a team effort. Then, when circumstances are right, both Democrat and Republican will cast party labels aside and move to correct our predicament.

"If you pace yourself, if you use that brilliant intellect you've been blessed with, and if you hold tight to those ideals which make you such a unique and valuable human being, the time will come faster than you imagine when you will be able to perform a service to this country comparable to the great patriots and statesmen in our history."

Hatch sat quietly for a moment, then he rose slowly and grasped Allen by the hand. "What can I say?"

A short time later, Hatch walked slowly to his office. As he entered he glanced at the clock It was 2:30 P.M.

"It's Friday," he said softly to his receptionist. "Tell everyone to go home. Cancel appointments."

"Senator Hatch," was the shocked reply, "are you all right?"

"Ah, yes, of course. Just tell them to go home."

Hatch entered his office and collapsed into his chair. He felt as if a heavy weight had been taken from him. His head leaned back and his eyes closed. For the first time in weeks he approached sleep without taut nerves and strained emotions. He dropped into a quiet, deep sleep.

Less than a year later Senator James Allen was dead and his protégé, Senator Orrin Hatch, had become a professional.

Part Three
The Professional

Chapter 6
THE MACE AND THE OLIVE BRANCH

History tells us that men and nations in general do not learn much from experience. Deleterious and degenerative practices tend to become habitual in men, and nations appear to persist in following age-old patterns of decline and destruction.

Progress, great and small, takes place when a few men have the character and foresight and the innate sense of careful reflection to see the large picture, and who, by their own keen sense of judgment and inherent courage are able to understand that the moral sphere, along with the scientific realm, is based upon fundamental principles. Political action and political decisions are in fact moral acts and decisions. Attempts to perceive political acts and decisions in terms of mere utilitarianism without a solid reflection on moral values that are both transcendent and ontological, inevitably travel a dark road.

Foremost among the men of Congress who live their lives and make their decisions in accordance with the traditional values of Western civilization with its Judeo-Christian underpinnings, Orrin Hatch began painfully to build a moral leadership role in the Senate. It was not going to be easy. His all-too energetic start had left many dismayed and his aggressiveness had left some noses out of joint. Those who needed his leadership most wondered if his unmatched drive would ever allow him to slow down enough to regroup, to gain stature, and to lead. His political enemies had already written him off long before the second year of his tenure had begun.

But Hatch was not to be counted out. Where all too often the ego of what might have become great men has caused them obstinately to perpetuate counter-productive behavior, Hatch humbled himself before the wisdom of Senator James Allen. Having swallowed the bitter pill of critical self-analysis he changed his modus operandi. With a new focus his perceptive mind mastered the characteristics of Senate leadership. His once feverish and sometimes uncoordinated activity now became calculated, organized, deliberate and weighted in accordance with the relative importance of the various tasks he set out for himself. He became increasingly more amenable to those, both Republican and Democrat, who had sought his leadership and had hoped he would step out front with more finesse, grace, balance and wisdom. He sought conciliation where possible rather than confrontation. As his second year of apprenticeship wore on, his political opponents began to see him in a new perspective.

"The new Hatch," as one prominent Democrat phrased it, was well on his way to becoming a substantial power in the Senate. His staff, his friends, and his fellow Republicans responded in ways that began to open numerous doors of potential leadership for him. It remained for Hatch to respond in a positive manner to these opportunities. Some of his most inveterate ideological opposites in the Senate began, often in spite of themselves, to show him respect. The most obvious example was his relationship with the leader of the Senate liberals, Senator Ted Kennedy. Although they were often at loggerheads, their legislative conflict was held within the bounds of gentlemanly exchange one would expect in such an august body as the United States Senate. The respect of each for the other grew as the months passed. Hatch became convinced that Kennedy was sincere in his beliefs and that his political actions were essentially compatible with his philosophical perspective. Again, Hatch could understand this and even respect it, although his own philosophy was more often than not diametrically the opposite.

It is not uncommon for men who share unusual skill, talents and abilities, to accord one another respect, though they be opponents, even enemies. This is true in athletics, it is true in war; it is true in a variety of men's actions where intense competition is the norm. As the battle rages, men pit their skills and cunning one against the other; and, if merited, gain and even acknowledge respect for each other. Such was the case with Hatch and Kennedy.

In committee, on the floor, and in private conversation, both Kennedy and Hatch matched wits. The skill, the fluency, the flair for the dramatic, the commanding physical appearance and the intelligence of these two protagonists made their confrontations fiery and fascinating, yet within the realm of good taste. By the beginning of Hatch's third year in the Senate, he and Kennedy were being photographed in friendly conversation. Referring to Hatch, Kennedy said, "I have a decent personal relationship with him." In Hatch's office hangs a photograph of him and Kennedy, in an obviously staged pose, their index fingers pointing at each other, and broad smiles on their faces. The inscription on the photograph was written by Kennedy to Hatch—"If Reagan could see us now." Significantly, Kennedy was to say of Hatch, referring to the latter's growing political clout, "He is the only Republican in the Senate I fear." To this man, one of the most powerful and influential leaders in the Senate, his statement was one of profound respect for Hatch. Significantly, Vera Glaser, a sharp reporter for the Knight-Ridder newspaper chain, wrote under the title *Hatch Becoming A Senate Power*, "Senator Orrin Hatch gets along so well with Senator Edward Kennedy that some Republicans complain about the friendly accord. Some complain that their relations are warmer than those Hatch has with the GOP." At a meeting of the Brigham Young University Women's Organization, Hatch raised a few eyebrows when he responded to a question about Kennedy, "Although we disagree on most major issues, as a legislator, I respect him; and, as a political opponent, I find him formidable." To another audience he remarked concerning his and the other six freshmen Republicans' position on the Senate Labor and Human Resources Committee compared to the veteran Democratic heavyweights led by Ted Kennedy (such as Howard Metzenbaum, Thomas Eagleton, and Don Reigle), "We're like a bunch of rookies up against the New York Yankees."

Yet, the cordial relationship between Kennedy and Hatch was not an aberration. More and more liberal legislators and lobbyists came to respect this young man from Utah. It was not that Hatch had become Caspar Milquetoast; he still stood on the principles that had encouraged him to run for the Senate. He still fought against major liberal legislation with an intensity that was both feared and admired, and supported with equal vigor legislation he favored. He retained the same dedication to the goal of turning America away from the welfare state. Although varying in some respects depending upon issues at hand, Hatch's voting record averaged about 90 percent in the conservative realm, according to the *Congressional Quarterly*. *The New York Times* described him as the "point man" for Senate conservatism.

But now he was in control. He led more than he pushed; he was respectful of others' feelings and beliefs; he was always prepared, always wide awake, yet his presence and delivery were now free of an overpowering urgency. He was still in a hurry, but now he was running the ball squarely down the field, picking up support from teammates, while gaining the respect of the opposing team, rather than running into the stadium retaining wall with his head down and his eyes closed.

His style of fighting for what he believed to be true with the intensity and skill of a gladiator while at the same time demonstrating respect and understanding for his political opponents, caused the prestigious *Congressional Quarterly* to describe him in terms of "The Mace and The Olive Branch." "Moments after Senator Orin G. Hatch, R-Utah, led the winning charge against the 1980 Fair Housing Bill, he went to the Senate anteroom and shook hands with every black civil rights leader he could find. From bitter debate rhetoric, he shifted to the sincere tones of a parent consoling his just-punished child. Though it was painful, he told the lobbyist he did what he thought was right. *It was vintage Orrin Hatch; in one hand the mace, in the other, the olive branch.*"

Referring to the above event, one labor lobbyist told a *Congressional Quarterly* reporter: "That took gall, guts and an awful lot of sense." Althea T.L. Simmons, head of the NAACP's Washington office said, "Senator Hatch, because he is so personable, makes you feel that he has your interests at heart. He is opposed to the social programs we favor. The fact that he is so personable about it doesn't make it more palatable. It just makes him more difficult to perceive as a staunch foe."

"Hatch can be abrasive," wrote Vera Glaser, "but the words come out soft spoken. When scorching an opponent, Hatch invariably opens with a compliment. Despite their differences with Hatch, liberals say they like and respect him." Richard Murphy, crack lobbyist of the Service Employees Union, described Hatch as "an honorable man," and Pat Reuss, legislative director of the Women's Equity Action League, said of Hatch, "He is someone we can deal with, although philosophically he is our enemy. We let him know when we disagree. He listens. He is not hostile. He is fair although patriarchal." One Senator said of Hatch, "He is a tough and rough opponent, but he is a gentleman. He does not use deceit. He does not hit below the belt. He is clever. He tries to stay a step ahead, but he has integrity. Using the biblical meaning of the term, Hatch is a just man." On June 20, 1978, the venerable veteran Senate Democrat Ed Muskie sent his picture to Hatch, and on it wrote, "To Orrin Hatch, whose performance on the Senate floor commands respect and attracts friends—even in the ranks of those who may disagree."

Hatch's other liberal opponents in the Senate generally see him in similar terms—a combination of respect and ideological opposition. Stern confrontation on the floor of the Senate or in committee is often relieved by friendly, humorous exchange in less trying situations. Once, when a group was being assembled for a television program, the director asked Hatch if he could move a little to the left. Liberal Senator Howard Metzenbaum responded in a jocular manner, ''I don't think Senator Hatch is able to move 'left'.'' ''To the contrary,'' answered the smiling Hatch, ''there is plenty of room for me to move 'left'. It is you, my friend, who cannot possibly move any *further* 'left'.''

The *Congressional Quarterly* commented about Hatch's style, as ''his willingness to work hard, his intelligence, and his outwardly sincere manner. Whether at committee meetings, in Senate debate or on television news shows, he generally turns in a smooth and articulate performance, and it is hard to penetrate the hard polish.'' The reader was warned, however, that ''he can project righteous indignation as well as anyone.''

Naturally, as Hatch finally rose to prominence, he was hailed by his fellow Conservatives, who had hoped that just such a thing would happen. He was especially recognized for his leadership in the Senate Western Coalition, an organization of Western Senators who stand at the forefront of the ''Sagebrush Rebellion,'' demanding an orderly transfer of public lands back to the states. Nevada's Paul Laxalt, a forceful member of the coalition, wrote that if Hatch would continue to ''ride herd'' on the ''Rebellion,'' it had ''a real chance of eventual success.'' ''Hatch,'' he acknowledged, ''has been the real leader in this effort.''

Significantly, it was Hatch's senior Senator from Utah, Senator Jake Garn, who was able to comment about his working with Hatch ''as a team to deal with issues that affect Utah and the nation.'' James Hansen, Utah Congressman replied to a query about Hatch by stating that ''our State is, indeed, fortunate to be represented by a man blessed with such integrity, decency and dedication.''

And from the East, New York Congressman Jack Kemp said of Hatch: ''Ideas are the key to good politics and progressive government, and it is in the world of ideas that Orrin Hatch is a champion. He, as much as any member of Congress today, is responsible for advancing bold, new ideas for tax, budget and regulatory reform that are so essential to getting our economy moving and making America great.''

On May 28, 1981, a grateful President Ronald Reagan wrote Hatch ''to express my continuing gratitude and esteem for your outstanding contributions. You have been eloquent in presenting our party's point of view and you have repeatedly demonstrated a keen grasp of the critical issues—not only those facing this country but those facing the state of Utah as well. I look forward to working closely with you as you continue to provide your rigorous and foresighted leadership in the United States Senate.''

Hatch had developed the ability to find a working model where extremes of an opinion or a proposed piece of legislation had so solidified the opposing sides that stalemate resulted. Hatch had learned by the clear lessons of experience that even a small step forward was preferable to no movement at all. He was often able to work out compromises which, while not totally satisfactory to either side, at least got the discussion moving again. And significantly, some of the firebrands that had come to Congress in this new wave of young, determined and dedicated politicians had gone through the same metamorphosis as Hatch, thereby greatly enhancing their prestige with their colleagues.

The painstaking "Holt Executive Advisory," published by the Holt Information Research, Inc., described them as "flexible." This "includes most of the GOP freshmen Conservatives on Capitol Hill, along with such veterans as Representative Phil Crane (R-Ill.), and Senators Hatch of Utah, Laxalt of Nevada and Lugar of Indiana."

It was, however, long after Hatch had become a recognized power in the United States Senate—indeed, his leadership extended to supporters, admirers and friends from both houses and among many who worked in the great government departments—that the press, both the national and, to a limited extent, that of his home state, Utah, began to acknowledge his growth in prestige and power. The national press is decidedly liberal in focus and tune. It was not going to readily acknowledge "the new Hatch." Nor was the media in Utah. It is interesting that in his Senatorial tenure, Orrin Hatch has appeared more often on the front page of the *New York Times* than on the front page of Utah's leading newspaper. In late October of 1981, Senator Hatch chaired a hearing on a health care bill he was sponsoring that would provide home health care at greatly reduced costs. The proposal, developed out of four years of study and preparation by Hatch, gained the endorsement of the American Hospital Association, the Multiple Sclerosis Society, the Amyotrophic Lateral Sclerosis Society, the American Cancer Society and nearly 30 other national health care organizations. WCBS-TV and WOR-TV in New York City editorially endorsed the bill. In Utah, the state's most prominent newspaper endorsed the idea of home health care but quoted the New Jersey Democrat, Senator Bill Bradley, who had nothing to do with the bill. *The editorial made no mention at all of Senator Hatch's work for the elderly,* although he wrote the bill and was singlehandedly pushing for its passage.

Ironically this local news black-out of Hatch is not unusual. While his name recognition is high in Utah, other areas of the country are much more aware of his achievements. With Jake Garn as Chairman of the Banking Committee and Orrin Hatch as Chairman of the Labor and Human Resources Committee, the state has never enjoyed such disproportional political power—nor have many other states. Yet few Utahns are aware of Hatch's profound political clout in Congress or his vital importance to the Republican Party in the Senate and to the state of Utah.

There may be reasons for this other than the fact that Utah is on the other side of the Continental Divide, while the national political electricity is plugged into the East. It is rumored that in crucial meetings in Salt Lake City to select a Democratic candidate to run against Orrin Hatch have sat Utah's current Democratic Governor, Scott Matheson, ex-Governor Calvin Rampton, Jack Gallivan, owner and editor of Utah's most prestigious newspaper, *The Salt Lake Tribune,* and George Hatch, owner of Utah's Television Channel 2, the *Ogden Standard Examiner,* radio stations and other weekly newspapers throughout the state. These men are the Democratic "king-makers" in Utah.

Hatch's predicament with both the local and national press is not an uncommon one. It remains the most serious, apparently insoluble, conundrum of conservatives at all levels of government: to sustain public support for their policies and themselves when those who daily report, explain, and analyze them are in profound disagreement. As Stephen Hess wrote in his *The Washington Reporters,* published by the Brookings Institute, those who control the media "are not simply passing along information; *they are choosing, within certain limits, what most people will know about government.*" According to former Secretary of the Treasury, William E. Simon, as far as the national press is concerned, there are only ultra-conservatives, rarely ultra-liberals; the latter are always "moderates." Conservatives are often far-right, liberals never far-left. Conservatives are often controversial, liberals rarely. Harvard political scientist James Q. Wilson, writes that "most members of the national media have views quite different from those of the average citizen. . . . The opinions of editors, executives, commentators, and columnists working for the largest papers, the news magazines, and the broadcast networks are significantly more liberal on all foreign policy questions and most economic ones. . . ."

In 1982, Robert Lichter, Assistant Professor of political science at George Washington University, and Stanley Rothman, Professor of Government at Smith College, published a work based on hour-long interviews with 240 journalists and broadcasters at the most influential media outlets. Their survey, "The Media Elite," reported that 81 percent of the media elite had supported McGovern over Nixon. They preferred Carter over Ford by the same margin. In 1964, they preferred Johnson over Goldwater by 94 percent to 6 percent. On the right-left spectrum, only 19 percent chose the right side.

In a time of political infighting, secularism and pragmatism, the political community and the media in general have become inured to both moral and constitutional principles and considerations. To the secular mind, both liberal and conservative, pragmatism, power, majorities, and political "one-upmanship" remain primary considerations, with basic Constitutional principles relegated to the realm of verbal window-dressing, while the crafty mind seeks ways to side-step its legal confines for momentary political advantage.

Hatch's mastery of, and devotion to, Constitutional principles has often caused him to lead out in legislative areas that even some of his fellow Republicans would rather have ignored. His firm determination in this regard has frustrated pragmatists of both parties, many of whom are the life-blood of the current political menagerie.

Furthermore, his strict moral conscience is looked upon by some of the press as "uncompromising." The fact that his legislative activities and his personal life, very much under scrutiny, tend to mirror his expressed moral code makes some of the media elite uncomfortable, since typically they are highly secular and permissive in philosophy. According to the study by professors Lichter and Rothman, media leaders are almost unanimous in their rejection of traditional sexual restraints. They uphold a pro-choice position on abortion and reject the belief that homosexuality is wrong (only 9 percent feel strongly that homosexuality is immoral). Eighty-five percent uphold the right of homosexuals to be teachers in the public schools, and a majority apparently do not even believe that adultery is wrong. Only 15 percent indicated the belief that extramarital affairs were immoral.

Obviously then, Hatch is not the kind of man these elite opinion-formers in the national media would call their own. To make matters worse for the Senator, the media elite belong primarily to the Eastern Liberal Establishment. Lichter and Rothman report that they are drawn primarily from Northern industrial states, particularly from the Northeast—two-thirds from the quadrant of the country extending from New England to Chicago's North Shore. Only 3 percent gave California, or the Pacific Northwest as their original home.

Furthermore, these highly educated and urbane media elites, most of them enjoying substantially above-average incomes, typically tend to look upon religion as irrelevant at best. According to Lichter and

Rothman, "only 8 percent go to church or synagogue weekly, and 86 percent seldom or never attend religious services."

Therefore, one would suspect that, on the one hand, Hatch, highly educated and urbane-looking himself, ought to be, as former Vice President Spiro Agnew described it—"an effete snob." Hatch's political conservatism, his expressed opposition to homosexuality and abortion, and his moral values, which are really more related to those of "average" America, have made him rather sort of a rebel to his own kind in their eyes.

As if all this were not bad enough, Hatch is a devout Christian and represents, of all places, the State of Utah. After all, to the Eastern Establishment, *nobody* lives in Utah. Even Hatch's Pennsylvania birth could not overcome this handicap. In January of 1982, this author attended a hearing on the extension of the Voting Rights Act in the Subcommittee on the Constitution of the Judiciary Committee while Senator Hatch chaired the proceedings. At the termination of the hearings an observer turned to a news commentator and offered, "Man, that Hatch is really good isn't he!" The commentator, irreverently and with noticeable vindictiveness, responded, "Can any good come out of *Utah*?"

Yet, surprisingly, from some of this elite group of media experts has come increasing respect for Hatch as his power position, his skill, and his legislative success have become obvious. Nor has his "mace and olive branch" style of leadership remained unacknowledged. Here again, often men with divergent philosophies will acknowledge extraordinary skill and accumulated power. But, in the last analysis, it is not in the East, but in his home state of Utah where Hatch's successes are least known and discussed.

The first nationally recognized commentator to describe publicly the growth of this political neophyte to senatorial stardom was Pulitzer Prize winner Jack Anderson. Anderson, perhaps more than anyone in the media, has an ear and an eye for delving into the inner workings of government. He is tough, perceptive, knowledgeable, thorough, sometimes cutting and even irreverent, but his observations are simply not passed off as being without substance. The man has stature. It meant something when he rated Hatch among the ten most effective Senators.

It was not until 1981 that the liberally-oriented, yet highly respected *Almanac of American Politics* (for its 1982 edition), recognized "the new Hatch." In two previous editions the *Almanac* had pictured him as "fervent and almost feverish" and lacking "flair and skill." Now Hatch was described as a man "with force of character." He was conceeded a "considerable influence on the conduct of government." Significantly, his having gone the extra mile in giving "due regard for the feelings and prerogatives of other Senators" was noted. The *Almanac* also rated Hatch eighth among his fellow Senators for impact on government. When such columnists as Kent Shearer began to editorialize the *Almanac*'s acknowledgement, Utah Democrats, hoping to unseat Hatch in 1982, were not happy. But, then, such information regarding Hatch's reputation would probably never be reported in Utah's media. Thus, many of Hatch's most important legislative battles would be unheralded in his home state.

It seemed to Hatch that from his first day in the Senate he had been pitted against the veteran Ted Kennedy. When Hatch became a member of the Judiciary Committee, Kennedy was already a substantial power there, and in the 96th Congress became that Committee's Chairman. Under Kennedy's leadership, the Committee began to crank out a series of what Hatch perceived to be serious anti-business proposals. Hatch became concerned not only with the content and the implications of Kennedy's proposed legislation, but as well with the fact that there appeared to be no one willing to "take him on." The realities of Democratic control of the Committee and the full Senate made it imperative to attack these measures with a highly skilled and well-organized opposition. And it wasn't happening. It looked as if Kennedy had smooth sailing.

So the freshman Senator from Utah became the focal point of an organized effort to thwart Kennedy—an activity that has since become a habit.

Kennedy was dedicated to the idea that the form of American business, small and large, be restructured and reconstituted to meet the nation's social needs, as he saw them. He was less concerned with the ability of American business to compete effectively and efficiently in the national and international marketplace. Instead, he sought by the power of government to direct the business establishment into meeting social welfare needs as he saw them.

Hatch, on the other hand, was a champion of the free-enterprise system. As he saw it, American business provided substantial social welfare benefits by its ability to put millions to work at favorable wages, by its tax base, and by its efficiency which allowed it to compete favorably in foreign markets. Hatch believed that government regulations had already seriously hurt the business climate in the United States and, hence, both the working man and the consumer. He saw Kennedy's proposals of additional application of government regulations not only unfair, but costly and economically stultifying, ones which would negatively affect the country at large. In philosophy, then, Hatch and Kennedy were natural adversaries.

It was in Hatch's attempt to block Kennedy's Illinois Brick Bill that the senior Senator began to recognize the existence of this brash newcomer from Utah. The legislation would have allowed for class action suits in the whole chain of product development and distribution. The potential effects and expense of this legal process was clearly devastating. Hatch called the bill the "Lawyers' Relief Bill," since, as he contended, the only people who would benefit by such legislation were myriads of attorneys whom small businessmen would have to hire in order to defend themselves against its effects. It would even stimulate energetic lawyers to instigate class action suits.

But the hour was late. By the time Hatch had come to the conclusion that he must lead out against Kennedy, the Illinois Brick Bill had already been voted out of committee, and was on the floor of the Senate.

At first Kennedy took Hatch's opposition activities rather good-naturedly. After all, what could he do? Hatch was not only greatly outnumbered, but he lacked floor experience. Furthermore, the freshman Senator could not begin to compete with Kennedy's resources. The Massachusetts Senator was flanked with a legion of lawyers, a veteran staff, and backed up by top liberal "think tanks" such as the Brookings Institute.

But Kennedy had misjudged Hatch's dedication and tenaciousness. He was also unaware that Hatch had made himself a rarely equalled expert on Senate procedure. This knowledge was to serve Hatch well as he used every maneuver one could imagine to stop Kennedy's legislation.

Against the formidable Kennedy and his impressive backup, Hatch took the field. At his side was Tom Parry, Hatch's "Chief Counsel." (Actually, Parry was his *only* counsel.) Parry, a graduate from the Brigham Young University Law School, had worked for Hatch's election and had been asked to come with the Senator to Washington. He was as wet behind the ears as Hatch, but he was indefatigable.

In order to stop Kennedy, Hatch had to out-maneuver, out-prepare, and out-hustle him. He used every legislative tactic and procedural maneuver available to keep Kennedy's bill from coming to a vote. Hatch believed that if he could hold on long enough he could educate enough of his fellow Senators to the morbific potentials of the legislation to cause its defeat. Backed by long hours of research, Hatch came to the Senate floor ready to debate every motion offered. He submitted amendment after amendment, with a dual purpose of keeping debate going, combined with the faint hope that amendments would be accepted that would take the teeth out of the bill. If all else failed, Hatch was prepared to filibuster in an attempt to talk the bill to death. Hatch referred to this as "extended educational debate."

It did not take Kennedy long to realize that he was in a battle, and that his opponent was not to be dismissed with a shrug. He began to counterattack with all the forces at his command. But at each step he was checkmated by Hatch. If he hoped to wear Hatch out, he was to be disappointed. Hatch was on the floor day and night so that Kennedy could not attempt to bring the bill to a vote without Hatch using his delaying tactics. Hatch and South Carolina Republican Strom Thurmond took turns, so that one or the other was on the floor at all times. Late one evening Kennedy attempted to attach his bill as a rider to another bill but Hatch and Thurmond intercepted him.

As the days passed, Hatch offered several hundred amendments to the bill. He kept the discussion going, going, going. Far into the midnight hours Hatch and Parry worked to prepare for the next day's legislative battle with the Kennedy forces. They were physically and emotionally drained. They had developed a siege mentality. At a moment's notice they had to be prepared to do battle on any aspect of the bill, or to counter any move Kennedy might make. They often commiserated that while they were working into the morning hours, Kennedy's staff and his stable of lawyers—about 15 of them working on the Brick Bill—were enjoying the Washington party circuit and the ubiquitous receptions. During one particularly rough midnight preparation session in Hatch's office, Parry suddenly looked at the harried red-eyed Senator and cried out: "Orrin what are we doing here? I mean, why in the hell are we doing this? We're out of our minds! Nobody cares!" For several minutes they laughed hysterically. Then they worked on until dawn.

But someone did care. The word was getting out to America's businessmen that they had a champion—"er, ah, Hatch, or something like that, from Utah." What political scientists call "grass roots" support began to back up Hatch and Thurmond in a growing crescendo. And from the ranks of Hatch's fellow Senators, more and more came over to the Utahn's side. His persistent attempts to educate his colleagues on the potential morbific results of the Brick Bill were beginning to register.

And, as Kennedy began to see the possible, then the probable, defeat of his efforts, he became furious. "I am tired," he told the Senate, "of one junior Senator controlling the legislation on this floor." That afternoon, he warned Hatch privately that he was going to "ram the Brick Bill down your throat." "Oh yeah," responded Hatch with a smile, "If you don't shape up, I'm going to turn you over to the Mormon missionaries.''

Kennedy never got a chance to "ram" the Brick Bill anywhere. Congress adjourned and the bill died before ever having come to a vote. Both Hatch and Parry went to their respective homes and slept the clock around.

But they had not heard the last of the Illinois Brick Bill. Kennedy was no lightweight. He believed in the principles of the bill. And his Kennedy ego had been blistered. In the very next Congress he brought the bill up again. He was now Chairman of the Judiciary Committee, but between the sessions of Congress support for the Brick Bill had seriously dwindled. Kennedy was going to have problems just getting it out of Committee. As a matter of fact, Kennedy went to the Committee mark-up session knowing he did not have enough votes. The swing vote was Indiana Senator Birch Bayh, who had remained undecided. Both Hatch and Kennedy were trying to secure his vote. On the day of the mark-up Bayh had been called to the hospital where his wife was dying of cancer. Kennedy called off the mark-up session, using Bayh's absence as the reason. Hatch wanted to make one last try at the wavering Bayh, but, under the circumstances, decided not to add to his burden. That afternoon Kennedy went to the hospital and secured Bayh's vote. A short time later, the Brick Bill was reported out of the Judiciary Committee.

Nevertheless, Kennedy might just as well have spared the effort. The bill was never given serious consideration. It died ignominiously.

It was the same with Kennedy's proposed Energy Anti-Monopoly Act and his Anti-Conglomerate Merger Bill. Both pieces of legislation were based upon Kennedy's philosophy that big business is inherently socially irresponsible. His philosophy does not allow for the economies of scale or efficiencies which allow these big businesses to compete on relatively equal terms within the international market. The Kennedy bills would restrain company mergers over a certain size, and restrict economic diversification. They would have, for instance, prevented the top oil companies from acquiring any other energy companies or concerns. Hatch was certain that, in practice, these two pieces of legislation would penalize companies for being superior competitors in the marketplace, for producing a superior product at a competitive price.

Hatch, once more resorting to his marathon Brick Bill tactics, engineered the defeat of both bills. Again Hatch had faced one of the most powerful forces in the United States Senate and come out the winner. Furthermore, Tom Parry, Hatch's lone legal counsel, had faced Kennedy's stable of lawyers and had emerged unintimidated and scratching.

It had been an exhausting experience, but a peculiarly emotionally rewarding one.

Through his senatorial term, Hatch incessantly picked up steam as his personal influence increased. Fresh into his Senate career, beginning in 1977, he played a major role in the attempt to defeat the ratification of the Panama Canal Treaty. Also in 1977, he was instrumental (curiously, in the House as well as the Senate) in defeating a proposal to expand a union's picketing power to secondarily boycott and shut down construction sites (the *common situs* picketing bill). In 1978 he led the battle to defeat the Labor Law Reform bill that had been promised the unions by Jimmy Carter and which Hatch felt would mean the end to any hope for responsible unionism in the United States.

It was in his battle to defeat the Labor Law Reform Bill that Hatch earned the bitter enmity of the labor union bosses. With the election of Jimmy Carter as President, and the Democrats enjoying a substantial majority in both the House and the Senate of the 95th Congress, organized labor saw a golden opportunity to pass what was their acknowledged number-one legislative priority. As Hatch saw it, the Labor Law Bill was hardly reform. It had an easy organizing, quickie election provision slanted completely against the small business to be organized. If a business owner talked about the union organizing effort to his employees, on his own premises, on his own time and cost, under the bill's equal access provision, he would have to open up his premises at his own expense and allow the union organizers to come in and preach their doctrine to his employees. The bill would have stacked the National Labor Relations Board almost completely in favor of the Unions by adding two more positions for Carter to appoint. Those businesses which do business with the federal government would have to capitulate to union demands or be contractually debarred from federal contracts for up to three years. Finally, it was pointed out that the businessman might be denied his Constitutional due process rights to have unfair labor practice charges by the NLRB tested in a court of law. This bill would have allowed the wholesale unionization of America against its will.

While the AFL-CIO argued that the current procedure had given unfair advantage to business to thwart unionizing activities, Hatch saw it differently. To him the intention was clear—increased unwarranted union power to move in on small business. The muscle of organized labor would increasingly be able to use intimidation that couldn't be challenged in the courts to increase a declining membership, where blandishments had failed.

And as a matter of fact, union leaders viewed the legislation *exactly* as Hatch did. This made their confrontation with Hatch all the more vitriolic. They knew he knew, and they hated him for that. They fully realized how much the legislation would tip the delicate balance of power in labor-management relations. It would, for all intents and purposes, solidify the Department of Labor as an entity largely controlled by a minority of labor czars who direct the nation's work force that is unionized. Had the bill been enacted into law, it would have, for all practical purposes, made it mandatory that targeted businesses organize or else face being "clubbed to death." Hatch was certain that the final result would be increased debilitating labor-management conflict, forced unionization, intimidation, the shutdown of great numbers of small businesses, fewer actual jobs and more corruption among the labor czars.

Having been a laboring man and a union member, Hatch felt deeply for the working man. He supported the idea of unions. In fighting the Labor Law Reform Bill, Hatch was, at least in his own eyes, declaring war, not on the working man, but on the big labor bosses, whom he felt had corrupted the labor movement, and were launching one more attempt to gain personal power at the expense of the working man and the country as a whole. Hatch was convinced that the decline of union membership in the United States could be attributed in great measure to the corruption and dictatorial power of certain national labor bosses. As far as he was concerned, the Labor Law Reform Act would be detrimental to the overall job market and worker freedom, while increasing the already frightening power of national union leadership.

During earlier common situs picketing hearings, some of the union testimony was directed against Hatch, attempting to paint him as anti-labor. "The trouble with you, Senator, is that you don't know anything about construction," charged AFL-CIO buildings trade official Robert Georgine, the former president of Hatch's own union, the Wood, Wire and Metal Lather's Union.

"Now just a minute," Hatch shot back, "I worked ten years with my bare, bloody hands as a metal lather. By the way, Bobby," Hatch glared at the obviously well-fed Georgine, "I could probably tie more lath now with one hand tied behind my back than you could with both of yours on your best day." The union men in the audience chortled over Mr. Georgine's discomfort, and the clearly union jibe which could only have been made by one fellow union craftsman to another.

In his naïveté, Hatch could not understand how anyone who supported the rights of working men and the free enterprise system could support the bill. He was unaware of the intense, uncompromising pressure these labor leaders, their coffers bulging with political action funds, could exert. Well-financed propaganda organizations such as the AFL-CIO's Committee on Political Education (COPE) could make or break many an aspiring politician, and could materially affect the re-election of more than a few incumbents. In many states, being labeled by COPE an "enemy of labor" could mean political suicide. They reveled in this power.

The Labor Law Reform bill had breezed through the House in 1977 by a 257-163 vote. The same easy road was predicted for the Senate, and Carter's hand was poised ready to sign it into law, and thus pay off his election promise.

In January of 1978, the Senate Labor and Human Resources Committee considered the bill. Hatch worked feverishly to block it in committee. He failed miserably. It was reported out on January 25, by a 16-2 vote. Only Hatch and Hayakawa voted against the bill.

Now Hatch moved to try and win converts in the whole Senate. Again he was rebuffed. The bill had easily enough solid votes to pass the Senate. Some Senators who were opposed to the bill—who, indeed, actually saw it in the same light as Hatch—were nevertheless, like the timid House members, fearful of not supporting it. Hatch knew the only protection for the minority was a very carefully planned filibuster—an ancient rite of the Senate which gives a numerical minority the opportunity to try to "talk a bill to death."

Hatch's mentor, the venerable Democrat, James Allen, although critically ill, agreed to help him lead the filibuster. The organization of a filibuster that has any chance at all of success is not child's play. This is a job for an experienced veteran. Just as plans were being laid out, Senator Allen was stricken and died.

This was a double blow for Hatch. He loved this statesman with the devotion of a son for his father. And, with the death of Allen, the filibuster was denied one of its generals. It did not take Hatch long to ascertain that if there was to be a filibuster, he must lead it. In the few days before the debate, Hatch questioned other veterans of filibusters and studied intently the rules of the filibuster until he had mastered them.

Full debate began on the Senate floor in May. In the meantime, Hatch was quietly working fervently behind the scenes with some of the Senate "untouchables." He was not going to give up on this one.

Hatch and the indefatigable Lugar, whom Hatch had recruited, organized teams of Senators to engage in what was to become one of the most intense filibusters in Senate history.

The Senate majority appeared to be unprepared for the tenacity and dedication of Hatch and his little band. Senate majority leader Byrd had elected not to use the "two-track" system, under which part of the Senate's day is allotted to the filibustered bill and part to other bills. This meant that Hatch, Lugar and the rest of the crew had to be on deck practically around the clock to keep their hold on the floor, thus preventing the bill from coming to a vote that would surely be a victory for the labor bosses.

By this tactic Byrd had hoped to wear out the "filibusterers." At the same time, his decision had in effect shut down the United States Senate for, while the filibuster raged, no other business could be transacted. The debate went on for three weeks before Byrd gave up and sought the first cloture vote.

All the while Hatch was working almost without sleep. He was kept on the floor answering questions for hours each day. From endless talk on the floor of the Senate, he slipped behind the scenes—to confront, to plead, to argue with some of his fellow Senators whom he hoped to pull away from voting for cloture. In addition, Hatch had given upwards of 300 speeches all over the country to rally small business groups and other free enterprise organizations behind the cause.

Nose to nose he pled with his colleagues to vote their consciences rather than their fears. To a number of these, this was exceedingly painful. No one who knows that his own actions are unprincipled likes his nose rubbed in the fact. Some of those who suffered Hatch's stinging rebuke may never forgive him.

As the days passed and the filibuster retained its gruelling pace, some of the nation's top labor leaders began to appear in the gallery overlooking the Senate, and more than one Senator cast furtive glances in their direction. On the last day, labor czar George Meany was there. The full force of union pressure was being exerted. Individual Senators were being pressured unmercifully—from both sides. Whenever a Senator was approached by the unions, Hatch was waiting in line to counter.

Finally, Hatch himself was approached. A labor lobbyist who had been friendly with Hatch tried to appeal to his better judgment. "If you had a chance," he reasoned, "I wouldn't come to you. You have a right to fight against the legislation if you feel it's wrong. But this baby is already packaged with a ribbon on it. You have had your say. Now back off. I know your re-election is a long way off, but the people I represent are as stubborn as you are. They never forget. And they have long arms. Be smart, Orrin. Fight another day."

There was a noticeable rumble in the gallery when Byrd's first attempt at cloture failed. Hatch's behind-the-scenes exhortations were paying off. Interestingly enough, a number of Senators who more than likely would have voted for the bill had it ever reached that point were courageous enough to vote against cloture of the filibuster, thereby helping to prevent the issue from coming to a vote. Hatch and Lugar figured they would easily get one cloture vote win because Byrd did not want to leave a bad taste in the mouths of some Senators by crushing two freshman Senators too early in the game.

But the fillibuster lasted five, gut-wrenching weeks. And when it was over it had withstood a total of six cloture votes, one of them by a single vote. This was the most cloture votes ever recorded in the United States Senate on a substantive issue.

The Labor Law Reform Bill was dead. It did not appear again in the 95th or the 96th Congress.

Something else had happened of which Hatch was unaware at the time. This filibuster had served to reduce markedly the influence of union leaders over Congress. The loss was a blow to Carter who had promised its passage. But even more, the "mace" had fallen heavily on the union leadership influence. For the near future, at least, someone had let the air out of their balloon. And they wanted revenge against someone—they wanted it badly.

Hatch was exhausted after the gruelling marathon. He had lost so much weight he had to cut a new hole for his belt buckle in order to keep his pants up. He wanted nothing more than to rush home and collapse in bed. But he had promised to make an appearance that evening at a reception hosted by John Sherman Cooper, former Senator from Kentucky.

As Hatch was led into the living room he was surprised to see George Meany sitting alone on a couch, looking as worn out as Hatch felt. He walked over to where Meany was seated.

"Good evening, Mr. Meany." Hatch extended his hand. "I'm Orrin Hatch."

"I know who you are," Meany growled back. "Sit yourself down here, I'd like to talk to you."

Hatch sat down beside Meany on the edge of the cushion, his hands folded on his knees.

"Yes, sir?"

"Well, Mr. Hatch, I want you to know that I think you are a man of great courage and energy. Oh, we underestimated you. We did not believe for a minute that you could pull this off. I have to say I respect you for what you have done and for your dedication to your beliefs.

"Now," he shifted around to look Hatch straight in the eye,

"now that that's been said, I must tell you that we cannot tolerate you in your present position. You are a danger to our purposes. There is nothing personal in this, but I must see to it that you are a one-term Senator. We are going to defeat you out there in Utah in 1982 if it costs us $4 million." (Vera Glaser wrote in the *San Francisco Union,* that Hatch's response was, "That would be wonderful. If you spent $4 million in Utah, it would double our gross product.")

That day the Democratic Party of Utah gained an unexpected boon in their dedication to beat Orrin Hatch. With their campaign coffers seriously depleted, they could now look forward to a fortune from organized labor to defeat their Republican rival. Hatch was to learn that the union leaders were not going to forget, and that their political arm could indeed reach even Utah.

"Orrin Hatch," wrote labor writer Paul Shinoff for the *San Francisco Sunday Examiner,* "is a blue-collar construction worker, retired. He now reads law books instead of blueprints, swings a gavel instead of a hammer. He is organized labor's primary target in the 1982 election, and the late George Meany once said labor would raise $4 million to defeat him."

Although the so-called "full-employment" bill (Humphrey-Hawkins) was passed the same year as the defeat of the Labor Law Reform bill, it survived only as a particularly watered-down philosophical expression, which, in actuality, was largely due to Hatch's efforts. In a variety of amendments, the main thrust of the legislation was turned from federal government-guaranteed make-work jobs to primary reliance on free enterprise and the private economic sector.

Hatch's ubiquity, his zeal, his bulldozer tactics, and what appeared to be his crass arrogance in those early months of his tenure were adding to the frustration of certain liberals, both Republican and Democrat. Already stung by Hatch's success in blocking and amending their pet bills, they were particularly bitter over Hatch's blitzkrieg style.

It was, however, during the 95th Congress that the metamorphosis of Hatch began to be clearly seen. Senate leaders began facing the reality that this tireless, young Senator was not to be taken lightly. Even if, in the future, he would "burn out," at present his fiery thrust was, in fact, making a substantial difference in the Senate. Like it or not, they were going to have to take seriously this Senator from the *West* (that made it all the worse!) who in their view seemed to trample generations of Senate customs and mores in his stampede to set the world aright.

Hatch's influence, combined with his growing reasonableness, patience, and his crucial understanding of the legislative realm in which one must judge "what will go" at any period of time coincided with the increasing willingness of Senate Democrats to negotiate with him.

During the 96th Congress, Kennedy brought up new legislation for the National Science Foundation concerning "Women in Science." Hatch was not opposed to the concept in principle but saw mischief in this particular proposal. Hatch *negotiated* with Kennedy in an attempt to remove what he believed to be the legislation's most objectional parts. The original proposal called for the creation of several new bureaucratic institutions to promote opportunities for women in science. As Hatch saw it, this proposed distribution of $23 million would have the effect of decreasing the available funds for direct grants and scholarships for women.

Through negotiations Hatch undertook with Kennedy, some of the emphasis on institutional support was eliminated in favor of more money for direct research grants and education programs, that is, money going to women themselves. His efforts also succeeded in integrating the Women in Science programs with the existing research directorate, a system of management which allows for a high degree of accountability, tight management of funds, and professional evaluation of research proposals.

In this way, Hatch was satisfied that funds would be well managed, programs carefully evaluated, and the individual "women in science" would be recipients of the grants rather than new bureaucratic institutions. On the other hand, Kennedy was willing to accede to these stipulations in order to avoid a marathon confrontation with the man Senator Strom Thurmond had called the "Tarzan of the United States Senate."

Hatch's remarkable leadership in the restructuring of the Civil Service Reform Act of 1978 offers another example. This act was touted by the Democratic leadership as a bill to streamline the Civil Service. Hatch and others, however, saw it as a particularly bad piece of legislation that not only irresponsibly allowed improper union domination of the Civil Service but also permitted singularly inappropriate behavior in the Commission's personnel activities.

Assessing the situation and realizing that there was no hope that this bill could be defeated, Hatch marshalled his political forces and laid siege to the bill in an attempt to dismantle its most objectionable parts.

Hatch attacked the bill on three fronts. One was private negotiations with Abe Ribicoff, one of the most respected powers in the Senate and chairman of the Government Operations Committee. Simultaneously,

Hatch had alerted his colleagues to be ready in reserve to attack, frustrate, and block the bill should it reach the Senate floor.

Now, Ribicoff, analyzing Hatch's strengths and anticipating his delaying tactics—including even the possibility of a filibuster in the Senate—all of which could impede the passage of the legislation for some time and perhaps permit amendments to the bill that were unacceptable, began to negotiate.

Out of this personal negotiation with Ribicoff, combined with Hatch's dramatic exposé of certain negative elements of the bill during committee hearings, and reinforced by the threat of stall in the Senate which hung like the Sword of Damocles over Ribicoff's head, the freshman Senator was able to tag no less than seven amendments to the act. The Hatch amendments accomplished what the liberals feared. Among other changes they eliminated the obviously "written in" acquiescence to union representation, and provided for the automatic decertification of an exclusive bargaining unit if it failed to prevent a strike or other illegal job action.

It was out of these private meetings between Ribicoff and Hatch that mutual respect and accommodation grew until Ribicoff put his arm around Hatch and said, "Orrin, you are a great man and the Senate needs you. You are a true gentleman."

New factors had come into play which made these friendly exchanges possible. For example, Kennedy and his colleagues had come to the agonizing conclusion that Hatch was going to have to be reckoned with and that he was not a "flash in the pan." Also it had become obvious that before Hatch made a move in the legislative arena, he had mastered the subject matter at hand. Before he could, for instance, cause Kennedy to modify his proposal for Women in Science, or accede to amending the Civil Service Reform Act, he had to demonstrate that he not only had developed an expertise with regard to the programs but also could see them in their total environment, even to the point of knowing the tangential facts that affected them and were affected by them. Finally, the ability to take such a position demonstrated mature judgment on Hatch's part. Just as diagnosis is both the key to effective medicine and its most difficult task, so to the member of Congress his assessment of "what will go" in a given legislative situation is both his most valuable asset and his greatest deceiver, for it dictates his actions. Some have an uncanny ability to guess right in this regard. Hatch is one of these.

Thus, if Hatch felt he could kill what was to him an objectionable piece of legislation, he went for the jugular vein. If he was relatively sure he could not stop the legislation, his modus operandi was generally to attempt to negotiate change of the most objectionable portions. That failing, he would attempt to get it amended during the committee hearings or later on the floor of the Senate during the general debate on the measure. Then there was always the filibuster—used sparingly for crucial measures.

Some measures to Hatch were either profound moral or critical Constitutional issues. Here he refused to negotiate compromises or to attempt to amend. He fought the measure on principle. There is no quarter given. Win or lose the battle was just as intense, as witnessed by his losing battle against the Panama Canal Treaty and his winning effort against the 1977–78 Labor Reform Act.

Some of the most intense battles fought by Orrin Hatch have been over Constitutional questions involved in the legislation being considered by Congress. The fact is that there is an abysmal lack of understanding and concern with the fine points of the Constitution by many on the Hill. There is, perhaps, among most Congressmen, a college freshman's understanding of the basic concepts of our federal Republic. When an issue involves intricate areas of application and probable result, however, Constitutional sensitivity begins to break down. All too often, not even the Congressman's staff will catch these fine points.

To add to this problem is the reality that members of Congress are so pressed for time, so under the gun to meet relentless schedules, that they often simply do not have time to dissect a piece of legislation in the proper manner. One of the greatest complaints of the solons to the professional political scientist and critical observer, David B. Truman, is that they often must vote on legislation with incomplete information. All too often the critical information is discovered by the Congressman's staff or forwarded by a lobbyist or a constituent *after* the legislation has become law.

Then, too, some members of Congress do not take the time to investigate legislation thoroughly. They find it more comfortable to take their cues from party leadership or favored interest groups or even from their estimate of what will be the majority vote on the issue.

This demonstrates the critical importance of that small cadre of Senators on the Hill, of which Orrin Hatch is a conspicuous member, who are in command of the situation, who are tapped into the complex communications grid that works unofficially but nevertheless with effectiveness. They are Democrats and Republicans, liberals and conservatives. They are men who take their elected positions with all seriousness. They are catalysts—they make things happen. They are informed; that is, they make themselves informed. They are aware of, and sensitive to, the maelstrom of political decision-making. They have a fine sense of perceiving the larger picture and those issues or points of discussion which will, or will not, affect those things that are of great or lasting import.

When Hatch joined forces with other Senate conservatives in their unsuccessful attempt to block ratification of the Panama Canal Treaty, his was a deep concern that transcended the usual arguments that the treaty was a strategic blunder and an economic disaster.

Hatch typically had read the history of the Canal in greatest detail and had dissected the Treaty word by word. He was convinced that the United States was sovereign over the Canal Zone.

Although a major concern of Senator Hatch's about the proposed Panama Canal treaties was the wisdom of the United States giving the impression of retreating once again from its international commitments, equally important in his mind were a variety of fundamental constitutional problems with the treaties.

Under Article IV, Section 3, cl. 2, of the Constitution, "Congress' shall have the power to "make all needful rules and regulations respecting the territory or other property belonging to the United States." Although he recognized that international treaties could be entered into with the unilateral approval of the Senate, Hatch did not believe that such a treaty could overrule basic Constitutional precepts, including the obligation of "Congress," that is, both the Senate and the House, to have a voice in the disposal of properties belonging to the United States. In Hatch's view, there was no question that the Canal Zone fell into that category. There was no Constitutional basis for the transfer of property of the United States without the approval of both Houses of Congress.

Related to this issue was the question of whether or not the Canal treaties were "self-executing" treaties or "non-self executing" treaties. If of the latter sort, they would be in need of implementing legislation. Such implementing legislation would have to be approved under normally specified Constitutional procedures. This determination is a difficult one that depends upon interpreting a number of earlier Supreme Court decisions that have not always been clear in their implications.

The other major Constitutional issue involves the role of the House of Representatives in the Canal treaties to the extent that such treaties involved the disbursement of monies from the U.S. Treasury to Panama. Under Article I of the Constitution, monies are to be drawn for the Treasury only in consequence of appropriations "made by law."

The passage of the Panama Canal Treaty by a margin of one vote was, of course, disappointing to those many Senators who saw the Treaty as a serious strategic blunder with dangerous economic overtones. To Hatch and other of the Treaty's opponents in the Senate, the passage of the Treaty was doubly reprehensible, since it also violated the Constitution.

It was the same with the proposed legislation to eliminate the electoral college. The proponents of "direct election" argued that the elimination of the electoral college would make the system more democratic, and preclude the chance of a President being elected with a majority of electoral votes and a minority of popular votes.

Because of the simplistic appeal of the "direct election" system, few observers saw any real obstruction to its passage. After all, a similar effort several years earlier in the House of Representatives had been approved by a margin of 5 to 1. Predictably the press was overwhelmingly supportive of the proposed amendment to the Constitution. Senator Birch Bayh, the leader of the "direct election" forces in the Senate, looked forward to an easy passage.

In the summer of 1979, one of the most significant, yet largely unheralded, Constitutional debates of our time was led in Committee and on the floor of the Senate by Orrin Hatch, in an attempt to defeat the "direct election" measure in the Senate.

Under the electoral college system, the nation's chief executive has been selected since 1804 through a process in which candidates prevailing in each of the 50 states earn the electoral votes of that state. With each state being entitled to a number of electoral votes based upon the total number of its representatives in the House and Senate, the candidate winning the majority of total electoral votes becomes the President.

Critics of the electoral college had argued for many years that it was a defective system since it permitted candidates to win who did not have a majority of popular votes, although, in fact, this had only occurred on two occasions in the country's history (with even these instances being disputed). These critics wished to substitute a system in which the winner would be decided purely on the basis of which candidate captured a plurality of the popular votes, thereby entitling a candidate with as few as 40 percent of the votes in a multi-candidate race to become President.

Dissatisfied with the present "electoral college" system established by the Founding Fathers, opponents had introduced Constitutional amendments Congress after Congress to abolish it and to substitute the new system of "direct election" of the President and Vice-President. Finally, after years of efforts to force a clear vote by the United States

Senate on this issue, opponents of the present system were assured that in this year victory was in their grasp.

When Senate rumbling began to indicate a new effort to abolish the electoral college was in the offing, Hatch became concerned. In talking with his colleagues he found a number of them equally concerned. Others he found to be totally cavalier in their attitude about Constitutionalism and tradition. Many used the utilitarian argument—the current system wasn't working exactly the way the Founders intended anyway. And it was cumbersome. Why not be done with it?

Intense study and conversation with experts on Constitutional law served to vindicate Hatch's concerns. Organizing a group of Senate conservatives about him, the Senator from Utah set out to upset Birch Bayh's apple cart.

As distasteful as the realization was, Hatch and his supporters had come to the conclusion that many of their colleagues in the Senate were uninformed about the ramifications of the proposed amendment. Their tack, therefore, was to be one of education. They believed that if they could make enough of their colleagues informed about the subject, they could defeat the proposal. Of course, the now experienced Hatch also knew how to mobilize outside constituent groups to action.

Hatch made two lists; one with the names of those who were already opposed to the amendment, the other those who Hatch felt would respond to a proper education on the facts involved. Hatch and his defenders of the present Constitutional structure argued that the electoral college had worked well over the course of two centuries to ensure the election of Presidents who were generally decent and capable men and who were national leaders. They argued that the system ensured against the election of basically regional Presidents, men who might win heavily in one or two areas of the country and lose everywhere else. Such a system would also encourage a marathon of Presidential candidates, with the probability of incessant run-offs. In this respect, Senator Hatch argued that, "while the present system—which is not a perfect system—might involve the election every century or so of a candidate with 49 percent of the vote, the danger in the system of 'direct election' is that we will regularly face run-offs and elect a President who is perceived as the President of but a single region of the country. If I were to make a judgment on which of these shortcomings is the greater 'crisis' for our Constitutional system, I would unhesitatingly choose the latter."

Hatch, further argued that the present electoral college was important in preserving other fundamental objectives of the Constitution, such as the dual federalism role of the states in the selection of the national government, the protection of political minorities in the political process, and the consideration of the rights of smaller states in the constitutional structure.

Bayh was apparently unaware, or not sufficiently aware, of Hatch's behind-the-scenes contact with outside groups and members of the Senate, for he appeared complacent during several weeks when Hatch and his group were engaged in intense personal lobbying and the development of numerous Constitutional briefs and analyses for their fellow Senators.

The debate over the proposed amendment was initiated immediately following the Independence Day recess in Congress, and Senator Birch Bayh was, to say the least, taken by surprise. He had failed to anticipate one of the most carefully planned and successfully executed efforts in recent legislative history.

Following several days of heated debate, Senator Bayh still was unaware that the rug was being pulled out from under him. He filed a cloture petition, designed to cut off further debate on the issue and bring it to a vote.

Senator Hatch, however, had counted votes. Having conducted daily "head counts"—at times none too gently—of wavering Senators for at least two months prior to the final vote, he knew precisely how each of his colleagues was likely to cast his vote.

Instead, then, of fighting the cloture petition as was expected, Hatch agreed to move to an up-and-down vote as quickly as possible, baffling Senator Bayh in the process. In the only vote that the United States Senate has ever taken on the issue of abolishing the electoral college, proponents of its demise—who had earlier counted as supporters a number of Senators easily able to secure passage of the amendment—found themselves 15 votes shy of victory. Senator Hatch had placed every Senator but one precisely correct on his predicted vote tally.

As a result, the electoral college fight was won and won in such a convincing manner that few observers believe that the effort to abolish the Constitutional process is likely to arise again in Congress for many years. In a Congress sometimes focused only upon spending and tax issues, pork-barrels, and subsidies, Senator Hatch had engineered what was one of the most enduring Constitutional victories in modern times. As professor Charles Black of the Yale Law School observed, "The proposed direct election amendment, if it had become part of the Constitution, would have been the most radical amendment in the history of the country."

With the election of Ronald Reagan to the Presidency and the Republican capture of the Senate, Hatch was forced to make yet another important transition in his leadership style. In the 96th Congress Hatch began to shift from the skillful use of legislative roadblocks, from David of the minority party wounding, blocking and frustrating Goliath, to an effective sponsor of legislation and forceful avante garde for Reagan's economic program.

According to the *Congressional Quarterly,* "when Republicans won control of the Senate in 1980, Hatch like other GOP Senators, had to shift gears and learn the ways of the majority party. Instead of tossing legislative grenades at Democratic bills, he now is responsible for guiding Republican measures through the Senate." In the 96th Congress, "Hatch has been one of the more visible Republicans, taking advantage of two prominent positions he holds: Chairman of the Labor and Human Resources Committee, which created many of the nation's social programs, and Chairman of Judiciary's Constitution Subcommittee, which handles proposed amendments to the Constitution on such volatile issues as busing, abortion and school prayer, in addition to all other Constitutional and civil rights issues." In addition Hatch serves on the Budget Committee, a special defense technology committee, the Select Small Business Committee, and is active in the group of committee chairmen who meet with the majority floor leader, Senator Howard Baker, in attempting to influence party policy and priorities.

The very nature of those committees which Hatch chairs and in which he holds membership ensure him a controversial reputation. Through those committees flow some of the most important, volatile and controversial measures in all of Congress, and which touch virtually all Americans. It is significant, that after the shift of power in the Senate, Ted Kennedy chose to become the ranking member of the Committee on Labor and Human Resources, giving up a similar post on the powerful Judiciary Committee which he formerly chaired. Observers on the Hill are agreed that his reasons for giving up his position as ranking Senate Democrat on the Judiciary Committee to the same position on Labor and Human Resources, were, first of all, the crucial nature of that committee's responsibility, and second, because he believed himself to be the only Democrat who could prove effective in blocking Hatch, whose remarkable political skill was now bolstered by a committee chairmanship and a majority of Republicans on the committee, all but two of whom are conservatives. Seasoned Washington observers have stated to this writer that Washington labor czars actually "insisted" that Kennedy switch to Labor and Human Resources because they feared that Hatch would "tear their guts out'' as Chairman, and that since labor delegates will over-whelmingly control the 1984 Democratic Convention, lock, stock, and barrel, Kennedy had no choice but to switch, or forget about the Dem-ocratic Presidential nomination for 1984.

Kennedy has used his formidable experience and his awesome persuasive power to the fullest potential to unify the Democrats on the committee and to win over the two liberal Republicans on specific issues. It has not been uncommon for Kennedy to accomplish this task. Hatch is not always able to hold the Republican majority together. The wonder is not that on occasion Kennedy gets his way, but that in this unique switch of roles—Kennedy was once the kingpin and Hatch the spoiler—Hatch, still a freshman Senator, has been able to wield so much effective power in spite of Kennedy and his liberal majority.

It is a rare occurrence indeed for a freshman Senator to find himself chairing one of the standing committees, especially one with the prestige and power of the Labor and Human Resources Committee. With Kennedy relentlessly nipping at his heels and with a seemingly endless array of problems he was determined to attack, a monumental task was ahead of Hatch.

To Hatch, the circumstances of his rise to a committee chairman-ship, as a freshman, with the Republican control of the Senate was a little bewildering. To Goldwater he confided, ''I keep wondering what I'm doing here with all this responsibility.'' ''Hell,'' responded the Senator from Arizona with a twinkle in his eye, ''I used to think that about myself for the first few weeks I was in the Senate. Then, after getting to know my fellow Senators, I came to wonder how all the others got here.''

By rule of thumb, such a chairmanship, having to deal with a highly professional opposition minority during a period of radical change, will generally be under the direction of a veteran leader of great legisla-tive experience and tenure, one with substantial accomplishments and stature. Again, some of the so-called political ''pros'' on the Hill predicted that Hatch was ''over his head'' chairing that particular commit-tee. They predicted that Kennedy with his experience, would ''bury him.'' This turned out not to be the case; and Kennedy, above all, knew why. With the courage and determination of a seasoned general, Hatch launched his command into the legislative fray. According to the *Con-gressional Quarterly,* Hatch ''jumped into his committee assignments with both feet.''

But this was not the Orrin Hatch of five years earlier. This was veteran Senator Orrin Hatch deftly wielding ''the mace and the olive branch,'' coordinating and leading his team, mastering every phase of the jurisdiction that was now under his charge, memorizing the fine points of every piece of legislation that came under his purview, matching and more often than not besting Kennedy wit for wit, charm for charm, cunning for cunning, word for word, checkmate for checkmate, maneuver for maneuver. When he lost, he left his opponents drained and exhausted. And when he won, he remembered to be magnanimous.

Not many weeks had passed, with Hatch in his leadership role before the most inveterate ''Hatch-haters'' on the Hill were forced to concede that this Senator from Utah was in cool, deliberate command. As one Senator remarked when Hatch walked in one morning to chair this premiere committee, ''The ice-man cometh!'' On April 12, 1981, Margaret Engle, writing from the Washington Bureau of the *Des Moines Register,* stated what most Senators on the Hill already knew: ''Despite efforts of Kennedy and other Democrats, the committee has been transformed under Hatch.''

Generally, a committee chairman will develop a style that, while it can be compared in part to that of others, retains in its totality the individual stamp of his personality, ability, character, wisdom, intelligence, and philosophy. Official position will avail a member of Congress little if his authority lacks respect among his peers. If he does not possess the leadership skills essential to his position, he simply will not lead. Whether or not those skills are possessed and operative can be seen in the degree to which the official leader can influence the acts and decisions of peers and to the degree that their opinions are sought after as cues for the political response of others. It can also be seen in the respect, however begrudging, extended them by colleagues who oppose them. It was the wise Ghandi who once asked, ''For what does it profit a man if his status is raised and he himself is not?''

In the early days of Hatch's Chairmanship of the Labor and Human Resources Committee his integrity was severely tested; and Ted Kennedy came to know that Hatch was to be eminently fair in his powerful leadership position. At the same time, he lost any question, if he had ever entertained any, that Hatch was indeed the Chairman.

During the heated debates over an amendment (Sec. 2) to the Voting Rights Act during the Spring of 1982, Hatch's mace-and-olive-branch style was clearly visible. The debate was involved with another one of those sections which allowed charges of discrimination to be lodged against public officials without any evidence of *intent* to discriminate. In effect, this section would have transformed the Voting Rights Act and the Fifteenth Amendment of the Constitution from provisions designed to ensure *equal access* to registration and voting into provisions designed to ensure *equal success* in the electoral process.

Hatch was particularly upset over this provision, since he saw it as blatantly unconstitutional and a rape of the rule of law. Yet his leadership in the hearings before the Labor Committee were exemplary. He had assured those favoring the amendment that they would be given ample time to express their case, and he more than fulfilled his promise. The cordial response between Hatch and Benjamin Hooks, Executive Director of the National Association for the Advancement of Colored People, was indicative. When Hatch's penetrating cross-examination of Hooks was over, he threw out the olive branch to the civil rights leader as a gesture to keep communications open. "I personally am grateful that you have taken your time to come here. I respect you as a civil rights leader and one of the great people in this country. We do happen to differ on this issue."

In return Hooks let it be known that the lines of communication were still intact. "And I, sir, have appreciated your courtesy and kindness to me and in allowing me to freely express my point of view. I continue to recognize you as the very powerful chairman of this important Committee. I would like to talk to you further, not necessarily under all these lights."

Later that afternoon, however, Hatch's demeanor changed. At one point, during his testimony, United States Attorney General William French Smith had replied to allegations skillfully presented by Kennedy, which had implied racism on the part of the Republican Administration. Smith curtly responded adding that President Reagan did not have "a racist bone in his body." From the audience, made up primarily of "civil rights" activists, came hisses and groaning.

Out came the mace. Hatch brought down the gavel with such force that it startled many in the room.

"We are going to have order in this room, or I will have the room cleared! I agree with the Attorney General. This is too important a Constitutional issue to have more heat than light. I am not going to tolerate any sneering or any snide comments or remarks from either side in this issue. As long as I am Chairman we are going to show respect for the Attorney General, and, I might add, for the President of the United States, who *I* know does not have a discriminatory bone in his body. I resent some of the things that have been said. I think it is time to start talking about the real issues and cease trying to make this into an emotional camouflage game."

Later, a news commentator remarked, "When Hatch ceased to

speak, his countenance remained fixed on the audience, as if to dare an untoward response. Although the audience was made up primarily of radical civil rights activists who are masters of intimidating their opposition, the room remained quiet. One could have heard the proverbial pin drop. From that point on, the discussion proceeded in an orderly manner and, for the most part, on the subject at hand. To all in the committee room, it was evident that Hatch was the Chairman, and that the Chairman was in command.''

Chapter 7
PARTLY NATIONAL AND
PARTLY FEDERAL

From the beginning, the Senate Western Coalition, and Orrin Hatch especially, had made it known that they would not follow the Republican Old Guard into the predictable failures of the past. While they offered allegiance to the Republican Party leadership, they affirmed their primary devotion to traditional Republican principles. They would not consent to accepting a gutless retread of the New Deal on the specious theory that not to do so meant defeat at the polls. And so, rather than "playing it safe" and "going along," the Western Coalition have joined with others of the New Conservatism to reshape the modern Republican Party and perhaps the Democratic Party as well.

As Hatch developed his own particular legislative style, he found himself becoming particularly interested in certain areas of the political arena. This is not unusual; in fact, with thousands of bills pouring through Congress, it is essential. Committee membership focuses attention on the committee's subject-matter, and often the Member of Congress will become an expert in a particular area and subject-matter. His attitude toward, and interest in, a legislative category will be influenced by his position, philosophy, personal sentiments, and feelings, and may reflect decades of input into his habit background.

When Hatch came into the United States Senate, he brought with him a background of poverty and the scars and ribbons of success won against the odds by intense effort, full-hearted dedication, and his ability to start anew after meeting with failure. One could have perhaps predicted that he would be an enemy of "featherbedding," waste, inefficiency, fraud, and corruption. He could not abide dishonesty. He became convinced that the federal welfare system promoted dishonesty, encouraged waste and destroyed character, issues with which the modern secular liberal does not even concern himself. He was particularly concerned about welfare fraud, purported to cost the taxpayers many millions each year.

At the same time, Hatch's heart went out to the ill and the handicapped and to those who, through no fault of their own, were placed in a situation that required the caring help of others. At the beginning of his tenure he had been placed on the Subcommittee for the Handicapped, and it was not long before he became one of the nation's foremost champions of the handicapped and chronically ill.

Ironically, he found that, while there were many who would vote for a measure to aid the handicapped, they had few real champions on Capitol Hill. The fact is that many of the "high rollers" in Congress find little political advantage in spending their valuable time or effort as advocates for the handicapped. After all, there are far more powerful groups with far more political clout. And there is always another election just around the corner.

When Hatch was, for the first time, introduced intimately into this world of special people, he discussed at length the problem with other Senators, such as Hubert Humphrey and the venerable 50-year veteran of the Hill, Jennings Randolph, who had been chairman of the Subcommittee for the Handicapped under the previous Democratic rule. When his duties brought him into personal contact with handicapped and chronically-ill children, they won his heart once and for all. It was not long before he became their champion. He was the founder of Parents League For Emotional Adjustment (PLEA), established to help emotionally retarded children.

As he matured in his knowledge of this special world, he took particular notice of his home state of Utah and its institutions, using that experience to launch himself as a knowledgeable expert and proponent of handicapped problems and prospects for solutions. Not used to so much attention from elected officials, Utah's corps of professionals and volunteers working for the handicapped were delighted when they saw Hatch's attention was real, his love and concern genuine: "We sometimes wonder what our elected officials really believe and feel," wrote John E.B. Myers of Utah's Legal Center for the Handicapped, "but, as you held young Conar Kristenson (at a Hatch Report to Utah meeting at Cottonwood School), it was apparent beyond question that you care in a very personal way for the handicapped. That caring has made you a very special man in the eyes of many thousands of handicapped people and their families.''

Letters of appreciation for Hatch's concern and support for the handicapped began to flow into his office from Special Education officials. Typical in tone were such remarks as that of Mary Ann Williams, Special Education Supervisor for Utah's Davis County School District. ''Thank you for sharing your time, concern, expertise, and your support on behalf of the handicapped not only in Utah but in all of the states.'' Even letters such as that written by Salt Lake School District Special Education directors C. William Davies and Eugene Smith, Jr., expressing deep concern over possible budget cuts, added the P.S.: ''We are all aware of the fight you have led for handicapped monies.''

One morning a call came to Hatch from one of Utah's Special Education activists. She had in her care a young lad who had fought valiantly against a terminal illness but was now only weeks from death. He wanted to come to Washington and see the Congress and to see Senator Hatch. ''Bring him,'' responded Hatch, ''we'll take care of him.''

On the day the boy arrived, Hatch called the seriously ailing Hubert Humphrey. ''I have a young constituent,'' he said with feeling, ''who is terminally ill. I think you two ought to meet.''

''By all means,'' responded the elder statesman, his once robust voice weakened by the cancer that ravaged his body.

That afternoon Hatch and Humphrey, the frail body of an enraptured youth between them, walked into a committee hearing. Humphrey sat the wide-eyed youngster between him and Hatch, and conducted a two-hour hearing, all the while holding the boy's tiny hand.

When the hearing adjourned, Humphrey talked for some minutes alone with the boy in the committee anteroom. Later that evening Humphrey called Hatch on the phone. ''Orrin, I cannot tell you what today has meant to me. I have had my life, and it has been a full one. It is to that precious child who touched my life today for a brief moment to whom my heart goes out.'' His voice was at a whisper. ''Thank you, my friend.''

With the capture of the Senate by the Republican Party, Hatch became Chairman of the Committee on Labor and Human Resources and the nation's handicapped gained a powerful proponent. Hatch placed special emphasis on the handicapped. Under Hatch's direction, Ron Docksai, professional staff member of the Labor and Human resources Committee, and Staff Director of that Committee's Health Unit, restructured the whole office. With Docksai's help, Hatch searched for a new coordinator at full committee level. He selected Christine Lord from Logan, Utah. Christine matched Hatch's concern. She had worked with the handicapped at Utah State University and had acquired a Masters degree in Special Education from Kansas State University. She had been acknowledged the Outstanding Student in Special Education. She was co-valedictorian for the College of Education and had received the Robins Award for "Woman of the Year."

Christine was given the responsibility of becoming an encyclopedia on the handicapped for Hatch and a liaison between the subcommittee and the full committee. She was also charged to keep lines of communication open to state and national organizations dealing with the handicapped. She was to be responsible for meeting all the needs of the handicapped: Rehabilitation, Special Education, Special Institutions, and Developmental Disabilities.

No two people are more compatible in philosophy than Christine Lord and Orrin Hatch. "His efforts," she stated, "are to help those who can't help themselves, while at the same time overseeing the budget and making sure the funds are spent frugally. He is especially pleased with our rehabilitation program, since it is truly cost-effective. For every dollar spent in the program, $10.00 is returned to the economy."

It was with this intention that Hatch moved into budget hearings facing President Reagan's austerity program. Beginning in 1981, much of the brunt of President Reagan's economic program fell within the purview of the Labor and Human Resources Committee. In fact, Hatch's powerful committee posts, including his position on the Senate Budget Committee—combined with his own recognized and respected leadership skills, added to the prestige he gains from being a close personal friend of Ronald Reagan—make him the eye of the needle through which most key social legislation must pass.

Fully one-quarter of all the budget cuts that the President requested in March of 1981 and which were included in the Reconciliation, fell under the jurisdiction of the Senate Labor and Human Resources Committee. Hatch was able to bring the majority of the Committee into substantial compliance with these Reconciliation instructions.

Even before the Reconciliation, Hatch steered through the Committee a recommended budget for the Committee's programs that sharply reversed the trends of the past. "This committee," Hatch stated, referring to past liberal Democratic control, "was bankrupting the nation." Hatch's recommended budget called for a reduction of $13.5 billion in budget authority from the previous year's recommendations. From April until August, Hatch led exhaustive negotiations within the Committee, within the Senate, and with the White House. In nine laborious, emotionally taut Reconciliation conferences, he achieved legislative changes in over 200 committee programs, resulting in over $30 billion in savings in fiscal years 1982 through 1984, a prodigious and unprecedented accomplishment. Particularly grueling were the negotiations over the structuring of five block grants into which over 30 federal programs were condensed. While he worked to keep his narrow committee majority together, the hard-driving Kennedy and his forces exposed every inconsistency, capitalized on every hesitation, and augmented every break in pace. On some issues Hatch and Kennedy were in agreement, but Kennedy was not swayed, as were some of his colleagues, by the Republican landslide. His New Deal philosophy remained a consistent guide to his political behavior. He fought with the same intensity to preserve the costly, big-government, New Deal programs as Hatch did for change.

Naturally the Senate Budget Committee became a focal point of the 1981 budget battles. Here Hatch was able to assist in uniting both Republicans and Democrats in the support of the President's requested funding reduction. Working closely with Chairman Domenici, Hatch helped put together Reconciliation instructions calling for over $40 billion in savings in 1982. President Reagan was later to reaffirm what already had become evident: Hatch had been an absolutely crucial leader and had played a fundamental and intrinsic role in the budget that was finally sent to the White House for the President's signature.

Still, with all of these necessary reductions, Hatch fought to retain or to add back funds for social programs he considered essential. As a member of the Budget Committee, Hatch was successful in amending the proposed budget to restore $345 million to the program for education of the handicapped. He succeeded in retaining endangered current funding levels of over $61 million for the Developmental Disabilities program by an $8 million add-back. Later, in floor action, he co-sponsored measures with Senator Weicker which added back $44 million for Rehabilitation and $69 million for Education of the Handicapped.

He shaped the Preventive Health Services Block Grant Act of 1981 so that greater flexibility and responsibility would reside in the states in delivering health services, health promotion, and disease prevention programs. It was his intention to prevent the handicapped programs from being lost within the Administration's Social Services block grant.

Finally, by the time the finished budget was ready for submission to the President, Hatch had not only been able to ensure the continuation of all programs for the handicapped at current funding levels, but he was also able to secure a 5 percent increase for education and rehabilitation state grants in 1982 and 10 percent for 1983. In the same process Hatch succeeded in gaining the continuance of the Developmental Disabilities Act, which was destined for expiration on October 1, 1981. Then, in an action that touched his heart, the Administration on Developmental Disabilities granted, at his suggestion, a $100,000 Special Projects grant for Utah State University to fund an in-depth study of Utah's handicapped and to develop a model other states could follow.

Perhaps no other event demonstrates more vividly the awesome political power wielded by Senator Orrin Hatch than his ability to grind out budget cuts for the President while simultaneously protecting "his" handicapped programs from the avalanche of cuts that were to touch nearly every phase of the governmental process.

When the final administration budget was announced, leaders in programs for the handicapped, fearing the worst, were ecstatic. Letters of appreciation poured into Hatch's office from all over the United States. "I don't know how in God's name you did it," read one telegram from Texas, "but you did it." From the Director of the Bartholomew Special Services Cooperative in Indiana, "*Thank you* for all of your efforts on behalf of handicapped students"; from Dr. Robert S. Black, President-Elect, National Association of State Directors of Special Education, "On behalf of NASDSE, I want to express my sincere appreciation for your concern for our nation's handicapped children"; from J. Scott Marshall, Director of Governmental Affairs for the American Council of the Blind, a resounding "Thank you" to Hatch and Weicker; from the Nebraska Governor's Planning Council an expression of appreciation to Hatch and Chris Lord; from the Arizona Governor's Council on Developmental Disabilities, "Your sensitivity for disabled persons, the truly needy, and programs that meet their needs is greatly appreciated"; from Bonnie Jones, Manager of the Division of Vocational Rehabilitation, Tennessee Department of Education, "I thank you for your efforts on behalf of the disabled citizens in this country. You have made it possible for them to continue on their road to independence and a rightful place in this society".

But, most of all, Hatch appreciated the letters from his home state. It was more than a matter of personal satisfaction, more than a feeling of accomplishment, more than a sense that he had participated in something truly worthwhile. The American system of representation inevitably turns those for whom we vote into political animals. A Senator or a Representative may change the world from his Washington base; but, if his home constituency feels neglected, he is in trouble. American Congressmen are "partly national and partly federal (local)."

Fully understanding this phenomenon, Hatch was doubly grateful for the numerous expressions from Utah such as that from Harvey C. Hirschi, Administrator, Division of Rehabilitation Services, Utah State Office of Education: "You are providing dynamic leadership for the disabled of America. You are truly emerging as one of the finest statesmen in the halls of our nation's Capitol. It is difficult for me to express in words the comments I am receiving from the disabled people of our state concerning their appreciation for your untiring efforts in their behalf."

Recognition for skills and effort expressed by one's peers is also important, for they are indications that one is respected by those who know him best. Without such acknowledgement, a Congressman may find himself impotent in the legislative milieu. So it was that Hatch was warmed by the many responses he received from his colleagues—from both parties.

Problems of the elderly—senior citizens—also came under the purview of Hatch's legislative responsibility. As he studied and, true to form, mastered the subject, he became increasingly concerned with the major financial problem facing most of the elderly—*inflation*—which was cutting away at their fixed retirement incomes. To make matters worse, years of abuse by government had left the Social Security system in shambles, technically almost bankrupt, as an inheritance for the new Republican administration. It was multiple problems such as this, the progeny of virtually unrestrained spending by government, which met the new Administration in tandem and which reinforced the dedication of Hatch to be a standard-bearer for Reagan's economic recovery program.

Too, in his battle for home health care for the aged, one again sees the concerns and the style which motivate Hatch. First of all is his sensitivity to the situation where many of the elderly infirm would prefer to be treated at home in familiar surroundings which psychologically comfort them and where they maintain relative feelings of self-sufficiency. Then there is the economy of the program. It would, according to Hatch's best information, measurably cut the cost of medical aid.

In all of this is evidenced Hatch's concern for those who cannot take care of themselves, combined with his insatiable desire to bring down the cost, size and inefficiency of government, while tenaciously protecting or espousing programs in which he sees merit. There are only so many resources at the command of government, and resources spent in one area require sacrificing other alternatives which compete for these resources. Budget cuts in one program area may simply be a means of transferring funds to a preferred alternative one. Only the individual Congressman truly knows whether his battle for application of scarce resources relates to his belief that his choice is a valuable one for his home state, or the nation as a whole, or both, or whether that choice enters the realm of the "pork barrel," where the struggle for funds has a less noble motivation—that of paying off interest groups for their electoral support, or "buying" reelection from the "home folks" by the enticement of federal projects for the home state, some of which are unneeded. The process, of course, drains off scarce funds that might have been budgeted for alternative uses of greater value to another state or to the country at large. Here the line between nobility and chicanery is a thin one.

It is the same with issues with which the Congressman becomes interested, or feigns interest. Again, in the limited time, strength and resources of the Congressman, his choice of issues in which he chooses to become involved will be undertaken at the expense of other, alternative issues with which he *could have* become involved. Here again, the difference between true patriotic concern and opportunism in his amenability to certain issues is known best by the individual Congressman in the depths of his own conscience.

The fact is that Congressmen *are* both national and federal (local). While they are sworn to uphold and protect the national government, they are also charged to represent their states. They are expected to promote the welfare of their respective states, to be spokesmen for their states' interests and needs. It is a precarious endeavor to attempt to balance the perceived needs of one's state with those of the nation at large and vice versa, especially with the reality of insufficient funds and resources to service the incessant and competing demands.

The more powerful a Congressman becomes, the more he is able to serve his state. This is one reason why the great influence of committee chairmanships is so important. These power-related positions simply augment, in many cases, the ability of Congressmen to gain scarce resources for his state as an alternative to those resources going to other states not so favored with these positions or to other economic areas that would have been included in the national budget.

Here again, one struggles with the proper balance between national and federal. When Oregon Republican Mark Hatfield, Chairman of the powerful Senate Appropriations Committee, was criticized for using his position to benefit his state, his response was that it was his responsibility to represent his state as best he could, and that if his committee chairmanship facilitated this, well, "That's the way the system works. I can't help it if I am Chairman of the Appropriations Committee."

The *Washington Post*, with its decidedly liberal thrust and tone, was not at all pleased with the Utah Senator Hatch's awesome power, and his ability to steer the hated Reagan Administration's program through the Senate. So, when the newspaper's Washington reporters and its editorial board witnessed Hatch using his political clout to preserve his essential programs for his state from the budget cuts, they went into paroxysms of editorial invective against him.

On January 25, 1982, under the title "Congress' Budget Cutters Protect the Home Folks," Hatch was taken to task in an anything but gentle manner for fighting to hold on to the Central Utah Project, a vast water development project which includes 10 reservoirs, 3 power plants, and 140 miles of aqueducts. It was conceded that without Hatch's intervention, the Central Utah Project would have been axed in the first rounds of budget cuts.

To Hatch, however, there was no contradiction in his behavior. First of all he reasoned, "This particular water project is cost-effective. Over time it will pay for itself and then some. At the same time, its implementation will allow further agricultural and industrial development that will benefit not only Utah but the nation in general. It is a productive project that has positive national implications. Utah is rich in resources vital to our country. Now, the second driest state in the Union, Utah, with enough water, can become the 'breadbasket' of the West and the provider of critical natural resources in abundance for our nation's future development."

The above illustrates the peculiarly favored position of Utah in the Union of States, since its two Senators, Garn and Hatch, are chairmen of important and prestigious committees through which much of the nation's most important legislation passes. Furthermore, these legislators enjoy prestigious reputations on the Hill. This situation places Utah in a particularly advantageous position vis-à-vis her sister states. However, in the fluidity of America's peculiar political system, this advantage could be lost in a single election.

Should a national general election return the Democratic Party to control in the Senate, the whole power structure there would shift, and Democrats would chair all committees and subcommittees and enjoy a majority of members in each. Should Hatch or Garn be defeated in their home State, they would be replaced by new Senators with no seniority. The committee chairmanships would be lost to Utah. Other states would emerge to take what is now Utah's inordinately favored position. Such are the fortunes of competitive politics, and the peculiarities of Congressional organization where longevity—repeated re-election—is generally tantamount to authoritative position within that body.

In the real world of Congressional politics, members of both the Senate and the House of Representatives enjoy relative amounts of influence, and they use it. Frequently they abuse it. The importance here is not that Congressmen use their influence, but with what motivation and to what ends. One's influence is related to such things as the prestige of his home state, the committees and subcommittees to which he belongs or chairs, whether or not his party is in power, his relationship with the President, and his own personal magnetism.

Senator Orrin Hatch finds himself in a favorable position in all of these areas. He is powerful. He is not passive. He wields that power openly and without apology. He has mastered the mysteries of leadership, and he leads. For whatever reasons, he is, in an historical perspective, one of the great powers of the United States Senate, and one of the most powerful men in the country.

Few would question his importance to the Republican Party, especially after his pivotal performance on behalf of Reagan's economic recovery program. Who would suggest that his determination to succor those programs for the handicapped and the aged so dear to his heart, were not decisive in preserving their position? Senator Kennedy would be the first to admit that Hatch had been a formidable power in the defeat of a number of bills favored by the liberal Democrats and/or labor leaders. Few observers would suggest that there were many in the Senate other than Hatch who could have successfully launched a proposed Constitutional Amendment to balance the federal budget.

Without Hatch's influence, the Central Utah Project would most assuredly have gone down for the count. In another important move it was Hatch and Garn, along with the gentlemanly Democrat Gunn McKay, former Utah Representative, who forced the over-zealous Environmental Protection Agency (EPA), to back down, to modify its demands where its extremism would have forced the closing of the United States Steel (Geneva) Plant in Utah. And who would question that Hatch and Garn forced a far better discussion of the MX missile issue in their state than the Department of Defense would have? It was Hatch who was able to arrange federal medical and handicapped grants for the University of Utah and Utah State University. When it appeared that a substantial number of people in southern Utah had been contaminated by radio-active fallout that had years ago swept over the area from Nevada nuclear testing grounds during the 1950s and '60s, Hatch enlisted the help of Ted Kennedy to fund an investigation of the charges and opened the door for possible relief to victims and their families. In May of 1982, the University of Utah received $1.5 million to provide the necessary research to confirm the extent of the damage.

All Congressmen face the reality that it is finally the "folks back home" who are their source of re-election. The "folks back home" know this too, and they take every advantage of it. "Constituent Services" is an integral part of a Congressman's labor. Here again choices have to be made that relate to his unique position as "partly national and partly federal (local)." With the limited time and energy constraints that plague each Congressman, he must choose among competing national and local demands, for each decision will favor an expenditure of time, energy and effort, at the expense of an alternative expenditure in another sphere. Even at the local level his choice of which constituent demands he will service will be done at the expense of others which he must necessarily leave wanting. Considering the relative merits of his attention to national, local, or his own personal benefit, is a crucial and time-consuming effort for him in itself. And again, the relative power of a Congressman in his legislative role will generally affect the degree to which he is able to service local constituent demands. A referral to some examples of constituent services drawn from Senator Hatch's office files will demonstrate the breadth of problems a Congressman has to confront in attempting to help individual constituents.

Charles E. Wade, for instance, had wanted to serve his country in the Army, but was turned down because of a missing toe, although he was perfectly mobile. It finally took a personal call from Hatch to an Army Brigadier General to get Charles a medical waiver, and entrance into the Army.

During an interview with Senator Hatch, this author was privy to a phone conversation between Hatch and a Utah constituent. The gist of the conversation concerned the woman's seriously ill brother, who, although apparently eligible, was being denied entrance to a Veteran's Administration hospital. When Hatch hung up, a secretary put him through to the appropriate senior administrator at the National Headquarters of the VA. He received the promise that the problem would be resolved by the following day. "That's the bureaucracy for you," he said to me. "This is the second time this week I have had to make such a call."

Richard Carroll is a severely handicapped Utah citizen who contacted Hatch's office after several unsuccessful attempts to gain employment with the Postal Service. He was married with three children. He had refused welfare, wanting a chance to prove himself. He was repeatedly promised a chance and then repeatedly denied because of his cerebral palsy. Richard wanted a job as a janitor. It was the USPS position that his handicap would present a danger to himself and his fellow employees. He had worked as a janitor for several years at the University of Utah. He was unanimously recommended by all his former employers and several doctors indicated there was no reason he could not safely work.

Hatch had several letters written to various officials in USPS. He was promised cooperation, but several months passed with no action. Finally, on January 12, 1979, Hatch personally called the District Director of the Postal Service and said, "Please give this boy a job. I take responsibility. I would hate to have to make an issue of your discrimination in future Committee hearings." Richard was hired that week on a conditional basis and continues in that job with high ratings at this writing.

Then there was British citizen Sheila Gunderson who had visited her parents in England with her American husband and daughter, both U.S. and Utah citizens. When the time came to come back to their Utah home, her visa had expired and she was told she couldn't leave. Her husband, Mark, who had to come back to work, returned with their baby.

After the American embassy told Sheila it would take two years to process her visa, Mark contacted Hatch's office. Three weeks later, after the proper paperwork was wired to England and the details were ironed out, Sheila stepped off an airplane to greet a very happy husband and baby—and Senator Hatch.

"In England, I went to my local member of Parliament, but he couldn't help me," she said. "He told me they're not going to take much notice of a husband and baby, and unless I got someone with some say or some authority on the American side, they'd just keep stalling me. Hatch," she said, "was that someone." And one could go on and on with such examples.

It was perhaps inevitable that at least one other element of human life which appeared helpless would capture the attention of Orrin Hatch—the rights of the unborn. This was an issue that many of the wise sidestepped, or tried to. Whatever you believed, you couldn't win on this one. The issue of the rights of the unborn was intimately entwined with the emotionally-tinged and highly controversial issues of ERA and abortion. Both sides of these intertwined beliefs were well organized and angry—very angry. By becoming enmeshed in the fray on either side, one brought the wrath of the opposition down upon him.

In 1973, before Hatch had even dreamed about becoming a United

States Senator, the United States Supreme Court in *Roe* vs *Wade* and *Doe* vs *Bolton,* found that the due process clause of the Fourteenth Amendment contained a guarantee of a "right to privacy" that encompassed a woman's decision whether or not to terminate a pregnancy. This right to privacy became a "fundamental right." In effect, the *Roe* vs *Wade* decision created a regime of abortion on demand. It amounted to a national policy of abortion with no restrictions of any significant kind.

Hatch had been disturbed by the decision for a number of reasons. Its moral ramifications were obvious, but his legally trained mind perceived in the decision one more tragic example of a tortured misinterpretation of the Constitution by the Supreme Court—one more arbitrary decision based on contemporary "sociological law," and one expressing utter contempt for the sanctity of life. This obvious prostitution of the intent of the American Founders in writing the Constitution, to say nothing of the intent of Congress in launching the Fourteenth Amendment, disturbed Hatch's sense of legal balance and position.

But then, like most citizens, Hatch went about his busy life, only occasionally recalling *Roe* vs *Wade* and *Doe* vs *Bolton* to mind, with a disgusted shake of his head. From time to time, his anger was aroused as he saw one state statute after another pertaining to protection of the fetus go down under federal court decisions. In *Planned Parenthood* vs *Danforth,* the court cut down a statute which required the consent of the father of the fetus before an abortion could be performed. In *Belotti* vs *Baird,* the court decided that the state must provide alternative procedures for a minor to obtain an abortion should parental consent not be forthcoming. In *Calauttie* vs *Franklin,* the court, in effect nullified virtually all fetal protection statutes.

Then, as a United States Senator, Hatch was placed on the Judiciary Subcommittee on the Constitution. The issue of abortion was beginning to heat up. Pro and con petitions under "freedom of choice" and "right to life," saturated the committee's mail.

As time went by his interest was piqued over both the moral and legal ramifications of the current endemic practice of abortion. He was appalled at the authoritative report from the Center for Disease Control's "abortion surveillance" division which claimed that 615,831 legal abortions had been performed in 1973, and the total reached 1.6 million for 1978. The Alan Guttmacher Institute (research affiliate of Planned Parenthood Federation of America) reported 1.5 million legal abortions in 1979; nearly 30,000 a week, over 4,100 a day, with at least 20,000 abortions performed on women in their *seventh* month of pregnancy or beyond. Add to this the estimate that for every 18 legal abortions in the

United States there is 1 criminal abortion. It was estimated that in 1979, 30 percent of all pregnancies were terminated in abortion.

Hatch spent a long evening at home studying the statistics. He went over them again and again, reviewing in his mind the spiritual, moral and legal ramifications of the small amount of information he had collected. Most of all, he ached inside when he contemplated the relation between this wholesale slaughter of human life and the spiritual beliefs he held dear. A Scripture ran through his thoughts—"Suffer the little children to come unto me, for of such is the Kingdom of Heaven." How can a righteous God, in whose image we are made, he reasoned, not hold us accountable as a people and as a nation for this wholesale crime against the living unborn. The words of Thomas Jefferson he had memorized at the Memorial ran through his thoughts . . . "I tremble for my country when I reflect that God is just, that his justice cannot sleep forever."

Hatch paced the floor for hours. From time to time he stopped to re-read the reports.

Suddenly it was dawn. Hatch quickly showered and dressed and drove to the Capitol. He called Frank Madsen and Tom Parry into his office. "This is top priority," he stated. "I want everything written on abortion—every study, every article, every court decision. Get the staff popping!"

Madsen and Parry knew what was going through the Senator's mind. They had been through this routine before. Hatch was going to take on Goliath again, but he was not going to take the field of battle unprepared. Before he drew the sling and the stone, he would be one of the most informed Americans on the subject of abortion.

In taking an active position on the abortion issue, Hatch was becoming involved in a controversy that was centuries old. It was Pythagoras, believing passionately that the soul entered the body at conception, who vigorously opposed the Stoic's contention that abortion should be permissible up to the very moment of birth. Abortion and infanticide were common in a declining Rome, especially among the elite classes. Later, the influence of Christianity and opposition by some of the great writers of the time helped bring the initial prohibition of abortion during the reign of Severus (193–211 A.D.). The ancient Hippocratic Oath included a prohibition of abortion.

As English common law developed, the doctrine of "quickening" drew the line of *legal* culpability; that is, sanctions would be applied if abortion occurred after the first movement of the fetus within the mother's womb. At the same time there was strong *moral* pressure against abortion as a practice.

In 1948, the World Medical Association subscribed to the Oath of Geneva, which stipulated, "I will maintain the utmost respect for human life from the time of its conception." In 1959, the UN General Assembly declared that, "the child, by reason of his physical and mental immaturity, needs special safeguards and care, including appropriate legal protection before and after birth."

In America, most of the States adopted the *legal* philosophy of common law, while the *moral* philosophy of Christianity served more potently than any legal sanction to inhibit the incidence of abortion.

Since the Civil War period, the legal philosophy regarding abortion in the states, generally assumed prohibition in all stages of gestation, with legal tolerations of therapeutic abortion. This variously included danger to the physical and mental health of the mother, apparent severe fetal abnormality, and pregnancy from rape or incest.

With the High Court decision of January 22, 1973, in *Roe* vs *Wade* and *Doe* vs *Bolton* (and subsequent related decisions), all effective legal control over abortions was nullified. At the same time, *organized* Christianity had all but ceased to be a moral bulwark against abortion. (Notable exceptions are the Catholic and Mormon Churches and affiliates of the Moral Majority.) Modern Christianity had turned its back upon its spiritual heritage, and had become co-opted into the world of secular humanism, where man, not God was the measure of all things, and where morality and ethics had become slaves to man's shifting, relative ideas of right and wrong, which are typically devoid of any traditional or spiritual guidelines. In effect, the above Court decisions were but reflections of this phenomenon transferred to the legal realm. The result was that unborn children at virtually any gestation period were left devoid of protection.

Months passed, and as Hatch pored over the extensive literature on abortion, including stark photographs of aborted fetuses, he was introduced into a world of horror seldom seen by the average citizen. He spent many hours in consultation with both national and local pro-life leaders. He was especially aided by the wisdom of David O'Steen, Executive Director of Minnesota Citizens Concerned for Life (MCCL).

Hatch talked personally to a number of medical authorities on abortion. He studied a virtual library of medical books and articles dealing with the subject. He studied Dr. Bernard Nathanson's revealing book *Aborting America,* and Professor John T. Noonan's book, *A Private Choice*. He consulted with eminent doctors and psychologists who were experts in the field of abortion. He was like everyone else who thinks himself "decent," and what he learned so troubled him that he wanted to dismiss the whole torturous subject from his mind—leaving that dark world of carnage for others to worry about. But, as a United States Senator and Chairman of the Constitution Subcommittee it *was* his responsibility to worry about. Events had brought the subject under his purview and jurisdiction. He could not dismiss it with a shrug, or soothe his conscience with an angry retort as the rest of us do. The monster had been laid at his doorstep. He had to deal with it. He swallowed hard and continued his journey into the abyss the rest of us, like Pilate, would rather not think about.

From a myriad of reports and studies he learned that "repeat" abortions probably accounted for nearly 30 percent of abortions performed, and that in 1978, approximately 21,000 abortions were performed on women who had three or more previous abortions. He was not surprised to learn that the highest "repeat" abortion rates (34 percent) occurred in the District of Columbia and New York City, which report more abortions than live births annually.

"How is an abortion performed?" Hatch asked a prominent physician and close friend. In the hospital laboratory the doctor, a cynical old cuss who had refused to perform abortions after his first experience with the operation, lay before Hatch numerous sequential photographs of abortions being performed. The Senator was unprepared for what he saw. He was sickened, both spiritually and physically.

"Let me explain these to you," continued the doctor in a sardonic tone. "The most common method of abortion is 'suction' abortion. This process tears the embryo or fetus apart like a vacuum pulls debris out of the rug. Then there is this, the 'dilation and curettage' method. This involves the pleasant practice of dismembering the fetus, a bloody piece at a time. Then there are 'saline' abortions, which kill the fetus with salt poisoning. Look at this picture. After a saline abortion this fetus is born alive and frightfully burned. You did not know, did you, that a fetus has fully human form by eight weeks, fingers toes and all, and that at just four weeks is sustained by his or her own beating heart?"

Hatch's eyes welled with tears. "I have seen enough," he said, his voice cracking, "I don't want to see any more."

"Oh no," cried his friend bitterly, "You ain't seen nothin' yet! I want you to take the full story back to those fools on the Hill who pretend to be keepers of the public weal. Abortion, as barbaric as it is, is just the beginning. Any psychologist worth his salt who has been involved in the abortion milieu will tell you that the whole bloody process brutalizes us—all of us who are remotely involved with it. Once we reach the point of accepting wholesale abortion, then we have little conscience left. Albert Schweitzer was right when he warned that 'If a man loses reverence for any part of life, he will lose his reverence for all of life.' Did you know that we are now practicing *infanticide* in many of our hospitals?''

''What?''

''Oh yes. As far as I know, the first case was in Johns Hopkins in 1970. A child was born with Down Syndrome and a throat condition— *escoageal atrisia*—the latter easily corrected by surgery. They put the babe aside. They did not feed it. It took 14 days to finally die. And do you know something else? This was done with the permission of the parents.

''Look at this article by Drs. Duff and Campbell from the *New England Journal of Medicine.*'' He slapped the piece angrily in front of Hatch on the table. ''These doctors agree with infanticide. They claim to have done the same thing many times, after consultation with parents. In their way of thinking the life or death of a newborn child can now be based on the *quality* of that child's life.''

''My God,'' exclaimed Hatch.

''Oh yes, *your* God—*their* God too, *those little babes*!''

The old doctor was gritting his teeth. ''Let me tell you that if this crime against humanity continues, we will one day brutalize ourselves into oblivion. Our hearts will be hardened against the most elementary claims of compassion. The Germans thought they were really forward-looking when they began wholesale abortion. Then came infanticide; then euthanasia; then, under the Nazi state, declaring certain groups as less than human—the insane, then Gypsies, then Jews.''

Thus did Hatch force himself to become an expert on both the clinical and moral aspects of abortion. And with his education grew his resolve to do something about it.

Nor was the Senator ignorant of the Constitutional ramifications of the ''Roe and Doe'' decisions. Here were problems related to federalism, to the separation of powers system, and to the intent of important Constitutional provisions. For a time Hatch researched the problems with the same intensity he had exhibited as a young law student. Too, he consulted with some of the leading authorities on Constitutional law in the country. Again, all he learned served to reinforce his antipathy to the ''Roe and Doe'' decisions. Hatch agreed with Harvard Law School professor John Hart Ely: ''It is . . . a very bad decision . . . . It is bad because it is bad Constitutional law, or rather because it is not Constitutional law and gives almost no sense of an obligation to try to be''; and with the angry Charles Rice of the Notre Dame Law School, who claimed that *Roe* vs *Wade* was "the most outrageous decision ever handed down by the Court in its entire history."

Hatch was convinced that the Court erred in making *abortion* a Constitutional right. "No such right," he informed Congress on September 21, 1981, "has ever been thought to have existed previously." He quoted from Judge Rehnquist's dissenting opinion: "To reach its result, the Court necessarily has had to find within the scope of the Fourteenth Amendment a right that was apparently completely unknown to the drafters of the amendment." He quoted University of California (Berkeley) Law School Professor, John T. Noonan: "The liberty established has no foundation in the Constitution of the United States. It was established by an act of raw judicial power. Its establishment was illegitimate and unprincipled."

On the other hand it was inconceivable to Hatch that the Fourteenth Amendment should not protect the life of the unborn. What the "Roe and Doe" decisions had, in effect, accomplished was to shift the decision-making authority away from the public forum and place it with the pregnant woman and her doctor, by encapsulating them within an alleged Constitutionally protected zone of privacy, while relegating to them the decision as whether an unborn child should live or die. In effect, what the Supreme Court had done was remove a class of human beings from the purview of the law, solely on the basis of their biological age and development, holding that the unborn are not "persons" under the Fourteenth Amendment and at the same time preventing any public control or scrutiny over the decision of abortion. Therefore, to Hatch, the "Roe and Doe" decisions were ipso facto an unwarranted distortion of Constitutional law and a clear attack on the Constitution.

Nor did he believe that abortion should be classed with other medical procedures, since abortion alone involves the purposeful, deliberate termination of human life.

Hatch's authoritative knowledge of the American Constitutional system convinced him as well that the Court had unjustly usurped powers, which in the federal system rightly belong to the states, thereby overriding most existing state abortion statutes, simultaneously annihilating any protections whatsoever for the unborn fetus during the early stage of pregnancy. He believed this denial of state authority to legislate on abortion to be an unprecedented legal blunder by the Court.

Hatch further believed that regulation of abortion practices was exclusively a legislative matter, within the general constraints of the Constitution, and subject to the traditional representative process, rather than judicial fiat. His knowledge of Constitutional law led him to believe fervently that the Court's decision in "Roe and Doe," holding that state and federal legislatures could not restrict or prohibit abortion, was a legal and Constitutional travesty.

A little over two years after his election, Hatch added Stephen Markman to his staff, one of the few top officials of his organization not from Utah. Markman is softspoken and smart. A graduate in law from Duke University, he was a practicing attorney and a member of the Michigan Bar Association. His knowledge in the realm of Constitutional law has proved to be an important aid to Hatch, since he serves as his Counsel on the Judiciary Committee. In Committee hearings which involve matters of Constitutional law, Markman can be seen sitting on the dais close to Hatch. As points are covered by the Committee, Hatch and Markman frequently put their heads together in discussion.

Markman, his mind a legal encyclopedia, was invaluable to Hatch on such issues as the successful efforts to preserve the electoral college, the proposed Balanced Budget Constitutional Amendment, and the Civil Rights of Institutionalized Persons Act.

Normally, after digesting Hatch's initiatives in Constitutional areas, Markman will attempt to stake out a position for the Senator, research the issues, prepare memoranda for him, maintain contacts with outside interest and lobbying groups, coordinate hearings, and attempt to market his proposals to the media and other Senators.

After Hatch and Markman spent long hours in attempting to design a logical approach to the abortion controversy, Hatch was armed for battle. To a professional, however, the direction and method of attack were crucial to success. Many times had Hatch, by dear experience, vindicated the wisdom of the late James Allen that intelligent *deployment* of one's limited forces must be basic to the overall campaign. Nor was a correct assumption of "what will go" with this highly controversial issue any less important to the outcome.

After much contemplation and "testing of the waters" by innumerable conversations with people whose opinions Hatch considered to be informed, the Senator came to the conclusion that in the present polemic that raged over abortion, any attempt to bring about an ultimate solution—that is, to bring to pass a national prohibition of abortions per se, was doomed to failure. After what he had learned about abortion, it was frustrating for Hatch to contemplate how ill-informed much of the American public was over the issue. He was not at all certain that there would be enough support in the United States to end the carnage inflicted upon the unborn. This grieved him, but he had to face the reality of the situation. Somehow, something had to be done to nullify the tragedy that was the offspring of "Roe and Doe," but that "something" had to have a chance of success; and, at the same time, it would have to comply with his purist's regard for the Constitution. Hatch's pragmatism did not take him beyond principle. He would not, as he interpreted an action, do damage to the Constitution—even in a worthy cause. Hatch remembered his frustration with many of his fellow Senators over the vote to extend the deadline of the Equal Rights Amendment. Some had told him that they knew the extension was an affront to the spirit of the Constitution but that the worthiness of the cause outweighed that consideration. He would not now place himself in the same position he had criticized others for taking, even in a worthy cause.

But there was another consideration. Hatch was Chairman of the Judiciary Subcommittee on the Constitution. His entire thrust had been to restore that Subcommittee to the position of a defender of Constitutional principles. Were he now to sacrifice that standard, over the long term his action would come back to haunt him as other issues came before him.

It was these sentiments that placed him in a frustrating position with one of his most respected friends, Senator Jesse Helms of North Carolina. Helms had sponsored "The Human Life Bill," Senate Bill 158. Essentially, S. 158 would overthrow the "Roe" decision by giving Congress the authority to unilaterally interpret, in a different manner than the Supreme Court, certain provisions of the Constitution. Specifically, by legislative enactment, S. 158 would reverse the Supreme Court's decision by declaring that the live unborn were human and therefore worthy of protection under the Fourteenth Amendment to the Constitution. It would also limit the jurisdiction of federal courts to hear and decide cases relating to abortion.

As unprofessional as many of the recent Court decisions have appeared, Hatch still accepted the Constitutional principle that it was the jurisdiction of the Court to interpret the law, however foolishly it had done so in "Roe and Doe." For Hatch, there were strong Constitutional reasons for opposing the overturning of a Supreme Court decision by legislative fiat. He was concerned that S. 158, if passed, could establish a precedent that would undermine the central role of the judiciary as the final arbiter for defining the terms of the Constitution. In effect, S. 158 would overturn a Constitutional decision of the Supreme Court by simple statute. Hatch did not believe Congress had the authority under the Separation of Powers principle "to interpret the Constitution in direct contravention of a previous Supreme Court decision."

Hatch further saw a negative impact of S. 158 on the principle of federalism, specifically on the central role of the state governments in the federal system. He feared that the long-term impact would be increased federal intervention at the expense of state authority. If Congress is empowered to overturn a Supreme Court decision and then define "person" in relation to the Fourteenth Amendment, then what would keep the Congress from defining or redefining the terms "equal protection" and "due process," given the potential expansive interpretation of these terms? Here there was potential for mischief. Before the Judiciary Committee's Subcommittee on Separation of Powers, Hatch cautioned, "If Congress can define what constitutes a 'person' for purposes of the due process clause of the Fourteenth Amendment and impose that definition upon the states and obligate the states to abide by that definition, then Congress would equally be empowered to interpret and define other substantive provisions of the Fourteenth Amendment." Hatch agreed with Professor William Van Olstyne of Duke University Law School that the acceptance of this principle in S. 158 had the potential of transforming Congress into a superstate legislature.

The more Hatch discussed the legal and Constitutional problems with Stephen Markman and other authorities on Constitutional law, the more he came to realize that the only method that had a chance of "making it" through Congress at this time, while remaining faithful to the Constitution, was a carefully worded Constitutional Amendment.

At length, after weeks of consultation, Hatch introduced an amendment—called the *Human Life Federalism Amendment*—that few, other than a number of approving legal scholars, fully understood. It read, *"A right to abortion is not secured by the Constitution. The Congress and the several States shall have the concurrent power to restrict and prohibit abortions; Provided that a law of a State which is more restrictive than a law of Congress shall govern."*

Immediately upon the formal announcement of the amendment, Hatch and his staff began a grueling crusade to educate interested parties to its intent and purpose. "In removing the abortion controversy from the federal judicial branch," Hatch told the Senate, "the proposed amendment would place the debate within those institutions of government far better equipped to deal with the issue. I believe that it is important to re-enfranchise all the people in fashioning a solution to the abortion controversy. That can only be done by placing this issue back within the representative branches of government, where it should have remained all along."

In effect, the Hatch amendment would remove the abortion issue from the courts where the pro-life movement has found little support, to the legislative and political arenas where the movement has been decidedly more successful. Yet, at the same time, it avoids the "states rights" dilemma in which abortion legislation would be left up to the individual states, thereby allowing the possibility of some more liberal states becoming abortion "havens." While the proposed amendment clearly authorizes Congress to pass a single national standard to protect life, the individual states may also legislate anti-abortion measures. These measures may provide *stricter* prohibitions than the federal statute, but they may not detract from it.

Just as Hatch and his staff had surmised, the first reaction to the *Human Life Federalism Amendment* (S.J. Res. 110), was almost universally negative. Initial favorable responses came only from some in the academic world, primarily the law faculty. Senator Kennedy had to chuckle over this one. "He is the only Senator I know who can get *both* sides of an issue angry with him."

Several of Hatch's senatorial colleagues, with but a rudimentary knowledge of Constitutional law, erroneously supposed that where the amendment gave concurrent power to the states and Congress to restrict and prohibit abortions, "provided that a law of a State which is more restrictive than a law of Congress shall govern," it was a violation of the Supremacy clause and therefore unconstitutional. Steve Markman spent many hours instructing those who were concerned about the wording of S.J. Res. 110. From the very beginning, Hatch's main concern was going to be one of education.

Naturally, Senator Helms was deeply hurt at losing Hatch's support of S. 158. In order to demonstrate the merits of his amendment, Hatch was forced to state the reason he opposed S. 158. In so doing Hatch was forced to stand against one of his closest friends, one who shared much of his ideology and his concern, one who had stood with him as a faithful ally during many great battles in the Senate. Both men were devastated by the confrontation. The press didn't make it any easier. On December 25, 1981, one Washington tabloid headlined "Hatch vs. Helms: Right to Life Goes Down For The Count." When Hatch and Helms met in private conference, the atmosphere was strained. With lesser men their friendship would have ended there. In this case, each was man enough to accept the other's dedication. In the end, neither asked the other to back off. When the meeting was over, their handshake was warm and real. They would join forces another day.

During hearings in the Judiciary Subcommittee on Separation of Powers, Hatch, a knot in his stomach, brought out the "mace" against S. 158. In a surprising move, however, Hatch did not attempt to kill it in subcommittee. He let it live. He had thrown the "olive branch" to

Helms. "I have," stated Hatch, "reluctantly voted it out of the Subcommittee in order to sustain the debate on its provisions. I will continue to maintain an open mind on this proposal. I am favorably disposed to virtually any measure to save the lives of the unborn, even if it is not my first or second or third choice at this point. However, I cannot state my support for the legislation."

Civil Rights and ERA lobbyists on the Hill were vocal in their opposition to S.J. Res. 110. One ERA activist was able to gain an audience with Hatch in his office. There was no cordiality in her tone. For several minutes she berated Hatch for his "male ego" and his "unconscionable attitude toward discrimination," as evidenced by his proposed amendment.

Hatch let her talk until, fairly out of breath, she stopped.

"Are you quite finished?" he asked.

"For the moment," she replied.

"Fine; now you listen to me! Your diatribe of a moment ago is typically untrue and unreasonable. You but serve to illustrate the 'tendency of the Left to become so enthusiastic over what is called reform that you fail to think the issue through.'

"Are you really unaware that abortion exploits women? So many of you 'are pressured by spouses, lovers, and parents into having abortions you do not want.' Can it be that you are not aware that 'most women who obtain abortions are under great stress, that they are usually ignorant of the humanity of their unborn child and unaware of the alternatives available to them?'

"Have you not considered how 'abortion allows a man to shift total responsibility to the woman? He can buy his way out of the accountability' by simply footing the abortion bill. 'The man's sexual role then implies exactly nothing, no relationship.' What happens here to your coveted right to choose? It becomes simply 'to serve man's right to use.'

"You talk to me about women submitting to abortion to preserve their lifestyle or economic or social status. Do you not realize that in so doing 'they are pandering to a system devised and run by men for male convenience?'

"Cannot you see that 'accepting short-term solutions like abortion will serve to delay the implementation of real reforms like decent maternity and paternity leave, job protection, child-care, and community responsibility for dependent people of all ages?'

"Of all the things which are done to women to fit them into a society dominated by men, 'abortion is the most violent invasion of their physical and psychic energy. It is a deeper and more destructive assault than rape.'

"Again, you speak to me of discrimination. Can it be that you are not aware that 'exclusion of the unborn from membership in human society and from the protection it entails is among the worst contemporary instances of discrimination?'"

Hatch became aware that he was beginning to raise his voice. He stopped speaking and sat down. His visitor was now somewhat subdued.

"Well, you have made some interesting points. But . . . ."

"*I* didn't make them," interrupted Hatch.

"I beg your pardon?"

"I mean to say that I am quoting from others—from *feminists*—Meehan, Loesch, de Jong, and Olivarez; and from Northwest University Law Professor Victor Rosenblum, a liberal Democrat who is dedicated to the cause of those who are discriminated against."

Hatch passed two xeroxed copies of articles into her hands. (Mary Meehan, "Abortion and Consistency," *The Human Life Review*, Winter, 1981, and Victor Rosenblum, "The Hatch Amendment: a Legal Analysis," *Studies in Law and Medicine*, 1981.)

"Oh," she looked intently at Hatch, and repeated the sentence Hatch had heard a hundred times before on a hundred different issues, "I had no idea you were so well informed on the subject."

"And I," Hatch responded, "am concerned that you are so *uninformed* on the subject."

But it was from a limited faction of the "Right to Life" camp particularly that Hatch was hit with the most concerted invective. It came from those whose views on abortion were similar to his but who were not prepared to consider the Constitutional implications.

He was branded a traitor to the "Right to Life" movement and to his good friend, Senator Helms. He was accused of ignoring short-term solutions that would end abortion for a method that might be years in ratification and still did not prohibit abortion.

For months Hatch, Markman, bolstered by a number of professors—from Lynn Wardle of Brigham Young University, and John T. Noonan of the University of California, on the West, to Northwestern's Victor Rosenblum and Amherst political scientist, Hadley Arkes, from the East—sought to educate their friends. If his amendment were to have a chance, a whole host of conservative groups and organizations would have to be brought into line. They had to be sold the Constitutional importance of the amendment, plus Hatch's firm belief that once the proper power of this issue was returned to the nation's legislatures, restrictive legislation would be forthcoming. In the meantime, he assured his detractors, other measures could follow, even a new amendment. But for now, he had to convince them that his amendment was the only measure that had a chance of survival.

"Once we can establish in the Constitution the principle that abortion is not an ordinary routine medical operation," he pled, "we can begin to re-educate all the American people to the cruel realities of abortion.

"I believe that abortion involves the taking of a human life. It is morally and ethically, and—I believe—Constitutionally wrong. Should my amendment become part of the Constitution, I would be among those seeking the most restrictive state and federal laws with respect to abortion.

"When a greater consensus exists in this country on the repugnance of abortion—which consensus I believe will be promoted by this amendment—I will be among those seeking a direct constitutional prohibition on abortion."

Slowly Hatch's alienated natural supporters began to come back under his banner. A series of speeches on the subject, media coverage, and mountains of letters and briefs mailed throughout the nation began to have some effect. By early 1982, the two most prominent "Right to Life"groups—The National Right to Life Committee and the United States Catholic Conference—had endorsed the amendment. They were followed by the National Pro-Life Political Action Committee and The National Committee For Human Life Amendment, Inc. On the 22nd of January 1982, a massive rally for "Right to Life" took place in Washington, D.C. In the march on Capitol Hill, made up of citizens from all over the country, scores of signs and placards read "Hatch Amendment."

And, significantly, Hatch began to see the beginning of a united front against abortion which transcended political ideology. Standing before the Subcommittee on the Constitution, a prominent law professor said to Hatch. "Let me commend you, Mr. Chairman. You have embarked upon a noble enterprise to protect the weakest among us." The words were uttered in all seriousness by the liberal Democrat, civil rights activist, and Vice-Chairman of Americans United for Life Legal Defense Fund, Victor Rosenblum.

Chapter 8
BUDGETS AND DEFICITS

As a political neophyte, Hatch came to Washington without a complete understanding of the potent bias to spend money that had developed in the Congressional legislative process. He was only relatively aware of that alliance of Congressmen, administrative agencies and special interest groups called the ''Iron Triangle''—the menage a trois that kept this bias energized on a continual basis. Like most citizens, Hatch knew that government spent too much money and provided too little in results. He knew that an unbalanced budget generally meant fiscal irresponsibility and that government deficit spending and inflation were frequently related. Likewise, he was frustrated because, although government leaders must assuredly be aware of the problem, nothing substantial ever seemed to be done about it. To be sure, the spending spree was somewhat alleviated by President Ford's consistent use of the veto. But it was business as usual under Jimmy Carter, who was to become the greatest ''spending'' President in history. (The seven largest peace-time deficits in the history of the country occurred during the 1970s.)

Despite campaigning as a Senatorial candidate on the premise that government was spending wildly and ineffectively, Hatch was to be stunned by the realization of how far this process had actually encumbered the body politic. By September of 1981 the federal government debt had reached an historic high of one trillion dollars. ''It took the government 199 years to roll up a deficit of a half trillion dollars,'' reported Hatch. ''It took six years to double that figure.''

At the above level of debt, interest payments total over $100 billion a year, which has now become the third largest item on the national budget, behind only social programs and defense. And, as Hatch has noted, "Interest payments do not feed the hungry or protect the nation."

As Hatch studied the politics of budget development and became aware of the intricate and oppressive pressure system that weaved its way throughout the governmental process, he acquired a practical education in the real political world one does not get in political science classes. What he discovered was a well-entrenched *psychology of spending* which tended to resist the most fervent and sincere attempts to economize. Its impact and influence were everywhere present throughout the governmental structure and process. A realization of its potency gave every indication of imperviousness to reform.

It was not difficult for Hatch, with his wide knowledge of history, to see that modern politicians had seriously defaulted on traditional U.S. concepts of fiscal responsibility and political science. Throughout most of the nation's history, traditional American fiscal policy required a balanced budget during normal economic circumstances. It prevailed as part of our "unwritten Constitution." "The balanced budget rule," observed University of Virginia Professor William Brent, "which served as part of the Constitution was, of course, not in the form of a written statement that every expenditure had to be balanced by a tax. But it nevertheless had Constitutional status. For expenditures in excess of receipts were considered to be in violation of moral principles. The imperative of the balanced budget was an extra-legal rule or custom that grew up around the formal document. It existed outside the precise letter of the Constitution on all fours with the system of political parties, the Presidential cabinet, the actual operation of the Electoral College and of judicial review."

"The public debt," Jefferson had warned, "is the greatest of dangers to be feared by a republican government." "The consequences arising from the continual accumulation of public debts in other countries," added John Adams, "ought to admonish us to be careful to prevent the growth in our own"; and James Madison agreed that it was essential to "liberate the public resources by an honorable discharge of public debts."

This doctrine, which was annunciated by our Founders, remained public orthodoxy through the years, through good times and crises, to the present time. If wars or other crises threw the national budget out of balance, the situation was regarded with great consternation, and every effort was brought to bear to alleviate the condition. "The balanced budget norm," writes Professor Brent "was so deeply ingrained during this time as to form a constraint of considerable power on the actions of government. . . . The unwritten Constitution maxim of the balanced budget . . . had the result of chaining Leviathan.''

Yet, by the end of the 1930s this intregral doctrine of the unwritten Constitution, had been seriously eroded and was to become almost completely abandoned after World War II. It was an era that gave rise to *modern liberalism* which differentiated markedly from *traditional* (''classical'') liberalism. Relegating to the past a skeptical view of government and an intellectual attachment to constitutional principles and norms, *modern* liberal practitioners—at first primarily academic intellectuals— inaugurated a new ''public philosophy'' which captured the imagination of both the American people and their representatives.

Democratic government was presented in the most uncritical terms. The idea that the traditional concern over government growth and political usurpation could now give way to a deliberately *positive* role by government (the ''affirmative state'') in our enlightened and progressive age was an exciting one, fraught, people began to think, with possibilities.

The Depression, followed by World War II, only served to convince millions not only of the appropriateness but also of the necessity of an interventionist political system in a time plagued with so many problems and blessed with so many possibilities.

At first, almost imperceptibly, the idea of a balanced budget inherent in the ''unwritten Constitution'' began to give way. From Europe the doctrines of John Maynard Keynes convinced social scientists, economics professors and presently politicians by the thousands that debt was not necessarily a bad thing and that, under certain circumstances, it was a positive good. When some of the ''old timers'' objected to the growing national debt, they were told what many students in America were being taught: ''We only owe it to ourselves,'' and ''Inflation generates jobs.''

The new liberal progressive felt himself the harbinger of a new era of economic growth, social justice, indeed, and an ordered democratic society sustained by a positive and benevolent political system geared to a purposeful challenging of the nation's problems. Correct planning on the part of an expanding federal government would stimulate, said Arthur Schlesinger, Jr., ''the growth of public conscience.'' Noted labor leader Walter Reuther saw the process as one of the federal government injecting ''a rational sense of direction into private decisions.'' The renowned economist John Kenneth Galbraith enthusiastically referred to it as ''The New Socialism.''

Many others of liberal philosophy, while not comfortable with the extreme direction advocated by Schlesinger or Galbraith, sought, in varying degrees, to bring about social reforms. While they remained attached to Constitutional forms, they too became advocates, or if not, at least gave tacit approval of the growth of the federal government and the extension of federal powers to accomplish their desired results. In the final analysis they, too, contributed significantly to the unchaining of Leviathan.

By and large, these modern liberals sincerely and honestly believed that the new direction of government—though largely unrecognized as yet by an unsophisticated general public—would eventually be justified by its fruits. The motivation that underlay their exuberance and their often selfless dedication was the belief that modern intellectualism combined with modern government could produce a happier "brave new world." They were, insists University of Pennsylvania sociology professor Albert H. Hobbs (emeritus), "convinced of the goodness of their end." Their conscience was "insulated by a shield of unshatterable self-righteousness. They were positive that history and science had proved them right."

In contemplating this zeal and self-assurance, one is reminded of the statement by Daniel Webster concerning human nature and political power: "Good intentions will always be pleaded for every assumption of authority. It is hardly too strong to say that the Constitution was made to guard the people against the dangers of good intentions. There are men in all ages who mean to govern well, but they mean to govern. They promise to be good masters, but they mean to be masters."   .

By the end of the 1930s, the new liberal orthodoxy had so permeated political thinking and practice that it had assumed the proportions of an ideology. A Constitutional revolution had taken place in the United States. Its dimensions were not generally recognized at first, but it was nevertheless a revolution. During this period the traditional meaning of such Constitutional provisions as the general welfare clause, the commerce clause, and the necessary and proper clause were, under strong executive pressure, gradually, but steadily and continuously expanded and changed by a definitional process of Congress and allowed to stand by the Supreme Court.

As Constitutional restraints, once considered sacrosanct, began to be relaxed, a great pressure system was created as powerful interest groups, many of which owed their existence, growth, and influence to government beneficence, found ways to penetrate the centers of decision-making, there to find political support, and, participation in that quid pro quo political relationship called "The Iron Triangle."

At one and the same time, great political conduits had been

opened through which the central government could now reach out and regulate and manipulate the interests and priorities of society in ways not possible since the country's founding, while providing direct access to government institutions by the more powerful and the better-organized interest groups seeking to forge beneficial alliances within the governmental system.

This conduit system, also at one and the same time often served the immediate purposes of both the government and the subsidy-seeking special interest. The interest group got the subsidy, and in return, through that subsidy, the government now penetrated the special interest with its regulations. For, it was reasoned, and sustained by the Court—that which the government subsidizes, it may regulate.

In all of this one is struck by the surprising and alarming lack of understanding of either the nature of man or the vagaries of democratic government. This Constitutional metamorphosis was allowing an ever-increasing distribution of the nation's wealth to powerful special interests and to the massive government bureaucracies organized to "regulate" them. But the fact was scarcely mentioned as the decades passed. Those who did express concern were often branded as "unfeeling," "lacking compassion," and "behind the times." In America's universities, those few students and professors who questioned the ruling orthodoxy were branded as "unintellectual."

As the years passed, the oppressive political pressure system and its offspring, The Iron Triangle, grew to proportions that no one could have anticipated. National legislators in growing numbers were both willingly *and unwillingly* ensnared in a process that made economy in government an impossibility.

From the beginning it was not hard to realize the fortuitous political relationship a powerful interest group could provide a Congressman, or even a President. The most dedicated liberal reformist could not avoid the reality that benefited interest groups could significantly aid in the election or re-election of its benefactors. Nor was the most pristine conservative—battling what he believed to be the drift toward socialism—left unaware of the political liability to be suffered from angry groups who saw him as a threat to their favored positions.

It was not difficult for the politician to see the relationship between tax revenues spent on programs related to powerful interest groups and electoral success. To Harry Hopkins, aide to Franklin Roosevelt, was attributed the statement, "Tax, tax, tax, spend, spend, spend, elect, elect, elect." Through this formula, not just a few politicians entrapped themselves into perpetual political servitude.

As Professor Roger Freeman of the Hoover Institution has observed, it is often not that members of Congress "do not wish to" economize, "but that under the circumstances, they can only do so at a great political risk to their survival." "Our legislators," concurred Hatch in his statement before the full Senate on March 27, 1981, "operate in an institutional environment which encourages deficits, which encourages high levels of spending, and which encourages high levels of taxation."

The political process thus became skewed toward artificially high levels of spending, that is, levels of spending that do not result from either a genuine demand or desire on the part of the body of the American people. In such a political climate members of Congress are motivated and pressured to spend money in behalf of favored interests with little concern over the relationship of such decisions to the availability of revenues, or the wishes of the unorganized masses of taxpayers.

Economists refer to this phenomenon which exacerbates the *psychology to spend* as "concentrated benefits and dispersed costs." It describes a tendency, a bias, if you please, toward ever-increasing levels of government expenditure, since it pits a relatively small, highly-organized group seeking "concentrated benefits" against a large, highly-dispersed and unorganized taxpayer who bears the dispersed cost. "Because spending interests tend to be visible, articulate, and intense in focusing their attentions upon individual spending bills, that are likely to accrue to their benefit," Hatch told the Senate, "and because they are able to reward or punish legislators with their electoral support or non-support, it is to the advantage of such legislators to be sensitive and responsive to their concerns. There is normally no similar constituency in opposition of such spending programs. Those who would logically be most concerned about higher levels of expenditures—the taxpayers—are diffused, unorganized, and particularly inarticulate. They have no lobbying organizations as do the spending interests."

According to University of California Professor Charles Baird, "Whenever government programs are considered one by one, there is a bias toward government growth. Each program has a well-defined constituency that receives positive benefits therefrom. In many cases, the *benefits* from a particular program to a particular person represent a large part of that person's total income, while the tax *cost* to the beneficiary of the program is miniscule. Such direct beneficiaries of program A, therefore, are strongly motivated to organize, work, and lobby for the adoption and growth of that program A in isolation, because any individual taxpayer's share of program A is miniscule. Since elected representatives inevitably respond to lobbying efforts, there is a high probability that program A will be adopted even if the sum of the benefits therefrom are less than the sum of the costs.''

Former Chairman of the Federal Reserve Board, Arthur Burns, adds: ''The proximate causes of this governmental bias are quite clear. In general, spending programs are more popular with people than higher taxes. The potential beneficiaries of a spending program are often a numerical minority, but they have a stronger incentive to keep informed, to organize, and to lobby for their favorite program than those who bear the cost have to oppose it. The rising cost of political campaigns and the concurrent proliferation of fund-raising committees put intense pressure on legislators to vote for spending programs favored by such groups. We may, in fact, be entering an era in which governmental processes are overwhelmed by the naked demands of increasingly well-organized and effective interest groups.''

And so, the ''psychology to spend,'' grew in intensity, with the only restraint on the tide of spending and governmental growth being the availability of tax revenues. Notice that the tradition of relating *spending* to *income* still rankled. The idea was hard to shake even amid the taunts of the ''new public philosophy'' advocates.

So it was ''Tax, tax, tax, spend, spend, spend, elect, elect, elect.'' A public eager to believe that government was the national benefactor went along—but not forever. As taxes began to grow and the unorganized masses of Americans began to feel the pinch on their incomes, with little compensating benefit as they saw it, the first rumblings of taxpayer anger began to register on government. Even those whose membership in preferred groups entitles them to government benefits resent having to pay taxes.

In spite of Harry Hopkin's supposed formula, there developed the spectre of diminished political returns as the increase in taxes began to be perceived as excessive by the populace. Yet the propensity of Congressmen to spend was not diminished. Neither were demands for government resources by special interests assuaged. The political costs of heaping further tax burdens on the public conflicted with the ''psychology to spend,'' ever-growing in intensity. By this time, it was probably too late to curb spending on a long-term basis. The addiction had already set in before the 1960s were out. New sources of wealth had to be found outside the taxing realm. It was as simple as that.

For a period, Congress turned to *borrowing* to finance current programs and other expenditures. This required annual increases in the legally imposed national debt limit. Because of the problems associated with a growing federal debt it was felt expedient to finance part of it by printing money; that is, the Federal Reserve was prevailed upon to purchase the securities resulting from the deficit. This caused money-supply growth to exceed the economy's capacity to produce, resulting in inflation and its attendant problems.

This method of deficit financing provided a means for ever-increasing levels of federal government spending by a back-door method of taxing which allows the government to absorb an ever-mounting share of the nation's financial resources, while leaving a decreasing percentage for productive use by the private sector.

As a result, deficit spending has provided Congressmen access to an ever-growing supply of funds. With deficit financing, the nation's legislators are no longer constrained in their ability to increase spending by the expectation of increases in revenues. "In consequence," reports the Senate Judiciary Committee, "permissible levels of spending no longer are defined. . . . Members of Congress are free to satisfy the demands of particular spending interests, and to obtain the resulting political advantages, without having either (a) to reduce spending for some other spending interest and incurring the resulting political disadvantages in doing so, or (b) to increase tax revenues and incurring the resulting political disadvantages in doing so. Members of Congress do not have to reduce levels of spending for one program in order to accommodate increases in other programs because there is no effective limit as to how much Congress may spend in its budget."

There is a day of reckoning for such economic profligacy. History is riddled with accounts of nations which have spent themselves into destruction. But it is human nature to concentrate on present benefits, deferring the piper's pay to some future time. "In this respect," continues the Senate Judiciary Committee Report, "the availability of unlimited deficit spending allows the political [and the economic and the moral] costs of spending measures to be deferred in time, while enabling the political benefits to be enjoyed immediately. While the benefits of the measure usually will be understood immediately by its beneficiaries, the costs—in the form of higher future taxes, higher future inflation, and higher future interest rates—usually will be evident at some future time." Also, since deficit spending financed by the central bank eventually causes inflation, salaries of the American people spiral upward with the increased cost of goods and services. This automatically provides additional revenue for Congress to disperse, since millions of Americans, with their increases in salaries and wages, are pushed into higher tax brackets. Thus, inflation provides an additional source of revenue for government use. In this unequal interaction between inflation and real economic growth, the *public* sector will consume a higher share of the national product each year, since the citizen, in earning more dollars, whether real or nominal, pays a graduating increasing share of these dollars to the government in taxes. This means, according to William E. Simon, "As people get pushed into nominally higher income brackets, their tax rates go up even though their purchasing power doesn't."

Economists call this "tax-flation," or "tax-bracket creep." According to Professor Baird, "with 'bracket creep' it is possible for members of Congress to raise taxes by doing nothing, which is considerably less painful than raising taxes by voting to do so." Add to this the fact that past Congresses, in creating the numerous "entitlement" programs that support the massive social welfare system had added acceleration clauses that allowed the cost of these programs to increase automatically without new authorizing legislation—and one can contemplate the magnitude of these hidden taxes.

The aggregation of these individual spending programs during the Carter administration finally hit the taxpayers with the simultaneous impact of both inflation and economic slowdown or recession—called "stagflation." Their fear and anger were reflected in the Reagan landslide, the Republican victory in the Senate, the electoral defeat of some of Congress' most prolific "big spenders," and the relatively bipartisan support for the Reagan economic recovery program in its early stages.

But the special interests have remained politically visible and articulate. They remain, for the most part, both willing and able to disperse rewards to friends or to punish their political enemies by their organized support, non-support or opposition. At the same time, the taxpayers, as the Senate Judiciary Committee report points out, "remain politically inarticulate, and barely able to perceive their self-interest in the contest of isolated pieces of legislation. . . . Thus, it is only natural that legislators, however sincerely committed to fiscally responsible public policies, should be sensitive and responsive to the concerns of lobby for new or expanded spending initiatives."

The more Hatch grew in knowledge and wisdom about the vagaries of government economics, the more he came to the sad conclusion that the process of The Iron Triangle had gone beyond the point of any possibility of reformation; that the infestation of special interest into the whole fabric of governmental decision-making had become virtually immune from correction. It was not an exaggeration to suggest that the "rage to spend," as one Senator put it, was "clearly out of control!" Even Reagan's forceful determination to storm the battlements of waste, fraud, and self-interest with his faithful crew of conservative Republicans and Democrats was doomed in the long run unless some way was found to alter the present system of pressure politics. If what was begun as a crusade by Reagan in 1980 was to be more than a brief interlude, something had to be done to alter the spending bias, to clip the wings of The Iron Triangle. Hatch was reminded of James Madison's warning in the *Federalist* no. 10, that the paramount responsibility of that new experiment in self-government was *"to break and control the violence of faction."* The far-sighted Madison ominously defined factions as a "majority or minority of the whole, who are united and actuated by some common impulse or passion, or of interest adverse to the rights of other citizens, or to the permanent and aggregate interests of the whole." "How Madison would hang his head in shame," Hatch said to Frank Madsen, "if he could see our day. His worst fears of uncontrolled special interest have become a reality two centuries after he uttered them."

And so Hatch became determined to fight what to many seemed an insolvable problem. It was clear to him that the only answer to this problem was to change the rules of the game, to somehow alter the conditions so that the *psychology to spend* was alleviated. Somehow, before it was too late, Hatch reasoned, the traditional limitations upon federal spending had to be re-established in such a way that the genuine will of the people would be re-enthroned. Members of Congress must once again be held ultimately accountable for their spending and taxing decisions. As Hatch put it, "The entire psychology of the Congressional spending process must be altered." He agreed with Professor Allan Meltzer of Carnegie-Mellon University, that "only by changing the ground rules under which spending decisions are made can we expect to obtain the outcome which people desire."

The Senator spent many hours conversing personally or through their writings with a number of professors in whom he had faith. "The simple arithmetic of politics," Professor James Buchanan told Hatch, "suggests a regime of permanent and continuing deficits in a democratic society where there exists no constraint that dictates some balancing of the costs and the benefits of spending programs. 'To spend without taxing'—this stuff of politicians dreams must somehow be held in check by rules of fiscal prudence. We must," he continued, "restore some rule that will restrict politicians in their natural, understandable proclivity to spend and to refrain from taxing. Budgets will tend toward chronic deficits until and unless politicians are constrained by some Constitutional rule which requires that the taxing and spending sides of the fiscal account are balanced."

"Some Constitutional rule!" The phrase stuck with Hatch. Ironi-

cally, as a Senatorial candidate Hatch had felt that a Constitutional amendment might be the only way to stop the government's spending binge. But as a new Senator, he began to see the difficulties of even approaching such an entrenched and protected problem. It seemed futile. But by early 1981 Hatch had reached that point in his Senatorial career where he held the political power and influence to lead out in attacking the previously impregnable Iron Triangle without the inevitability that his action would be a lost cause. As Chairman of the Labor and Human Resources Committee, and the Judiciary Subcommittee on the Constitution, Hatch was in a position where his determination and political savoire faire packed enormous clout. Combine this with his personal friendship and influence with some of the most respected leaders in Congress, with numerous conservative and other organizations outside of Congress, plus the respect and personal warm friendship he enjoyed from the President, and it is no wonder that Orrin Hatch had become recognized by his peers as one of the most powerful men in the United States.

Hatch began a series of meetings with other Senators, both Republican and Democrat, who were also determined to "chain Leviathan." He spent many hours with the gutty Republican Chairman of the Judiciary Committee, Strom Thurmond. Many additional hours were spent with the sophisticated Arizona Democrat, Dennis DeConcini. It is interesting that among the first five men to roll up their sleeves and begin to hammer out a Constitutional Amendment were three Republicans—Hatch, Thurmond and Al Simpson of Wyoming—and two Democrats—DeConcini and Howell Heflin of Alabama (former Justice of the Supreme Court of Alabama). As indicated in a previous chapter, the past few elections had brought to Congress a new breed of legislator who was dedicated to change, and willing to put party aside if necessary. In this case, freshmen worked hand in hand with some of the old workhorses with a dedication that was as curiously refreshing as it had been rare.

As Hatch made himself an expert on economics and fiscal policy, his course of action began to crystallize in his mind's eye. Typically, the road he took was an unencumbered one, for he had mauled and mulled all the variables involved before he took a step. Every consideration—moral, legal, constitutional, practical—had been thoroughly and exhaustively tested with experts and colleagues and analyzed by his own perceptive reasoning. When Hatch was ready to move, his decision was to the point, remarkably astute, and workable. It was not offered as "pie in the sky," nor was it an exercise in grandstanding. Such had never been his style.

The proposed amendment—Senate Joint Resolution 58—like the

abortion amendment, was short and to the point. There was no attempt to read economic policies and formulas into the Constitution or clutter it up with complex economic jargon. It represented a unique approach simply by making it possible to overcome and neutralize biases within the existing political framework that worked in favor of higher levels of public spending. As the Founding Fathers had before him, Hatch was astutely working with human nature.

Section I re-establishes the balanced budget as the norm of federal fiscal policy. It requires a $^3/_5$ths vote of both houses of Congress to break this norm. Therefore, deficit spending would require approval by 60 of the 100 Senators and 261 of the 436 representatives, regardless of the number of Congressmen present and voting.

Section II requires that the balanced budget in Section I cannot be achieved at a level of taxing or spending that grows faster than the economy as a whole. It requires members of Congress to go on record in support of necessary taxes before they can take advantage of increased levels of revenue. "The key to this section," Hatch pointed out, "is the requirement that the big spenders and the budget-busters in Congress be made more clearly identifiable by the public by requiring them to go on record whenever they favor deficits or increased levels of public spending. If Congress wanted more programs and higher spending, it would have to raise taxes, and then it would have to face the political consequences. No longer could these representatives evade and avoid responsibility by engaging in fiscal exercises that make it difficult for even sophisticated observers to pinpoint responsibility for the budget."

"In seeking to reduce the spending bias in our system—the unlimited availability of deficit spending and the access to automatic tax increases—," reads the Judiciary Committee Report, "the major purpose of the Resolution is to ensure that, under normal circumstances, votes by Congress for increased spending will be accompanied either by votes (a) to reduce other spending programs or (b) to increase taxes to pay for such programs. For the first time since the abandonment of the traditional balanced budget requirement, Congress will be required to cast a politically *difficult* vote as a pre-condition for a politically *attractive* vote to increase spending." As a result, not only would federal spending generally be matched by federal revenues, but revenues would not be raised without political cost to members of Congress by a majority public which is increasingly concerned over taxes, inflation, and government spending.

Before Congress could make available to itself greater amounts of revenue for new spending initiatives, it would have to stand up in view of the public and place itself on record in behalf of such increased revenues.

Nor would Congress be able any longer to just simply remain silent and allow taxes to rise automatically by the insidious forces of "tax-bracket creep." An express vote would have to be cast in full public view.

The genius of this proposed amendment is that it deals realistically with human nature. While on the one hand the measure dampens the "psychology to spend" on the part of the Congressman, the special-interest groups, on the other hand, find themselves in competition for *decreasing* rather than *increasing* financial resources and each special interest is now placed in competition with taxpayers "to raise the total ante in the federal Treasury." There would now be an external constraint on Members of Congress "to exercise fiscal responsibility in making their policy decisions. There would be an external constraint, something beyond their own ability to resist the importunings of spending interests, upon which they could rely." According to Professor Roger Freeman, "Congressmen need a defense against excessive demands which allows them to say 'no' to a multitude of pressure groups. Such a defense cannot be built by statute because any act of Congress can be amended or repealed by this Congress or the next. Only a Constitutional amendment can impose credible and effective spending restraints."

Under the aegis of one Constitutional amendment, Hatch and his band of "untouchables" had covered all the bases. Structurally, the proposed amendment was a masterpiece. Contextually it brought together the previously diverse ideas of Congressmen who believed in the route of the Constitutional amendment to regulate the problem, but could not agree on whether it should require a balanced budget, or a tax limitation, or a spending limitation, or some combination. Senate Joint Resolution 58 combined all of these viewpoints under one roof and in a way that was remarkably consistent, compatible, and Constitutionally sound. As Orrin Hatch told the Senate, "the proposed amendment is a combination balanced budget-tax limitation-spending limitation. It is a balanced budget amendment through the express provisions of Section 1. It is a tax limitation amendment through Section 2 which prohibits increases in revenues as a proportion of the national income without a vote; it is also a tax limitation amendment in the sense that it eliminates the indirect tax of deficit spending—a tax that is reflected either in future inflation or future interest limitation as a result of the conjunction of Sections 1 and 2."

So the amendment was ready. It was both politically and legally respectable. But the task of bringing it to the point of becoming the 27th Amendment to the Constitution of the United States had just begun. It faced a battle that might take years.

The first step was to shepherd Senate Resolution 58 through the

Judiciary Committee. This was the easiest step, since its primary sponsors formed a bipartisan majority on the committee, its Chairman included. In March of 1981, this became the first such proposal ever to be approved by a full committee of either House of Congress. It became known as The Balanced Budget/Tax Limitation Amendment.

But there remained the task of carrying it through both Houses of Congress and then guiding it through at least 34 (⅔ majority) state legislatures. As the American Founders had intended, it was to require a monumental effort to amend the Constitution.

So, the process began to attempt to develop a consensus of support for the amendment. This is the part of the legislative process least seen and understood by the general populace. Led by Hatch, the co-sponsors began the trial by fire of any substantive piece of legislation—to educate and convert a majority of their fellow members of Congress to the point that they will support the amendment.

This sequence transcends the regular debates that take place on the floor of Congress, and even the committee hearings. Here there is one-on-one personal discussion and exchange that takes place on a daily basis on the Hill. In effect, Hatch, Thurmond and the others were advocates of the amendment before their colleagues, and this often exhaustive process requires contact on an informal as well as a formal basis and in private as well as before the collective.

Simultaneously, it is important to build support from prominent and influential people outside of government whose endorsement will add both legitimacy and publicity to the effort. If the legislative product is to be "sold," a great deal of organized support must be developed, and this takes talent, dedication, and pure tenacity. The importance of the Balanced Budget/Tax Limitation Amendment, and the sense of responsibility its sponsors had taken upon themselves engendered in them great portions of the above.

At the helm was Senator Orrin Hatch, his apparently inexhaustible fountain of energy turned to full force. *The Wall Street Journal* described him as the "parson" who was presiding at the marriage of diverse interests over the amendment. By the spring of 1982, the Balanced Budget/Tax Limitation Amendment boasted 54 Senate co-sponsors and nearly 200 co-sponsors from the House of Representatives.

Hatch was pleasantly surprised to see some members of Congress declaring their sponsorship of the amendment whom one would not expect to see supporting such a cause. While more than likely some did so only to give the appearance of fiscal responsibility, others frankly welcomed an opportunity—some with near desperation—of breaking away from the entangling alliances that stimulated the "psychology to spend."

Too, support for the amendment began to appear from important sources outside of government. This kind of support, of course, is indispensable to the promotion of a Constitutional amendment. A timely Gallup Poll found that about 75 percent of those surveyed favored a balanced federal budget amendment. According to Gallup, support for such an amendment is substantial in "virtually all demographic sectors of the public."

Support and assistance was also forthcoming from such organizations as the Chamber of Commerce, the American Farm Bureau Federation, the National Cattlemen's Association, the National Federation of Independent Businesses, the National Tax Limitation Committee, the National Taxpayers Union, and a host of others.

Hatch was particularly pleased to receive the endorsement of the noted economist and Nobel Prize winner, Professor Milton Friedman. This was a doubly important event, since the Professor had been critical of other proposed amendments. "Both the concepts of balanced budget and spending limitations are right and are combined in Senate Joint Resolution 58," the Professor stated. "It is more sophisticated than it appears on the surface. Sections 1 and 2 together achieve a limit on total spending and a balanced budget statement. It is an effective measure, in my opinion to limit government receipts and spending, on the one hand, and to produce a balanced budget on the other." While President Reagan waged a "tremendous fight to get what reforms he has come up with through the Congress," added Friedman, "you cannot keep on doing that year after year. Maybe he can get one or two more victories along the way. But we need to pin those down." And the "most effective way to do it" is through this amendment.

Then, on March 31, 1982, the icing on the cake—President Ronald Reagan endorsed the concept "as the answer to uncontrollable government spending. Excessive Federal spending and deficit," the President continued, "have become so engrained in government today that a Constitutional amendment is necessary to limit this spending. I shall continue to emphasize the need for such an amendment."

Another factor which may well benefit the chances for the Balanced Budget/Tax Limitation Amendment is the threat of a Constitutional Convention. The Constitution provides that two-thirds of the State legislatures can direct Congress to call a Constitutional Convention for the purpose of considering and recommending amendments to the Constitution. At this writing, 31 state legislatures have approved petitions calling for such a Convention for the purpose of drafting a balanced budget amendment—just three short of the necessary two-thirds. Since most Congressmen are uneasy about the prospects of a Constitutional Convention, its threat could encourage many lawmakers to opt for the Balanced Budget/Tax Limitation Amendment as a more favorable alternative.

The proposed Balanced Budget/Tax Limitation Amendment has thus become the first such an attempt ever to be given serious consideration by Congress. Similar measures have been introduced in Congress 52 times since the 1960s. The Hatch Amendment has been the first to reach the Senate floor and the first to have any chance of becoming the law of the land. Noting the growing number of the proposed amendment's sponsors, Professor Friedman remarked that "if it ever gets out of the House and the Senate, three-quarters of the States would adopt it like wildfire."

The fate of this one single proposed amendment could well determine the future of the United States.

Chapter 9
OVERSIGHT

The excitement over the initial success of the Balanced Budget/Tax Limitation Amendment was dimmed by the realization that there was a long, rough road ahead. This was not just a piece of legislation, it was a Constitutional Amendment.

Thus, this long-range project carried with it the same frustration as Hatch's Abortion Federalism Amendment. While the process of each was both logical as well as Constitutional, Hatch had asked himself, "What do we do in the meantime?"

It was this feeling of frustration that kept Hatch from actively fighting against some other forms of anti-abortion legislation which he believed to be far less adequate. At least, he reasoned, there would be continued discussion and activity on the subject.

Now, while he was certain that nothing but a Constitutional Amendment would inhibit the spending bias of Congress, he was willing to consider other methods, such as encouragement of members of Congress to exercise spending restraints, and promotion of new members to Congress who carry such a resolve. But all of these alternatives have been attempted in the past with limited results. Actually, a large number of statutory restraints on spending have been proposed over the years. Some have been enacted into law. But none has succeeded over time since no Congress can bind a succeeding Congress by a simple statute. All a succeeding Congress has to do is adopt a budget which is in conflict with the earlier measure. Since the new budget is in effect a new statute, the previous statute is overridden.

Also, experience in the American legislative process dictates that expectations that fiscal conservatives will be elected in appreciable numbers over time in a modern "hyper-democracy," or that once they are elected they will consistently resist the blandishments and the political opportunities offered them by the omnipresent political pressure system, are chimerical. Nevertheless, such alternatives, while little more than a finger in a dike needing an arm and a shoulder, do provide at least some counter-pressure on the legislative spending environment. Organizations such as the Washington-based Free Congress Foundation, directed by the remarkable Paul Weyrich, have done wonders in promoting conservative causes through information dissemination.

At the same time, the new conservative Political Action Committees (PACs) have, interestingly enough, made an impact on the political accountability of a number of members of Congress whose actual voting record and the economic implications of that voting record have in the past been largely unknown to their constituencies. The practice of exposing their voting records to a wide home audience by the extensive use of the media apparently cost more than one Congressman his job in Washington. For a number of legislators, the practice of talking one way to the "folks back home" and then voting the opposite way while in Washington without fear of being exposed was over. No one really knows to what degree the PAC media campaigns have been effective, but, judging from the cries of anger against them, there has been some substantial impact.

Then, there is a legislative process called "oversight." Depending upon a number of factors related to the political configuration of the Congressional committees, plus the character, determination and relative power and influence possessed by the member of Congress directing the oversight, this process has the potential of a substantial impact on accountability and responsibility with the leadership structure of the great administrative agencies into which the greatest proportion of government resources flow—augmented by 44 independent regulatory agencies and 1,240 separate boards and commissions, each with its own ideas about how to solve society's problems.

To assist in its broad powers of legislation, the Congress, over the years, has assumed substantial authority in overseeing the administration of its legislated programs. This function has been officially assigned to the Standing Committees of Congress since 1946. The General Accounting Office, headed by the Comptroller General, is an important investigative arm of Congress, especially in its oversight of executive fiscal management of the National Budget. Therefore, with its "power of the purse," augmented by its investigative and oversight powers and supplemented by the GAO, the Congress possesses the opportunity and means to exercise substantial "watchdog" scrutiny and investigation of the Administration, should it desire to do so.

The fact is, however, that there is little actual oversight exercised by Congress or the committees. Some so-called oversight investigations are little more than shams. Others are carried on primarily for publicity. A few have real substance, but these are the exception.

Real oversight is nasty, tough and difficult. It has political overtones that shake the system. Vested interests in the organization targeted for investigation have various means to retaliate against those who would disturb the status quo. It is the sad truth that few members of Congress have either the courage, the tenacity, the moral commitment, or the stomach to launch a serious oversight investigation.

It is not that the members of Congress do not know and understand that much of the federal bureaucracy has grown inefficient, arrogant and slovenly. Most simply do not have the fortitude to attempt to do something about it. Others just plain lack the moxie or the qualified staff to carry out sustained oversight of the bureaucratic citadel. Still others choose not to do so for political reasons.

Nor do the top administrative management of the great bureaucratic agencies lack self-policing powers. In many instances, Congressional oversight would not be needed if effective controls were applied by the bureaucratic leaders. The fact is that many decide not to do so. With this knowledge, Hatch was doubly grateful for those men of integrity in the administration who honestly attempt to "run a tight ship," and who are conscientious and dedicated in overseeing the economy of their particular operations.

The degree to which a committee of the House or Senate will exercise the prerogative of oversight is dependent on a number of conditions. Like all aspects of this, the grandest of all governmental systems, those whom we the people elect to manage it affect its functioning by their style and their integrity. Therefore, while some functions of the executive branch feel the relative weight of Congressional oversight, others fester in incompetence, corruption, and worse, with virtual carte blanche. Some Congressmen will go to great lengths to protect favored programs, and the strength of certain departments and bureaus, backed by related powerful interest groups, and supported by influential Congressmen, and even committees or subcommittees in a mutually supportive coalition, is well known on the Hill. Nor has it been out of the question in the past for certain Congressmen and even committee Chairmen to resist oversight of certain departments or departmental functions for other, political reasons. There is an unwritten rule among many who serve in Congress that one does not embarrass the party, especially if one's party is in control of the Executive Branch.

The ability, character, personality and interest of those who wield power and authority in Congress will affect both the degree and the quality of oversight extended. A few assume committee chairmanship with extraordinary dedication to principles which override politics and which tend to motivate concern over not only the administration but the appropriateness of a program under their jurisdiction.

When the Republicans gained control of the United States Senate after the general election of 1980, one such Senator became Chairman of the Committee on Labor and Human Resources and of the Constitutional Subcommittee on the Judiciary Committee. He was Orrin Hatch from Utah.

Overnight, but not without a toe-to-toe fight with Kennedy, Williams, Metzenbaum, and "the boys" who once controlled the Labor Committee, Hatch revolutionized its focus, its direction, its very character. He dusted off and oiled the oversight machinery. But he did not do it alone. He was joined by a number of courageous Senators, both Republican and Democrat, and sustained by a team of dedicated staff members.

A Congressman's staff is his right arm. The most gifted lawmaker will be ineffective if his staff does not complement him. As indicated, such stalwarts as Frank Madsen and Tom Parry, whose dedication to their boss is unexcelled on the Hill, have been an integral part of Hatch's extraordinary success as a freshman Senator.

One prominent legislator stated that "the real cut of a member of Congress can be measured by the quality of his staff. That's right! The really top people in this place have the most qualified, professional, and loyal staff members. You're just plain ineffective without them. Our offices have to be well-managed. There has to be constant interchange and flow of vital information from your specialized staff hired to help you with your Committee assignments. And that information has to be accurate. These people have to be loyal. They have to be willing to work late hours. The staff of a member of Congress worth his salt doesn't leak information."

"Hatch?" he responded to a question, "I don't know anyone who has a more loyal staff."

In the almost total replacement of Chairman Hatch's support personnel, there were some conspicuous holdovers from the previous Democratic control of the Senate. One had been the Judiciary Committee's Chief Investigator under Senator Baucus. He was a life-long Democrat and a 15-year veteran named Frank Silbey. Silbey has investigated everything from faulty smoke alarms to Nazi war criminals hiding out in the United States to the exposure of a $300 million plan to adorn the federal phone system with what he described as "bells, whistles and tooters."

Silbey began with Senator Sam Irvin, the North Carolina Democrat of Watergate fame. He then worked for Representative John Moss, Democrat from California, and finally Montana Democrat, Senator Max Baucus.

But as time passed and Silbey became more and more knowledgeable about the inner workings of the federal bureaucracy, party labels ceased to mean anything to him. The enemy which consumed his life's endeavor was what he believed to be corruption, mismanagement, and inefficiency in the bureaucratic arm of the government. "There is a Democratic Party," he told the *New York Times,* "a Republican Party and a Bureaucratic Party, and the Bureaucratic Party runs the government. These people . . . look upon new administrations as birds of passage."

An ordinarily pleasant man with a sophisticated sense of humor, Silbey's demeanor changes when he picks up the spoor of inefficiency or corruption. An encounter with Silbey, wrote Joseph Spear for *The Investigator,* might well be "unsettling. Silbey is bald, bespectacled and, well, portly. But beneath this cherubic exterior is a dedicated, aggressive digger whose hair-trigger sense of outrage can turn him as mean as the proverbial junkyard dog."

By the time Silbey became acquainted with Hatch he was "mean" most of the time. He had become a well-known investigator on the Hill. ("The best advice a neophyte investigative reporter can get in Washington is this," wrote Spear, "Make a date to meet Frank Silbey.") "The federal government," Silbey reported, "is far worse in terms of corruption than it has ever been. In the past few years corruption has gone from a trickle to a torrent, and mismanagement has grown from a mushroom to a redwood tree."

As an investigator on the Democratically-controlled Senate Judiciary Committee, Silbey was doubly frustrated. There was typically little true oversight going on, and his investigations—some of them uncovering serious bureaucratic abuses—were shelved. At times, Hatch and Arizona Democrat Dennis DeConcini were the only members of the committee willing to pursue these tough cases which were brimming with political overtones. Time and again Silbey sent cases to the Department of Justice only to find that they had been shelved with no action or follow-up taken.

In the controversial Silbey, Hatch saw much that he liked. Silbey was dedicated. His bete noire was corruption and mismanagement, and he saw it as his life's work to fight the "beast" with all his energy. Hatch was to have his hands full in reining in Silbey's enthusiasm, his emotional and easily expressed sense of outrage. Investigators who spend their time uncovering *malfeasance* and *non-feasance* in government must often fight the tendency to become, oddly enough, both cynical and crusading in spirit. With Silbey, Hatch walked a narrow line, attempting to hold the reins in tight without damaging the man's sense of dedication.

At least as important was Silbey's personal integrity. As Silbey himself told *The Investigator,* the only money he ever took home from the Hill was his paycheck "I don't need lunches, vacations, or broads. I've never killed an investigation. I've never pulled punches. I don't deal, and I don't sell out."

Equally important was the fact that over the years Silbey had developed important contacts with the media, other government investigative organizations, and informers. Without these vital aids the investigator cannot be effective. According to the *New York Times*, "Mr. Silbey's politics didn't matter to the Senator [Hatch] because he knew he was getting a hard-driving investigator with good press contacts." Silbey is renowned for his ability to obtain virtually any document he goes after.

At the same time, Silbey saw in Hatch an "untouchable" who would, from his position of Committee Chairmanship, conduct "real" oversight. As the *Times* put it, "Mr. Hatch's politics didn't matter to Mr. Silbey because, as chief investigator for a major committee, he would have far more power than if he had remained with the minority of a minor subcommittee unable to use the majority's subpoena power or ever hold a hearing."

Other top investigators, some of them Democrats, joined Hatch's team. They knew that here was where the action would be, that this freshman Senator was not playing games. One was James G. Phillips, a big man and a former athlete. He had been chief investigator for the Senate Judiciary Committee's Anti-trust and Monopolies Subcommittee. He also specialized on energy uses and insurance. Prior to his service on the Hill, he had been an investigative reporter for *The Washington Post*. He knows his way around. He has a reputation of being tough, tenacious, uncompromising, and "untouchable."

Hatch investigator Dan Gill is a former FBI agent and was an employee of the Labor Department. After early retirement, he offered his services to Hatch. He had seen the pressing need for change and saw in Hatch that possibility. According to Phillips, "Dan knows where all the bodies are buried."

Then there is the young Ray Mollenhoff, son of Clark Mollenhoff, the Pulitzer Prize-winning journalist. Ray had been an undercover policeman in Bethesda, Maryland. As an investigator for the House Banking Committee, he was involved in the Bert Lance investigations. He is young, sharp, eager.

These investigators are singularly impressive. They have a personal code of integrity that appears to be followed scrupulously by most top investigators on the Hill. They put politics aside. They respect a tough, honest Congressman, and they become frustrated when they work for those who will not, or cannot, fight inefficiency or corruption.

The respect of an investigator for his boss is crucial. Investigators are feared and hated by those who would prefer that the conduct of their agency or office not be scrutinized or investigated. At every step of the way the investigator generally faces the wrath of that Iron Triangle to which the agency or office "belongs." Unless the member of Congress in charge is willing to suffer with his investigators the "slings and arrows" of "witch-hunt" charges, anger, recriminations and outright threats of revenge, oversight will not get off the ground. In short, if he is not willing to "back up his staff," there will be few if any effective investigations. Therefore, it was significant when Silbey said of his boss, "Hatch is marvelous. He really backs up his staff. You can't get back-doored working for Orrin Hatch. For an investigator, the Chairman is the key. You're only as good as the Chairman lets you be." According to Phillips, "Senator Hatch is a man of great integrity and courage. He not only has our respect, but he has the grudging respect of the authority figures in the bureaucratic agencies. They know he gets what he goes after, and that makes our job easier. We also know he'll stand with us and protect us. Remember we have no clout of our own. Sure we're loyal to him; he is loyal to us. It feels good to work with someone who is really accomplishing something. Look how this one man is changing the Labor Department around."

Still, Hatch was amazed at the number of cases pointing to an abuse by government agencies of their financial resources and their responsibilities. As he challenged the vast, labyrinthine bureaucracy so well-entrenched in the governmental system and having been so protected and coddled or ignored by previous administrations, Hatch came to understand more than ever before the intransigence and self-serving tendencies of many of these organizations. More than anything else he lamented the determination not to be examined, not to be changed or reformed. Often, any attempt at oversight was seen as an attack to be repelled, any criticism as an affront not to be tolerated. Often there was no perceived intention to be responsive to the Congress or to the public. There was often an obvious tendency to be a law unto themselves within broad and often ill-defined legal limits.

For instance, Frank Silbey stated that "The General Services Administration is in a mess and has been for years. Do you know that, although that organization is in charge of stockpiling vital minerals for the country, it hasn't conducted an audit for over 30 years of the stockpile it already has? It has been estimated by investigators who know their way around the Hill that from 10 to 20 cents of every tax dollar spent to keep the government going is lost to waste, fraud, non-competition in awarding government contracts (which guarantees paying the highest price for the service or the product) and related abuses." (To what extent Silbey's estimates may or may not be *technically* correct, they identify problems that do exist and have existed for many years.)

The situation is exacerbated by the fact that oversight, to be effective, often needs the assistance of agency employees. And it is not all that often that anyone will risk the sting of his superior's disapproval by submitting damaging information to Congressional investigators. There is an unwritten bureaucratic rule that agency employees do not expose negative information about their organization—or "rock the boat" in any other way, for that matter. When, for instance, General Accounting Office security officer, Ralph Sharer, uncovered embarassing evidence that the GAO had been penetrated by Soviet espionage, his superiors tried to muzzle him. That failing, he was transferred to a job *studying marine mammals*. The messenger was blamed for the message. It was Jack Anderson who exposed the incident in his column. "I have," wrote the Pulitzer prize winner, "dealt with dozens of informants who had the toughness and courage to blow the whistle. All came to the same end: they became the targets in place of the real culprits."

From the very beginning of Hatch's oversight campaign, it became obvious that this Senator from Utah was not going to follow the customary way of doing things. First of all, there were to be no "sacred cows." Oversight investigations exposed the shabby handling of welfare files in state welfare agencies, prodding the Social Security Administration into action on the subject. Hatch's investigators found that at any one time there are more than $200 million in uncashed Social Security checks sitting in the offices of the SSA. Furthermore, the SSA had made no effort to resolve the situation and characteristically wrote the money off as spent.

A government motor pool audit, once carefully suppressed, by the agency, showed not only waste and efficiency but outright fraud. A

Justice Department audit showed that backlogs of thousands of unde-livered warrants were allowing dangerous criminals to escape justice. A General Services Administration audit showed the United States was paying premium prices for office equipment. At least a half million dol-lars in overcharges were detailed and publicized. The typical practice was for officials of the GSA to award contracts without bids or competition to "sweetheart" firms who either charge the top prices or overcharge the agency for goods or services. It is common knowledge that the contracted firm will then "kick back" under-the-table payoffs to those who helped award the contracts. This seamy practice has apparently been going on virtually unabated for a generation. It was also found that the GSA was misspending millions of public funds on goods and services from firms under the Aid to Minority Enterprises Program, where overcharging and shoddy materials and goods and poor workmanship were the norm rather than the exception.

As the Hatch organization probed deeper into the GSA, things didn't get any better. It was discovered, for instance, that during 1979 and 1980, the GSA had spent more than $2.5 million to rent over 106,000 square feet of space at a Washington office, and then left it vacant. Hatch also found evidence of mismanagement by the GSA in other areas. "The Federal landlord," wrote Jack Anderson, "is woefully mismanaging of-fice space. . . . Senator Orrin G. Hatch (R-Utah) is poking into the GSA mess."

Hatch's investigation into the GSA was a boon to that organiza-tion's Director, Jerry Carmen, a Reagan appointee, who had been desper-ately working to reinstitute professionalism and accountability in this agency.

Hatch's long investigative arm reached even to the FBI, the Na-tional Cancer Institute, and the Education Laboratories Program, uncov-ering both minor and serious problems in the expenditure of federal funds, and questionable management practices.

Hatch and his investigators came down hard on the Directors of the National Cancer Institute with charges of mismanagement. When Hatch presented the evidence to the Labor and Human Resources Com-mittee, respected Democrat Howard Metzenbaum joined the critical evaluation. Recently appointed as the program director was Dr. Vincent De Vita, Jr., a noted cancer therapist, who had inherited the mess from the previous administration. Hatch left no doubt in Dr. De Vita's ringing ears that he was expected to put his house in order, and fast. "You must understand," he told De Vita, "how important it is to manage. I believe that you have the great qualities and abilities to do just that."

It seemed to Hatch that everywhere he directed his oversight team of investigators they returned with damning evidence. The list seemed endless. Hatch shook his head in disbelief when his investigators presented him authoritative evidence that the Department of Health and Human Services could not account for billions of dollars in previous budget expenditures. Having "broken ranks" from the HHS, an in-house investigator with an impeccable reputation told Hatch that the agency lost tens of billions each year in fraud, waste, and mismanagement. After studying reports from the General Accounting Office and other agencies, investigative reporter Donald Lambro estimated that waste, fraud, and incompetence in the federal government was costing taxpayers at least $100 billion annually. On May 16, 1982, the National Institution of Justice, the research arm of the Department of Justice, issued a study which estimates that fraud, corruption and waste in the multitude of the federal benefit programs cost taxpayers up to $25 billion a year. "Fraud in government benefit programs," stated the report, "is now widely viewed to be a serious national problem."

Thus, the new Reagan appointee as Secretary of Health and Human Services, Richard Schweiker, had his job cut out for him. Having someone like Hatch in the Senate was to be important for Schweiker.

Fifty years of reluctance—with some notable exceptions—to provide anything like oversight of the bureaucratic empire, had left a baleful legacy of waste, fiscal abuse, incompetence, fraud, empire building, and secrecy that astounds the imagination, a situation with which the average voter is virtually impotent to deal, and one which only the most dedicated Congressman will dare face. Yet it is this cancer, that threatens the very foundation of honest government "by the people." It is a singular danger to self-government. It stands as a near-impenetrable bulwark against economy in government, and its cost is a most virulent threat to the American economy. The lack of effective oversight of government operations and costs by America's elected representatives remains a serious default on the citizen-taxpayer, and on the legislator's sworn oath of office.

It was with Hatch's investigation of the Labor Department and the alleged misuse of labor pension funds by labor leaders and racketeers that Hatch moved into the most politically sensitive and dangerous part of his political career.

When Orrin Hatch turned his investigative focus to alleged corruption in the leadership of organized labor, particularly with regard to the misuse of labor pension funds, the sky fell in. The labor czars, already miffed over Hatch's successful filibuster of the so-called "Labor Law

Reform Bill,'' became enraged over this latest invasion of their turf by ''that arrogant (so-and-so) from Utah!'' At the first indication of Hatch's direction, they began to pull all of the Washington strings at their command to thwart him. He was one of the very few *effective* antagonists who could cause them any real trouble. From labor leaders, certain sections of the media, and certain members of Congress came renewed cries of ''anti-labor'' leveled at Hatch.

Hatch's activities fueled the flames of intensity with which both Democratic Party and labor leaders were determined to unseat this Lochinvar from out of Utah. During the week of January 18th, Glenn Watts, president of the Communications Workers of America, among others, met with Democratic Party strategists and joined them in declaring that Hatch would be a top priority for defeat in November 1982. Organized labor ''will spend all of the money we can get our hands on'' to get Hatch out, Watts warned.

One of the political action committees chosen to transfer funds to Utah in an attempt to defeat Hatch is the *Progressive Political Action Committee* (PROPAC), directed by political pro Victor Kamber, who heads a successful Washington Communications firm. ''Victor Kamber,'' writes Media General Services' Gene Marlowe for the *Richmond* [Virginia] *Times Dispatch,* ''aspires to be disgusting. He is determined to give the Conservative PACs a dose of their own medicine. Included among the Senators targeted for defeat was Orrin Hatch. The idea was to blast Hatch's traveling 'to exotic places on behalf of special-interest groups,' implying that the taxpayers were paying the travel tickets.'' (This ignored the well-known fact that Hatch does not use government funds for his offshore or personal traveling expenses.)

Continuing, Marlowe writes of his interview with Kamber, '''Nothing evil, nothing wrong with traveling,' Kamber says shamefaced. 'I find this disgusting. But I'm tired of losing—I'm sorry. The point of mudslinging,' he continued, 'is not just to raise the hackles of voters, but to raise money. . .'''

Referring once more to Hatch, Kamber, in a surprisingly candid mood, confessed that his modus operandi would consist of taking facts in which there is ''nothing evil—nothing to suggest evil—and planting the seeds in the minds of the people of Utah that Hatch is up to no good.''

Then there were the physical threats—two calls from Florida, and one from the D.C. area. (At this writing all are being investigated by the FBI). Hatch urged his family to leave their Virginia home and return to Utah. His wife, Elaine, reminded him that they were a team. They would all stay together.

To many, the image of the Congressional wife is one of meeting celebrities and attending parties and special events in beautiful gowns. Actually, this is a small part of Washington life. The Congressman's wife spends most of her time waiting. Congressional sessions spell countless hours for the law maker, most of which are not visible to the average viewers; that is, his time spent on the floor of the House or the Senate, and even in Committee, is but a fraction of his labor.

Most time-consuming and frustrating of all is just plain *preparation*. Hatch and his staff weathered months of painstaking investigation before hearings could be held on labor corruption. On the Hill, knowledge is power—hence the importance of the combination of a tireless professional staff and a tenacious legislator.

At the same time, a member of Congress must visit his home constituency often, which means more time away from his family in Washington.

Too, when Congressmen such as Hatch are promoting substantive pieces of legislation, it is often necessary to gain the support of important interests in different parts of the United States; hence more traveling.

To be successful as a wife of a dedicated lawmaker, the "Congressional widow" will have to have the patience of Job and the sense of humor of Erma Bombeck. For months at a time she will have to be father as well as mother. If she is sensitive, she will be wife, confidant, listener, comforter, encourager. She will sense his moods and learn how to react—most of all, learn when to be comforting and when to "back off."

The understanding and devotion that Hatch gets from his wife and family are vital to his own sense of proportion. The stability and love in his home are unusually important factors for one with Hatch's driving temperament. His family is a calming, soothing change of pace in his life. Since Hatch is a dedicated "family man," the tone of that institution is unusually important to him.

Nevertheless, he carries with him concern for their safety, and it weighs heavily upon him.

For over eight years, the Democratic-controlled Senate Labor and Human Resources Committee had refused to hold formal hearings, despite repeated complaints by, among others, ranking minority member, Hatch, that the Labor Department was not enforcing pension protection (The Employee Retirement Income Security Act), and that corrupt labor leaders with ties to organized crime were systematically bilking the pension funds of union members with the assistance of the pension fund fiduciaries.

During most of this time, the Labor Committee was chaired by Senator Harrison Williams of New Jersey, a Democrat who was loath to attack any subject related to labor. (In March of 1982, Williams, caught in the ABSCAM net and found guilty of promising to use his influence to obtain government contracts, was forced to resign from the Senate in order to prevent his expulsion.)

But during this period Hatch had been gathering a great deal of evidence. Now Williams was gone and the Democrats were in a minority. As the Chairman of the Labor Committee, Hatch, prepared for hearings, the "labor connection" braced for a battle.

But it was when Hatch and his investigators approached the Department of Labor that he learned just how far the "strings" of the "labor connection" had reached. It is not uncommon for bureaucratic agencies to be captured by their "clientele" interests. Now just add a member of Congress who supports those interests and, as a matter of course, the interest and the agency, both of which in turn support the Congressman, and an Iron Triangle is forged.

The Department of Education, for example, was, in effect, a bureaucratic entity within the federal government which acted as an advocate for the politically and financially powerful National Education Association (NEA), which counts in its ranks a large percentage of the nation's teachers. A separate Department of Education was a gift to the NEA by Carter and other "friends of education" in Congress. (Its function was once part of the Department of Health, Education and Welfare.) Whatever the Department of Education does or does not do for America's school children, it is primarily an advocate for policies and programs—some of which are highly controversial and unpopular—initiated by the NEA leadership, a special-interest group.

In spite of the fact that President Reagan selected a team of Republican political supporters charged by him to phase out this costly department which boasts few tangible benefits, many of its personnel, together with the NEA and a host of members of Congress, are fighting to maintain the department. Ted Bell, Secretary of Education, has been placed in the unenviable position of attempting to carry out the directions of the Reagan administration while servicing the legitimate needs of education and educators.

One of the most powerful and immune Iron Triangles of all, however, has the "connection" of organized labor, the Department of Labor, and substantial numbers of Congressmen. For many years this combination had been impregnable. The Department of Labor had become largely the promoter, advocate, and protector of organized labor from within the administrative arm of government; and, as is the custom, there was little representation there for the majority of American workers who are unorganized. Indeed, there was precious little representation there even for labor union *members*. The VIPs to which the Department of Labor career bureaucrats apparently paid homage were the union *leaders*. Now, a freshman Senator—from Utah, of all places—had dealt this combination a number of severe blows and appeared to be regrouping for another assault. Up went the defenses. When Hatch charged that the Labor Department had failed to keep labor bosses and underworld figures from misusing millions of dollars in employee pension funds, he abolished any possibility of willing official cooperation from its career leadership.

It was true that there was a new Republican administration. It was true that Secretary of Labor Donovan and the other top political appointees at the Department of Labor were Republicans. But it was also true that, with the bureaucracy at the Department of Labor, it remained virtually business as usual.

When Hatch made his move, the top career management, to whom the *political* leadership of the Department must defer on the organization's technical procedure, dug their heels in. The political appointees to such a department face a cadre of high-salaried bureaucratic career managers who are in command of the intracacies of the organization configurations, the communications grid, the paper flow, the filing, recording, and intelligence system. They are in short, the masters of using *procedure* as a substitute for *function*, should they wish to do so.

Therefore, when Hatch first asked for assistance and information from the Department of Labor, he met a stone wall. "Ronald Reagan's Labor Department," wrote Donald Lambro for United Feature Syndicate, "has zealously resisted Hatch's persistent efforts to dip into the agency's confidential files, claiming that such an inquiry would endanger ongoing cases or interfere with the Department's work." Innocent people would be hurt it was claimed, and some of the information requested was, well, "classified."

The new Labor Department Solicitor, Tim Ryan, was told that the sheer number of files and the excessive amount of information requested by Hatch would take months, maybe longer, to put together in suitable form. And everything that went out would have to be duplicated, and "there are 25 five-drawer file cabinets." They were "sorry" about all of this, "but what can one do?" Some were angry. "Are we supposed to bend over every time Hatch makes a demand? Do we want to make this

Department a stomping ground for Congress and lose our departmental integrity?''

The Hatch investigative team also found to their anger and frustration that a number of files had disappeared. One informant told Hatch that had he not used a subpoena when he did many other files would have been destroyed. ''We have evidence,'' Hatch told the *Washington Post,* that ''there have been people down there [at the Labor Department] who deliberately destroyed documents. We don't want that to happen to documents key to our investigation.'' Silbey told the *Post* that he had spoken with over 100 past and present government officials during a 3-month period and that he had compiled allegations ''from really good people about files being taken out of their hands and recommendations for prosecution'' being ignored.

It did not take long for Hatch's investigators to find that the primary bottleneck seemed to be the holdovers in the Labor Department's Solicitor's Office (Department of Planned Benefits). ''Too many cases,'' Senate investigators charged, ''ended up in Solicitor's and never went anywhere.''

There seemed to be a pattern here. Investigations of labor abuses were undertaken. Files were appropriately referred to officials for action. The Solicitor's Office had all of the material necessary, but nothing substantive was done. In some cases the statute of limitations was allowed to run out, including one highly significant potential criminal case involving Teamsters Local 299 in Detroit, Michigan. Department records indicated that time was about to run out on 36 other cases, a danger which some Labor Department employees suggested was avoided by the Solicitor's Office by administratively closing out 163 cases. ''Embarrassment was temporarily avoided, stated Hatch, ''but only through what appears to be concealment.''

Some of these cases had been shunted back to the Labor Department's Office of Enforcement, which had sent them to the Solicitor's Office in the first place. Hatch claimed that the Solicitor's Office directed Enforcement to seek *voluntary compliance* from many of the most notorious characters in the labor movement who had been accused of systematically abusing the worker's financial resources for years. There was evidence in some of these cases that ''dummy'' corporations had been set up to ''launder'' funds received from union health and welfare plans. In one case investigated by Hatch a $24 million loan had been extended by the trustees of the Southern Nevada Culinary Workers and Bartenders Union Pension Fund between 1972 and 1977 to a borrower with strong union ties. The loans were originally set up for investment in specific land projects. However, it had been alleged that large portions of the money had been siphoned off for other purposes, and the inherent value of the original projects had been brought into question.

In 1977, Thomas Kane from the Labor Department's Division of Reporting and Enforcement recommended that criminal litigation be instituted, that an injunction be issued, and that the borrower's notes be called due. Solicitor's refused. Instead, Solicitor's inaugurated a *civil suit*. Then, "independent" investment managers were selected by Solicitor's to oversee the pension fund and to manage whatever assets were acquired by the loans. The investment managers promptly spent $13 million *more* of the Fund's depleted wealth to embellish property estimated at only $11 million in value. By late 1981 the borrower owed the Fund $45 million, including interest. At this writing, none of the "borrowed" money has been returned; nor has the civil suit ever been brought to trial.

As Solicitor's continued to refuse to refer significant cases to the Justice Department for criminal action, Kane maintained that he persisted in pressuring that office to do so, but to no avail. Serious arguments ensued. Kane claimed under oath that the directors of the Solicitor's office told him "not to deal with Justice."

A substantial backlog of cases had accumulated, some of a highly significant nature, yet personnel from the Solicitor's Office claimed that there had existed no effective or computerized tracking system to identify the disposition of thousands of cases or any way to track or verify their status with respect to the statute of limitations. "It seems to me," offered Hatch, "that they are trying to fight modern gangsters with 19th-century methods." Jeffrey Clayton, Labor Department's Administrator of the Pension Program, submitted that in certain instances fiduciaries of retirement funds may have had little fear that their activities would be explored "because the chances were good that the Department [of Labor] would not sue."

As a matter of fact, when an insurance agent secretly revealed to the Solicitor's Office serious improprieties in the administration of one particular abused pension fund, a Solicitor's attorney promptly informed the trustees of the fund. The insurance agent's "cover was blown," and his life put in jeopardy. A United States attorney in Chicago, who was looking into the case, was so upset over the incident that he threatened to issue a grand jury subpoena for people in Solicitor's to explain their action.

On April 15, 1977, a blistering letter was sent from the Justice Department to Solicitor's stating that Justice was not getting the proper cooperation from them. The letter was signed by the Assistant Attorney

General, Benjamin Civiletti. "Several letters have come to my attention which I find disturbing," he wrote. "It appears that in one case we were not informed of matters obviously requiring investigation until after a civil suit was filed by the Labor Department and we read about possible violations in the newspaper. In another case, an attempt was made to interfere with the issuance of a grand jury subpoena for certain records which might indicate the payment of substantial kickbacks. . . . The recurrence of these types of situations is unacceptable."

Too, the *Los Angeles Times* reported the concern of the General Accounting Office that the Labor Department had failed to coordinate its inquiries into pension fund abuses "with the Justice Department and the Internal Revenue Service."

One could go on and on. As the evidence mounted, the Hatch organization worked to prepare for hearings before the Senate Labor and Human Resources Committee. But Hatch now faced a dilemma. He was in an awkward position. The nearly always "bridesmaid rather than bride" Republican party had an unwritten rule—"Don't attack the party or party members!" Now with a Republican administration in the driver's seat, it seemed to some Republicans a serious faux pas for a prominent Republican Senator to attack the Labor Department while its political directors and the Secretary of Labor were also Republicans. To some media writers Labor Secretary Donovan's untenable position vis-à-vis Hatch's investigations would be simplistically misunderstood. It could put the Republican administration in a bad light.

"Lay off for a while," one savvy prominent Republican urged Hatch. "Donovan hasn't had the time to gain control over there yet. Give him awhile. This investigation thing is going to make him look bad and the Party along with it. The most important thing now in this new rebuilding period is the Party."

"I'm sorry," responded Hatch. "Your way could take years. I know the Party is important; so is Donovan's image. But there are things more important. There is wholesale corruption out there in the labor movement and wholesale coverup of it, even tacit cooperation with it, within the Labor Department. I'm going after them. I am going to expose them. If I don't get some action there soon, I will use the subpoena. That will break the lock of secrecy over there, and I believe Donovan and Ryan and the rest of the people there will be better able to function."

So Hatch went before the Labor Committee and asked for permission to use the subpoena. He got it, but not without a fight. According to *The Washington Post,* "The Labor Committee approved the subpoena by a 15 to 0 vote, but only after more than an hour of partisan bickering about the secrecy with which Hatch and his investigators have handled the probe. Committee Democrats were first briefed two days ago on the investigation into organized crime's influence on union activities, and on the Labor Department's pursuit of such allegations. The probe began nearly three months ago, and in Hatch's words, is 'well advanced at this time' . . . . Senator Edward M. Kennedy (D. Mass.) maintained that, under the panel's rules, members must authorize an investigation before any subpoenas stemming from it could be issued. Hatch disagreed and finally won approval for the subpoena by a formal vote after promising to keep the Democrats informed of the investigation's progress.''

Hatch's prediction turned out to be true. To be sure, both Donovan and Ryan took their lumps in the media, and they didn't like it one bit, but the embarrassing focus of the media was on the bureaucracy of the Labor Department. Headlines, such as ''Sen. Hatch Accuses Labor Department of Failing to Protect Pension Funds'' from *The Washington Post,* began to appear in major newspapers across the country. The pressure was now shifting to the Labor Department. ''Sunlight,'' stated one of Hatch's investigators, ''is the best antiseptic.''

It soon became evident that no pressure was going to dissuade Hatch. The oversight investigation was ''for real.''

Then, when Hatch issued subpoenas for Labor Department files, the foundations of the citadel shook. According to the *New York Times,* ''Senate investigators noted that Congressional Committees often subpoenaed private individuals and their records, but had seldom challenged the Executive Branch in this fashion.'' Even Donovan was shocked by this action. He let it be known that he was miffed.

Still, it was clearly media exposure, plus the use of the subpoena to get files from the Labor Department, that broke the lock on the door. At the heart of exercising true oversight is the willingness to use the subpoena. Depending upon the situation, it may well be its use or non-use that tells one whether or not the oversight is in earnest.

The Labor Department's Solicitor's Office began to open up. Hatch's ace investigators, Jim Phillips and Dan Gill, found a steady increase in cooperation from within the Department. Also, the number of employees within Labor who were willing to talk sincerely with Phillips and Gill grew significantly.

Indeed, between the time the subpoenas had been delivered and the day Hatch had deadlined for the Labor Department to respond to his subpoena, that organization became revitalized in its legal responsibility to guard labor pension funds. Suddenly shelved cases, some of them close to dying due to the statute of limitations, were dusted off. ''It was something to behold," said Frank Silbey. "It appeared that someone had given the Labor Department a hot-foot. Someone had. The man with the match was Orrin Hatch."

It was an eager Jeffrey Clayton, Administrator of the Pension and Welfare Benefit Program, who stated, "To put it in the venacular, 'enforcement is in.' I don't think there is any question that there are going to be more people sued."

As the doors began to open to Hatch's team of investigators, many in the Labor Department and even union members gained the courage to fight the Establishment. As Jim Phillips put it, "When the word got around that the Senator was in the driver's seat and was not about to be dislodged, witnesses, who before were frightened to talk, began to open up to us. They believed the Senator would protect them." Even a number of individual union members had the courage to strike out on their own against labor corruption by filing law suits.

On April 22, 1981, *The Washington Star* editorialized under the title "U.S. Seeking to Add $270 Million to Teamsters Pension Fund Suit," "The Labor Department yesterday moved to add 9 allegedly improper transactions made by a Teamsters Union pension fund to a list of 15 dealings the government wants the fund's former trustees to pay for personally."The fact that this press release was issued by the Department of Labor almost simultaneously with Hatch's issue of the subpoenas is significant.

On Tuesday, February 24, 1982, the unbowed Chairman of the Senate Labor and Human Resources Committee, the "mace" bared, opened hearings on "Labor Department ERISA Compliance." He had met the "labor connection" head on, and had penetrated the armor of that once impregnable Iron Triangle. He had stormed the citadel.

During the first day of the hearings, through 10 hours of testimony, all Democratic members of the Committee were conspicuous by their absence. They charged through a spokesman that their boycott was caused because they had not received material concerning the hearing from the Chairman in sufficient time to become properly informed. "Where are all the 'friends of the working man' today?" asked Senator Thurmond, winking at Hatch.

C. Booth Wallentine, Executive Vice President of the Utah Farm Bureau Federation, was exuberant over this great victory for a "home state boy." "Modern politics may have no better example of political courage," he wrote in his column "Viewpoint" for the *Utah Farm Bureau News,* "than the relentless battle Utah's Senator Orrin Hatch is now waging against the mishandling of union members' pension funds by corrupt labor union bosses and their attorneys. The battleground is the Senate Labor Committee, chaired by Hatch. The Utah Senator says he'll spend a year, if necessary, in hearings to find out why the U.S. Department of Labor has failed to enforce Federal ERISA laws prohibiting special loans to union bosses involving millions of dollars of rank-and-file union members' pension money . . . . Orrin Hatch has the courage to tread where no labor committee chairman dared to tread before. Somehow, to me, all this doesn't deserve a partisan label.''

Top investigators on the Hill also hold respect akin to awe for Hatch. ''My gawd,'' said one homespun but brilliant investigator, ''ain't nobody but Hatch who'd take on big labor in an election year. He is either all man or a damned fool.''

Booth got the same response. One veteran Senate investigator told him, ''We've watched Hatch buck everybody to get this thing out in the open . . . . Hatch is the first labor committee chairman with the guts to take on a government bureaucracy that has traditionally been a labor union fiefdom—and in an election year, too. That's incredible!''

If anyone was left in doubt as to Hatch's intentions, his opening statement before the Labor Committee would clear up any misunderstanding:

> Today we open what I expect to be a year-long series of hearings into the Labor Department's handling of enforcement cases involving abuse of union pension funds by corrupt union leaders, corrupt businessmen, and organized crime figures.
>
> Our decision to initiate these hearings came last year when we discovered that the Labor Department had accumulated a backlog of 247 enforcement cases, many of which were becoming endangered by statute of limitations problems. We were concerned that an inordinately large number of these cases—163, to be exact—were closed out administratively in 1981.
>
> The committee is not in a position at this time to say whether each and every one of these 163 cases should have been placed in litigation or referred to the Justice Department for prosecution. However, my staff has reviewed enough of them to determine that a common theme runs through all too many cases—that the Labor Department's Office of the Solicitor, which in other departments is known as the general counsel, has refused to act meaningfully or vigorously against those who abuse these pension funds. This is true with respect to both Democratic and Republican administrations dating back to the Ford years.

Refusal by the Solicitor's Office to crack down on criminal elements was recently cited by the Senate Permanent Investigations Subcommittee as a major contributing factor to the problems that the subcommittee found with the Teamsters Union Central States Pension Fund. The same problem has surfaced in my staff's investigation of the Southern Nevada Culinary Workers' Pension Fund case, which we will be looking into . . . .

From our preliminary work on other enforcement cases, it is a theme I expect will be aired more and more extensively in this hearing room as our inquiry proceeds throughout the year. The stakes are high. Currently there are more than 50 million workers in 560,000 pension plans, and the present value of those plans is more than $550 billion. We must ensure that the Labor Department is adequately protecting these assets.

Let me say at the outset that I am not questioning the integrity of any Labor Department employee who has participated in these enforcement cases. We are simply looking at their job performance, and that level of performance has not been high with respect to protecting union pension fund assets which have been milked repeatedly by union leaders and outsiders, some of whom have reputed or known organized crime connections.

Those who would characterize these hearings or me personally as anti-labor are mistaken, and they know it. It is time that someone spoke up for the rank-and-file union member whose hard-earned retirement income is being systematically stolen by certain union bosses, business persons, and racketeers.

Entrenched politicians with incestuous ties to dishonest union leaders will not protect those rank-and-file members. The Labor Department has not and will not protect them either. Both these forces have been traditionally aligned with union leaders.

This, of course, is not to say that all or nearly all of these leaders are dishonest. Many are fine individuals. Nonetheless, the individual worker or retiree appears to be the forgotten man or woman in all this. I intend to do my best to protect them.

EPILOGUE

In Hatch's major legislative efforts, one sees the unmistakable love he holds for the American Constitutional system. It is not just the fact that in his energetic and tenacious oversight there lies the potential of saving the taxpayer literally billions of dollars, however important that is to our inflation-ridden economy. Nor is it just the fact that more professionalism and responsibility is appearing where his oversight has touched the federal bureaucracy, however important that is to "good" government. It is much more. With all the strength of his belief in Constitutional government, Orrin Hatch is a significant force in reinstituting vigorous and meaningful checks and balances back into the system where they have been neglected. His efforts signal the possibility of an enlightened and determined Congress once again bringing this enormous and powerful bureaucratic arm of the executive branch under some measure of control, some degree of restraint, some modicum of responsiveness. Indeed, if this is not accomplished, one foresees a repeat of the swollen bureaucracy of ancient Rome, which succeeded, by its own oppressive and costly weight, in contributing in a significant way to the collapse of the empire.

If Hatch's Balanced Budget Tax Limitation Amendment should become the law of the land, it would further enrich the checks-and-balance system so esteemed by the country's Founders in their wisdom. It is more, much more, than just the fact that the amendment has the potential of healing a fevered economy, which is clearly out of control, with the restraining influences inherent in aligning spending with income. This amendment would once again place the unorganized voter in a commanding position vis-à-vis government spending by ensuring that his representative could not spend without taxing and could not tax without being visibly accountable to his constituency.

The Budget Amendment would also insure greater competition for available funds between the great interest groups, while at the same time forcing them and their legislative friends into open competition with the taxpayer over taxing and spending levels. *One, of course, cannot legislate responsible behavior, but one can illuminate irresponsible conduct.*

No longer virtually disenfranchised with regard to government spending, the unorganized citizenry would be given a new infusion of self-government, a new influence on the taxing and spending practices of their representatives. The sad history of previous democracies suggests that the people may not take advantage of such an important opportunity, but the Budget Amendment would at least give them that opportunity.

Hatch's Human Life Federalism Amendment, if it, too, becomes an addition to the Constitution, will do more than open the door wide for those who seek the most stringent controls over the practice of abortion. It has the potential of renewing the strength of federalism. The amendment reaffirms faith in the representative process and in public debate, *both state and national,* while it just as vigorously condemns governmental usurpation, even by the Supreme Court.

It is no exaggeration to suggest that Senator Orrin Hatch's efforts carry with them the potential of making a monumental impact on our Republic and of engendering a revival of vigilance as well as respect and support for the Constitution of the United States.

Perhaps most important of all, this man from Utah, described by columnist Donald Lambro as an "articulate and well-liked freshman lawmaker whose impeccably tailored senatorial attire masks a tough rough-rider attitude," demonstrates to all of us the impact one totally dedicated human being can have in the face of overwhelming challenge.

David can still challenge Goliath.

"How stands the Republic?" you ask?

A little straighter than a few years ago.

Other Regnery Gateway Titles of Related Interest

Why Reagan Won, by F. Clifton White & William J. Gill. The only complete account of the 16-year effort that brought Mr. Reagan, and the ever-growing conservative movement, the Presidency. This account contains insights into Ronald Reagan the man, and anecdotes about the President's private life. Was $14.95. Now $6.00.

Phyllis Schlafly, by Carol Felsenthal. Revered as "the heroine of the right wing," denounced as "a traitor to her sex," Phyllis Schlafly, best known for her fight against ERA, has been called the most controversial woman in America. This lively and enlightening biography explores both the politics and the private life behind the public image. $3.95 (paper).

Target America, by James L. Tyson. This timely report reveals for the first time documentary evidence of the infiltration of Communist propaganda interests in the U.S. media. Was $12.95. Now $5.00.

Fat City: How Washington Wastes Your Taxes, by Donald Lambro. This chilling exposé on federal waste was distributed by President Ronald Reagan at his first Cabinet meeting. Lambro has provided the frightening particulars of bureaucratic fraud and federal boondogglery. Was $12.95. Now $5.00.

A Changing America, by Paul Laxalt, et al. A succinct, intelligent statement of the conservative agenda for the '80s. Written by seven senate leaders and introduced by President Ronald Reagan, *A Changing America* covers the essential areas of U.S. policy. $2.95 (paper).

Abuse of Trust: A Report on Ralph Nader's Network, by Dan Burt. The author demonstrates that the Nader network is no different in its essential constitution, its private control, methods of operation, and lack of candor than the worst among those it condemns. Was $12.95. Now $5.00.

- -